Endorsements for
The Happiest Man in the World

"I have known Jim Jackson for more than fifteen years. He has lived as exciting a life as anyone I have ever met, and I'm delighted to learn that he is recording some of these experiences for the benefit of others."
—Philip Yancey, Author, *What's So Amazing About Grace?*

"It is my pleasure to join the many other voices that praise the work of Jim Jackson and Project C.U.R.E. I am a firm believer that government alone will never be able to solve the most critical issues facing the most vulnerable of our society. Our best hope of overcoming these challenges will come when we harness the vision and dedication of non-profit organizations like Project C.U.R.E. and the outstanding people who lead them. This wonderful program does more than just provide medical supplies and services to children and families. It provides hope!"
—Bill Ritter, Jr., Former Governor of Colorado

"Through the dedication of Jim Jackson and the tireless volunteers of Project C.U.R.E., this Denver-based non-profit has been able to impact virtually every major nation in the world—without the help of government programs. Ordinary citizens giving out of the goodness of their hearts—that's where real change begins."
—Bill Owens, Former Governor of Colorado

"I have known Dr. Jim Jackson for over 20 years and served alongside him overseas on a number of occasions. Project C.U.R.E. has an outstanding record of effective and enduring health interventions in austere locations in more than 125 countries. Many of these contribute to US national security by helping to win "hearts and minds" in favor of the American people. Jim's generous personal example of medical humanitarian outreach shows a kinder and gentler face of the United States and is exactly complimentary to what we in the US military must do to protect our homeland."

>—Dr. James W. Terbush, Command Surgeon,
>NORAD/Northcom, Homeland Security

"Dr. James W. Jackson is a great pioneer of human altruism. There are few in history who have helped more than he has, through his work with Project C.U.R.E. *The Happiest Man in the World* is a must read for all who are concerned with helping the needy in the global human family."

>—Howard C. Self, National Executive Director,
>Universal Peace Foundation

"Jim Jackson's beautiful story about his journey from successful businessman to the realization of his call to serve, translates into a very basic tenet for establishing world peace. That is—to serve with no strings attached and with great love to all humankind. Mother Teresa's life was a testimony to this, as is Jim Jackson's."

>—Anna Maria Larsen, Larsen Consulting International

The HAPPIEST MAN in the WORLD

Life Lessons from a Cultural Economist

Dr. James W. Jackson

Winston-Crown
PUBLISHING HOUSE
DENVER, COLORADO

The Happiest Man in the World: Life Lessons from a Cutural Economist
Published by Winston-Crown Publishing House, Ltd.
PO Box 651
Evergreen, CO 80437

© 2010 by Dr. James W. Jackson
All rights reserved.

ISBN 978-1-61137-000-3

Scripture quotations are taken from the Holy Bible, New International Version.
Some names have been changed to protect identities.

Edit: Harold Fickett
Cover Photo: Jimmy Dozer
Cover Design: Linda Wood

Library of Congress Control Number: 2010941207

Published in the United States of America
2010

10 9 8 7 6 5 4 3 2 1

Dedication to

Dr. Anna Marie Jackson

My Pretty Cheerleader and
Precious Partner for Over Fifty Years

⁂

Contents

1. The Question 1
2. Snakes on the Road 5
3. Childhood Promises 17
4. I Was Afraid You Were Going to Ask 25
5. Hardball Banking 31
6. Making Money 39
7. The Garden of Gethsemane 51
8. Closing the Gates and Opening the Word 63
9. The Turning Point 67
10. Paradox and Reversal 77
11. Devils and Angels 87
12. Beyond Brazil 97
13. Up Close and Personal—Always 109
14. The Challenge of Neutrality 125
15. Avoiding the Pitfalls—and the Thugs 139
16. Partners and Networks 147
17. A Short Course in Changing the World 165
18. Cultural Economics 185
19. Despair 203

Contents

20	Cost of Petrol Just Went Up for You	223
21	Empowering Others	247
22	Darkness Comes to Call	271
23	The Final Surprise	279
24	A New Wave of Global Transformation	291
	Appendix	299
	Dig a Little Deeper: Reader's Discussion Guide	305
	Notes	311

1

The Question

Isn't it strange that princes and kings,
And clowns that caper in sawdust rings,
And common folk, like you and me,
Are builders for eternity?

To each is given a bag of tools,
A shapeless mass and a book of rules;
And each must make, ere life is flown,
A stumbling-block or a stepping-stone.

—R.L Sharpe, A Bag of Tools, circa 1809

like to tell people wherever I go, "I am the happiest man in the world." If that's not literally the case, I certainly must be among the few whose deepest desires have been fulfilled beyond what I could ever have imagined.

I've traveled to more than one hundred and fifty countries and have regularly experienced in any given thirty days the worst and the best of humanity. In the midst of squalor and within the private enclaves of plenty, I have seen both happiness and misery, and it's certainly not wealth that makes the difference. So what does?

Can we find happiness by pursuing our own dreams, or does human fulfillment depend upon our connection with others? Does our fate depend upon the world's destiny?

I was raised in a secure family and an active Protestant church. I was adamantly instructed that the church was the institution that dispensed happiness based on the notion—echoed by many faiths—that in loving God and one's neighbor lay the secret of happiness. Yet not many of those churchgoers acted happy at all. I quickly learned what the church was against, but it took me a long time to discover what Christians were for. We were instructed that we could find meaning in our faith—a meaning that embraced the individual and then spread outwards. If large numbers of Christians found meaning in their faith, they could have a transformational effect on the world.

The post-World War II era never really showed me much hard evidence of that. Historically, the church was at the forefront of the humanitarian reforms of western civilization. What has Christianity accomplished lately, though? Today, surveys indicate that many still "believe"—more people than ever, in fact—but all that believing isn't changing much of anything. Why is that?

When we think about people who are out happily changing the world, we think about a new class of "social entrepreneurs" like Bill Gates, Bono, Warren Buffet, or Bill Clinton. These folks are using what they learned building successful businesses, political machines, and huge followings to bring about meaningful change. They are helping to build a better world for people no matter what those people believe.

What agenda does the neighborhood mega church have for global transformation—for remedying the world's worst problems, like education, poverty, disease, and political corruption? Is it sending teenagers to far-flung locations to build houses over spring break? That's wonderful, but it lacks the scale and innovation that the world's problems demand.

I am an economist and a businessman, and I have learned the art of wealth creation. I have invested heavily in Christian education and once helped fund a megachurch, only to see my fellow Christians disappoint me beyond measure.

I finally traveled out into an unknown landscape where I discovered both the true meaning of my faith and the importance of global transformation.

During this voyage of discovery, I came to the conclusion that while the Bill Gateses of the world have very good ideas, without Christianity's understanding of the human person and the world, these very good ideas accomplish much less than they ought.

However, social entrepreneurship, carried out in the light of Christian principles, can have a transformational effect on us and the world for which we long. The active practice of love, toward our enemies as well as our friends, makes way for the reign of God in human affairs—for God's justice and peace. I know this because I've seen it at times and in places where only God's power could have proven greater than the barrel of a gun.

That's why I can say, there is a way for *you*, too, to become the happiest man or woman in the world.

2

Snakes on the Road

The war-torn pavement was peppered with potholes. Our driver, Malu-Malu, was successful in swerving to miss most of them. Snakes were a different issue.

The hot African sun had coaxed scores of large and deadly green and black mamba snakes out of their jungle lairs and onto the parched asphalt. The only road maneuver performed by Malu-Malu when he spotted a large snake on the roadway was to take deadly aim at the snake, even if it meant darting over to the wrong side of the road.

When the Toyota Land Cruiser was within striking distance, Malu-Malu would slam on the brakes and skid the tires over the body of the reptile rolling it up like a sailor's knot. But that wasn't good enough. Once the SUV had come to a screeching stop, our government driver would throw the vehicle into reverse and back over the snake again. Then for good measure he would yank the gearshift down once more into drive, and run over the snake once again.

I put my hand on our driver's shoulder and asked him, "Is wrapping up mambas into pretzels your most favorite sport?"

Malu-Malu looked over at me, his eyes stern, his jaw set. "A snake like that just recently killed my sister, and there is no reason to allow that snake to slither into a peaceful village and kill another innocent person!"

OK.

I was in the Democratic Republic of Congo in fulfillment of my duties as founder and chairman of Project C.U.R.E. (Commission on Urgent Relief and Equipment), a nongovernmental agency dedicated to providing lifesaving medical supplies to lesser-developed nations. The Democratic Republic of Congo certainly qualified, since war and governmental corruption had beggared the country and reduced its already rudimentary health care institutions to desecrated shells. My specific task was to perform Needs Assessment Studies on hospitals and clinics that might be restored, at least in some measure, through the aid of Project C.U.R.E.

Poisonous mambas were the least of my worries. I was in dangerous territory in the jungles of post-coup Congo. I was riding in the minister of health's Toyota through the great rainforest basin of the Congo River, on the road from the capital city, Kinshasa, to a remote settlement called Kimpese, an area with a population of approximately two hundred thousand.

Just weeks before, on January 18, 2001, one of dictator Laurent-Désiré Kabila's trusted army generals had assassinated the dictator in his home. A gun battle raged within the Kinshasa Presidential Palace for about an hour and a half before the coup succeeded in taking over the government.

It had taken Laurent Kabila, a Hutu and a protégé of President Yoweri Museveni of Uganda, nearly thirty-two years to overthrow Mobutu Sese Seko, the previous diabolical dictator of the Democratic Republic, under whose government the country was called Zaire.

As an insurgent freedom fighter, Kabila had wooed the armies of neighboring Uganda and Rwanda to help him overthrow Mobubu Sese Seko. As soon as he had the reins of power well in hand, Kabila double-crossed Uganda and Rwanda by cutting deals with Angola, Zimbabwe, and Namibia for diamonds, gold, and oil reserves.

Laurent Kabila's dictatorship lasted only thirty-two months. During his short and bloody stint, he oversaw the murder of nearly 4.5 million people. In those weeks of chaos, armed troops from Zimbabwe, Angola, Namibia, Uganda, and Rwanda were roving the countryside, pillaging the remnants of the country's resources and raping its women.

I had been asked to travel to Congo by one of Project C.U.R.E.'s strategic partners, Dr. Larry Sthreshley. The government of Congo had issued papers giving me authority to travel, and to assess the medical situation, at my own risk. Given a chance, the roving soldiers would have robbed me, held me hostage for ransom, or killed me on a whim.

It was a six-hour motor trip from Kinshasa to Kimpese. Dr. Larry would have accompanied me personally had it not been for critical meetings he needed to attend in the politically unraveling city of Kinshasa. Despite the chaotic situation, Dr. Larry insisted that I see the hospital in Kimpese, where he reported extraordinary things were happening. Dr. Larry knew the staff there to be extremely dedicated, providing health care with virtually no resources. He thought Project C.U.R.E.'s supplies could hardly be better used in any other area of the country.

The journey stands as one of the most dangerous I have ever taken, even with the health minister supplying his official car and driver. The government had also sent along a righteous man of the cloth, the Reverend Pastor Fidele Bavuidinsi, who, I was informed, was the deputy president of the ACBCO, RDC (whatever in the world that meant). He was to take care of any travel logistics and indigenous conflicts that might arise. He spoke all the local languages and came equipped with a pin-striped black suit, a Desmond Tutu-style purple bishop's shirt with a white plastic collar, and a huge red Bible that he kept continuously in hand.

I undertook the journey because of my respect for Dr. Larry Sthreshley, the son of a retired Presbyterian missionary. In the early 1900s the Presbyterian denomination had performed remarkable mission work throughout the sub-Saharan Desert in Africa. Their work had included the building of outstanding hospitals, medical clinics, and teaching compounds. I loved visiting these old facilities. They were built like campuses, with the different departments situated in crisp and sturdy stone buildings connected by flower-lined walkways and pleasant gardens. Even now many of the buildings stand as classic examples of turn-of-the-century African architecture.

Beautifully quaint stone and wood houses with rambling verandahs and screened-in porches were situated close to the hospital and teaching compound. Outside the houses and missions buildings were old garden spots where fresh vegetables and fruits had been grown for the workers.

During the 1960s and 1970s pressure groups within the denomination had applied political and social criticism over the church leaders' policies of managing the medical mission endeavors from the United States. The opposition's argument was that it was paternalistic, patronizing, and just unfair for the denomination's leaders in America to think they had to be the ones to run the institutions and make all the decisions. After all, who knew better than Africans how to run African institutions? Eventually, it became enough of an issue that everything was turned over to the indigenous people.

But these high-minded attitudes concealed a hidden agenda. Cutting the nationalistic umbilical cords saved the sponsoring groups a lot of money, thus re-supplying discretionary funding for domestic programs. Predictably, the experiment failed miserably. By the 1990s the institutions were in deplorable condition.

That's when Larry Sthreshley got involved with a plan to rejuvenate the health systems and salvage the historic investments of the institutions. Although I visited much of West Africa with him on previous trips, I had always resisted visiting the Democratic Republic of Congo. I had never felt that the country was safe enough to run the risks. As I told him more than once, I thought the place was spooky and lawless.

Now, of course, I had arrived at one of the worst times in its history, which, given its history, was saying something.

The Democratic Republic of Congo was as big in size as Europe and possessed rich natural resources of gold, diamonds, copper, cobalt, magnesia, and zinc. Since the country gained independence in 1960, recurring tribal wars and forty years of leadership by criminal thugs had caused the former Belgium protectorate to unravel at its civil seams. Worldwide opinion had concluded that internal conflicts stretching back hundreds of years, and meddling by neighboring countries, rendered the Congo essentially ungovernable.

To stabilize the country, international forces put into place a leader named Mobutu Sese Seko. Mobutu Sese Seko quickly morphed into an inhumane despot. During the thirty-two years of his rule, the dictator diverted half of the state budget to his personal bank accounts. He stole most of the foreign aid given by the World Bank, the UN, the US, and other free countries trying to help Zaire. He amassed a personal fortune known to be in excess of $6 billion while saddling the government with another $10 billion in debt.

While Mobutu's friends, cronies, and military leaders lived the life of ease, the people suffered. Infrastructure crumbled. The roads degenerated; schools, government hospitals, and other institutions fell apart. The economy established during the time of Belgian rule fell into shambles controlled by thieves. Poverty and suffering exploded while Mobutu murdered his opponents, put them in jail, or corrupted them in other ways.

Laurent-Désiré Kabila packed even more violence and corruption into his brief four-year dictatorship.

Early in the day of our trip to Kimpese, I had wondered why the Reverend Pastor Fidele Bavuidinsi had been sent along—and how he had wrangled the assignment. His presence would have been more comic than not but for the dangerous situation. As we were loading into the Land Cruiser, the Reverend Pastor Fidele kept waiving his big red Bible around and barking out commands, telling each of us where to sit and that he was now in charge. "Thus sayeth the Lord!" he added, punching the air with the big book.

I looked over at our driver and rolled my eyes.

Pastor Fidele began barking even more orders to our driver, Malu-Malu, as we pulled out through the sagging wooden gates of the dilapidated old African youth hostel where I was staying while in Kinshasa.

Soon, following Fidele's directions, we were bouncing down garbage-strewn roads in dangerous neighborhoods of Kinshasa. Several times Fidele would have the driver go back and forth through the streets until he found the different men he was looking for. The reverend would pop out of the car, perform some sort of transaction with the men, and then bark more orders at Malu-Malu. Other times he would have the driver stop in a back alley. Fidele would jump out, run into a doorway, and soon emerge and climb back into the Toyota.

He kept us touring through the sleaziest ramshackle parts of Kinshasa for more than an hour and showed no inclination to head out for Kimpese. It was quite obvious the fellow was dealing in drugs or collecting payoffs. He was certainly not baptizing babies.

Finally, I became exasperated and told Fidele that we had an assignment and he would have to take care of his business dealings at some other time.

He threw what can only be described as a clerical hissy fit. "This is taking no time at all. You will have plenty sufficient time for me to get you to Kimpese. I am Pastor Fidele Bavuidinsi and I am doing the work of the Lord. What I do is important!" All the time he was hollering at me he was waving his big red leather Bible back and forth as if he might slap me with it.

"Take us to Kimpese!" I told the driver.

About two hours into our road trip we began to gain elevation and the landscape changed from broadleaf jungle foliage to rolling grasslands punctuated by banana trees and a few acacia and mango trees. Only about 1 percent of the fertile land held any sign of recent or former cultivation. But the view from the top of one of the grassy hills back toward the verdant rainforests begged for a photo shot.

The minister of health had requested that before arriving in Kimpese I make a stop at the Soto Bata Hospital. The facility reminded me of the campus-style hospital I had assessed with Dr. Larry Sthreshley a couple of days before in an area called Kajiji. It had been at Kajiji that I had heard detailed stories of how the American, Belgium, and British mission societies had accepted applications for young people to go into the troublesome areas of the Congo in the late 1800s and early 1900s.

The average stay—that is, *life expectancy*—of an early pioneer missionary was eleven months. New recruits to the Congo were instructed to pack their goods in a wooden coffin so that there would be a way to ship their bodies back home for burial.

Most would die of malaria, tuberculosis, respiratory illness, or intestinal ailments contracted through unsafe water or food. Waves of brave dedicated young Christian men and women volunteers traveled there and tried to research ways of coping with the health hazards so that those who followed might actually live long enough to do the work. I wondered whether our world would see such dedication again.

There was something disturbingly strange and eerie about the Soto Bata hospital. As we wheeled into the rutty circle drive I noticed that the facility was almost totally deserted. Only a couple of male nurses were there and one young male doctor who had just recently arrived. Fewer than a half-dozen patients were there sitting on the front stairway waiting around for help.

I quickly learned why. Until just a couple of days before, the hospital had been occupied by Angolan and Zimbabwean armies as a high-profile command post for their marauding troops. Now the doctor and nurses were trying to reassemble the staff and hospital helpers to make the facility back into a hospital. While the foreign soldiers were there they had raped every woman they saw and stolen from the surrounding villages.

When the foreign troops left they took everything of any value with them from the hospital. Anything that even looked like medicine had been carted away. They took all the bandages, utensils, microscopes, and operating room instruments, even the pens and pencils. They carted away all one hundred beds and mattresses for their next camp, and the unscrupulous thieves had even taken the surgery room scrubs and boots.

The old ambulance at the Soto Bata hospital did not run because of a broken engine, but the departing soldiers had stripped the tires, wheels, battery, headlights, and every other removable part from the ambulance and taken everything with them.

While they did not take the patients' paper medical files with them, they did scatter them over the office floors.

I quickly wrapped up my needs assessment study by taking pictures of the sad mess and writing "needs everything!" on my report.

We gathered out in front of the Soto Bata hospital for a photo op next to the health minister's new Toyota. As we parted, the young doctor and one of the male nurses took me by the arm and urged me, "Please, Dr. Jackson, be on the lookout for those roving gangs of soldiers. They are like crazy animals. They will see you as 'money' and they will kill you and have no one at all to answer to for their actions. It will be like the raping and murdering they have done here. No one will ever hold them accountable for their actions. You must be careful, and we will pray."

As we traveled on the road to Kimpese the countryside was a mosaic of virgin African splendor. The road turned from pavement into rutty red dirt, but the limitless view of open savannah was worth the bumpy ride. I had been traveling throughout Africa since the early 1980s, yet I never tired of its landscapes. I didn't much like the squalor of the urban chaos, but I was in love with the unspoiled Africa. Despite being in a war zone, I began to relax and enjoy the unique beauty.

I glanced over at "Pastor Fidele Bavuidinsi, deputy president of the ACBCO, RDC." He had slouched down in his seat with his head bouncing on his chest, drooling slightly onto his purple-colored clerical shirt. As he slept, his arm and hand muscles had relaxed, and his big red Bible had bounced loose and silently slid to the floor.

Suddenly, Malu-Malu slammed on the brakes! It wasn't another mamba snake. We had almost hit a huge truck that had overturned and was blocking the road. I braced myself. Pastor Fidele unceremoniously came to consciousness screaming out the Lord's Prayer and clutching for his red leather Bible!

Apparently, the driver of the monster motor truck had swerved to miss hitting another oncoming truck and had ditched his large sets of dual wheels in the soft, red dirt on the right side of the road. There were no more people at the crash site so we drove on. A car accident in such a land was one of my worst fears, as the people who show up—if anyone shows up—are not there to help like the auto club.

Before we reached Kimpese, I had an hour of silence in which to think about what I had already seen and heard on this trip. In Africa, one person dies of malaria every ten seconds. AIDS was then raging completely out-of-control. Three of every four babies were dying of AIDS before the age of two, and nine hundred children were dying every day of the disease. The estimates were that 1 million children would be orphaned and would have no one to take care of them. How would a country like the Congo cope with such a situation?

My stewing was called to a halt as we approached the gated compound of the Institut Médical Evangélique (I.M.E.), Kimpese hospital. I remembered Larry saying, "Something special is going on there. I would like you and Project C.U.R.E. to be a part of it."

As we drove onto the compound I was hit with conflicting intuitions. First, I thought the facilities showed great promise. I could identify where the old 1900s campus-style buildings had been built and were still standing. More recently there must have been an infusion of capital, as several new beautiful and well-designed buildings were nestled into the campus boundaries.

The buildings were a combination of one- and two-story structures painted in shades of tan and topped with bright red metal roofs. The buildings were generously supplied with large windows, which made the structures more inviting. The concrete walkways connecting each building were lined with well-trimmed hedges about three feet tall and sprinkled with colorful African flowering plants. I was encouraged.

Then came the second, conflicting intuition—this gut-wrenching feeling that Pastor Fidele had done nothing to set up meetings or even let the officials know that I was coming to their hospital. He could hardly wait to get me out of the Toyota so that he could commandeer the vehicle and "his chauffeur" and commence his own personal business enterprises, whatever they were.

I told the obsessed cleric to stay put and employed some of my own homegrown ingenuity to locate the medical director of the hospital, Dr. Meli Sanja. I also found Dr. Nsiangana Fele, the director general and legal representative of Kimpese.

When I filled them in on the strange situation, and the fact that I was the founder of Project C.U.R.E., they were terribly embarrassed, dropped everything they were doing, and graciously hosted me during the entire needs assessment study.

Dr. Larry Sthreshley had not led me astray. What I found thrilled me.

But I was still in Africa. Between the buildings the laundry had still been draped over the thorn bushes to dry. Racks of worn, unsterile, stained latex gloves were sitting out in the sun to dry so that they could be used over and over again. And just as I would see in any other African hospital setting, the patients' family members had gathered outside the buildings around their charcoal fires, preparing to fix meals for their loved ones. They had brought their goats for milk, their chickens and ducks for eggs and meat, and their wooden-pole sledges and stone bowls for pounding grain and rice into flour in order to make breads for the patients.

On the inside of the hospital the dedicated doctors, nurses, and laboratory techs were performing miracles with nearly nothing. I had visited thousands of hospitals around the world in developing countries, but nothing had impressed me more than what I was seeing in the creative determination of the doctors at the Kimpese hospital. In the orthopedic ward I watched as the staff worked together to assemble bits of discarded pipes and pieces of old chain to fashion traction devices that they attached with a rope to a water bucket filled with stones. They would drape the rope over the end of the antique hospital bed and add stones as needed for the traction procedure.

With curiosity I watched as they employed homemade bone-stretching devices that they screwed directly through the flesh and into the patient's bone. They were experiencing a high rate of success using procedures I had not seen attempted before in rural Africa.

I determined in my heart right there that, if at all possible, Project C.U.R.E. would donate hundreds of thousands of dollars worth of modern medical equipment and inventories of fresh medical supplies to assist those dedicated doctors and nurses at the Kimpese hospital. Working together we had an opportunity to change the health care delivery system of that whole Congolese region.

That night, since there had been no plans made for my arrival in Kimpese, I was shown to an old cast iron hospital bed. The staff was kind enough to give me a clean sheet and a mosquito net. I took out my trusty handheld charcoal-and-iodine personal water purifier, and dipped the end of the hose into a bucket of water that had been collected from the hospital roof during a recent rain storm, took a drink, and washed some of the dust out of my eyes.

As I crawled into the bed and carefully tucked the mosquito net under the lumpy old mattress, I asked the good Lord to protect me from any of the hospital-borne diseases and viruses rampant in an institution like that.

As my weary body began to relax on the bed I listened to the unique sounds of the African night far, far away in the heart of the old Belgian Congo. I thought of the snakes on the road, the soldiers raping and pillaging in the surrounding countryside, the political chaos in Kinshasa, the skullduggery of the Reverend Pastor Fidele, and in the midst of it all the heroic efforts of the doctors, nurses, and other staff members running this life-giving medical institution. That was the world. A war zone. A power grab. Rank hypocrisy comically parading around in clerical garb. At the same time—in the very same place—there were people doing their duty and showing care and compassion for others.

I was there to make a difference, to lend a hand, and I thought, to a degree, I knew how. I had to wonder, though, at how I had come to be there. It was hard to think of anywhere farther from the Boise Valley in Idaho, where I grew up.

3

Childhood Promises

So much of my destiny, I realize looking back, lay in a handful of stories, a few that were personal and others I found in books.

My parents taught my two brothers and me that doing well in business and doing good deeds in the world should be inseparable. They instilled in the three Jackson brothers an entrepreneurial spirit that looked forward to philanthropic ends. I was taught how to create wealth in order to practice virtue.

"I will never be able to give you anything and never be able to leave you anything," my father, Richard W. Jackson, told his boys. "But, I can show you how you can get anything you want." These messages might seem strange coming from a young energetic minister who had more talent than he knew what to do with: stranger yet, because they were addressed to me before I was old enough to attend school.

"You can take anything you have and make it into what you want," he would say. "But in order to accomplish this, everyone involved has to end up 'better off.' Find someone who has what you need and give him in exchange something that he wants even more than what he has, and you will both end up with exactly what you wanted."

As far as I can remember our dad formally demonstrated that concept only once. One day he brought home a New Zealand white rabbit. It was a large female rabbit with pink eyes and soft fur, who was pregnant. Soon she delivered a skad of the cutest, fuzziest little bunnies imaginable. He then told my two brothers and me to trim the grass along the edges of the sidewalks until we had enough to fill our bright red Radio Flyer wagon to the brim.

When we were finished he came out of his study and took the irresistible bunnies and nestled them into the fresh green lawn clippings. We didn't know he was teaching us marketing, but there they were: white bunnies, green grass, and red wagon.

He went with us on a walk through the neighborhood. Kids began to follow us and ask if they could hold the bunnies. Soon the kids were demanding that we let them own bunnies for themselves!

As I recall, we bartered our first bunny for a marble collection including "cat's eye" shooters and even a couple "steelie shooters." We then took the rare marble collection and another fuzzy bunny and traded for a tricycle. We took the tricycle and another bunny and traded for a slick new scooter with a drag brake on the back wheel. On a little farther, surrounded by a lot of kids and some smiling parents, we took the scooter and another irresistible bunny and traded for a very handsome bicycle.

When we arrived back home we all agreed, "Today, everybody in our adventure ended up 'better off.'"

By the time my brothers Bill and Dave and I were in junior high and high school we were trading for automobiles. The major downside was none of us was old enough to have a driver's license. We would have to call home and explain that we had just traded for a Pontiac and needed some help driving it home.

I think my dad enjoyed seeing us grow into budding businessmen. He didn't say much about it, but when we would put a good deal together he would grin a lot.

My father was a dynamic speaker and a popular writer for the area newspapers. People loved his original oil paintings. In fact, he traded an oil painting for the mother rabbit he had used to teach us rabbity economics. Believe it or not, he could preach a supercharged sermon and paint a beautiful oil painting at the same time. He would give the picture away to someone in the congregation.

While World War II was winding down my dad got involved in the new radio business and had seven shows a week including the regional *Coca-Cola Hour*. Many times I would go to the studio with Dad, and he would have me sing to his unseen audiences. People would actually phone in and request to hear more of that "kid who sings."

Located on the outskirts of the towns where I grew up were Mexican labor camps where migrant workers lived. Local farmers built the camps to accommodate the seasonal crop workers and their families. My dad became fluent in Spanish, and in the evenings he would go to the camps and eat with the people. He would talk to them about spiritual things and ask them about their families back in Mexico, and then he would stand me on a box or a table and have me sing some songs—in Spanish—while he played the harmonica. I didn't know what I was singing, but I had learned lyrics phonetically and the people clapped and cheered.

When I was about five years old I even sang at a very large church in Berkeley, California, in front of a crowd that I thought was at least a "million" people. It was scary.

I loved the evenings at our house as my mother, Josie Jackson, created a soothing atmosphere that eventually sent us to sleep. After dinner, once all of our chores were finished, my mom would relax for half an hour by sitting down at the piano and playing her favorite songs. Josie Jackson was a dedicated school teacher and my father's church musician. She had started playing for church services at twelve years old when the regular piano player died suddenly. When her playing stopped, we kids all headed for the sofa. We would curl up around her and she would begin to read to us. Our home was always full of books and usually we got to choose the evening stories. It was in that setting that I first began to hear about other young boys who had overcome incredible obstacles to become great successes.

I learned about the Adventures of Andy, the Little Highlander boy, who had come to America from Scotland when he was twelve years old. He got a job running a small steam engine at a bobbin factory near Pittsburg. Soon he was keeping the company's books while going to night school. At age fourteen he became a runner for a telegraph office and then a telegraph operator. Sensing his promise, a rich man allowed him to use his books and personal library to study.

This highlander boy, Andrew Carnegie, worked very hard and became rich. He did not forget his origins, though. Everywhere he manifested sympathy for the poor, and deep interest in the happiness of his fellow men. Toward the end of his life he spent all his energy and riches building hospitals, schools, and scores of public libraries where other men and women and children could study and learn.

As a young boy, hearing such stories, I determined that I would be a millionaire by the time I was twenty-five years old. During my teen years I had read books, like Napoleon Hill's *Think and Grow Rich* and W. Clement Stone's books, *Success through a Positive Mental Attitude* and *The Success System That Never Fails*. My childhood vow took deeper root and would eventually become, for a time, my life's primary motivation.

I had the stories of Henry Ford, Cecil Rhodes, and William Carey nearly memorized, but something made my heart pound when I would listen to mom reading about John D. Rockefeller and Dwight L. Moody.

I identified right away with young Rockefeller because he had done with turkey eggs what I had done with bunnies. At age nine Johnny had gone into the forest and collected wild turkey eggs, and, with his mother's permission, had tended them until they hatched. He was able to take them to market and trade them for what he needed.

At age fourteen John's family moved to Cleveland, Ohio, and he attended good schools and graduated from Folsom's Commercial College. He told his family, "I must get involved in a church. I must find some way to become a useful member in a church."

At age fifteen he took money from his earnings and decided to help his church pay off its debt. He would stand at the entrance of the church as the members came in and encourage them to contribute toward paying off the debt. By the time he was twenty, John was on the church's board of trustees.

John started his career as an assistant bookkeeper at four dollars per week. Within three years he was promoted to head bookkeeper at a salary of five hundred dollars a year. "Work was honorable," he said, "and neither time nor money should be spent foolishly."

When he was twenty, John and a friend started a produce commission firm with their savings. In the neighboring state of Pennsylvania the first oil well in the United States was drilled. John and his friend went to view the well with the idea of starting a refining operation. Near the well site they had to cross a rotten log that spanned a mushy area. John fell off the log and came up completely covered with thick black oil tar. "Well," said his friend, "I see that you have plunged into the oil business head over heels."

Instead of spending his time idly with wild friends, John D. Rockefeller continued inviting people to his church where he served as Sunday school superintendent. He also continued to learn and invest in the new oil industry, eventually becoming president of Standard Oil Company, and the wealthiest man in the world.

In later years he focused on giving away his millions, not carelessly, but thoughtfully. He founded many organizations, including the Rockefeller Institute for Medical Research, to cure diseases.

I wanted to be just like those young boys who did well and loved God. One day on the way home from a morning at the radio station, I asked my dad if it was possible that Jesus wanted to come into *my* heart. On the radio program he had been talking about the love of Jesus. My dad pulled the big blue Buick over to the side of the road right then and prayed with me as I accepted Christ into my heart.

Dwight L. Moody's story had similarities to those of Carnegie and Rockefeller, but then swung from entrepreneurship in the business world to Christian mission. Dwight was born in 1837 in Northfield, Massachusetts.

His father died at the early age of forty-one, leaving his widow in poverty with the care of nine children. Their home had been heavily mortgaged. After the father's death, creditors swooped in and grabbed everything of value including the kindling wood.

Dwight's mother tried to keep her family together, and on Sundays they walked over a mile to get to church. To save wearing out the shoes, the children carried shoes and stockings in their hands until they got within sight of the church, then put them on.

Dwight left Northfield when he was seventeen in order to find work in Boston at a shoe store. He was an excellent salesman. One day his Sunday school teacher stopped by the shoe store. In the back room, surrounded by shoe boxes, Dwight accepted Christ. He wanted to get involved in the church, but the leaders suggested that he did not have enough education or experience.

Later, he moved to Chicago and became a successful shoe store owner. At his new church he began to invite people to go with him and even rented four church pews and filled them with his friends. He volunteered to teach a Sunday school class, but the leaders would not allow it. They told Dwight that he would have to go out and bring in brand new students if he wanted to teach.

Eventually, he went across Chicago to a poor area and started his own Sunday school class in a rented hall. He went into the neighborhood and visited families, offered to help them, and then invited them to his Sunday school. Within a short time his flock grew to one thousand six hundred members.

Dwight L. Moody sold his successful shoe business and went into religious work full-time. He was thirty years old. Other churches invited him to speak, and he even traveled to England, Scotland, and Ireland, attracting crowds of thirty to forty thousand. No fewer than 100 million people heard of the love of Jesus from the lips of Dwight L. Moody in his lifetime.

Moody never forgot sitting on a park bench in Dublin, where a man named Henry Varley told him, "The world has yet to see what God will do with and for and through and in and by the one man who is fully consecrated to Him."

Moody replied, "I want to be that man."

Why did that story thrill me every time I heard it? A lot of the old ladies in my dad's church received God's call for me that I was to be a preacher—and they all accepted! "Yup," they would say as they patted the top of my head, "that's Jimmy, our little red-haired preacher boy!"

I thought that might not be such a bad idea, since I knew the ropes, and where else could I get a job where I'd only have to work one day a week?

Later on, when my dad switched from preaching to teaching at a Christian college, our family traveled as a musical quartet with Mom playing the piano.

My greatest fan was the cute little Johnson girl, a beauty I had known since grade school. In fact, we had been born in the same hospital delivery room. We dated throughout high school. I played all the sports, and Anna Marie was the pretty cheerleader.

When I asked her to marry me, the only contingency to her acceptance was that I would sing to her at the altar in our marriage ceremony.

With her "yes," I had to get her dad's permission and blessing.

I went out to his farm not far from the Snake River in western Idaho. I found Keller Johnson in the barn with his head in the flank of a Jersey cow, stripping out the last squirts of milk.

"Hi," I said, awkwardly. "I'd like to talk to you about marrying Anna Marie. Would you give us your blessing?"

He reeled back on his one-legged milk stool and looked me in the eye. "You know, there's a lot of responsibility that goes along with that! Take finances for instance. And part of that is the cost of college education."

Her dad was about to paint me a picture. "You know her older siblings; we put away money for their education. Now Erma, her older sister, we paid for her private high school education, her college education, and her nurse's degree. Her older brothers, Howard and Floyd, we paid for their private high school education, college education, and their medical school costs as well, even their internships in orthopedic surgery. Mother and I have set aside money for Anna Marie's total education, but if you choose to marry her then all those responsibilities are totally yours. You make your bed and you lie in it!"

"I know," I said with a grin, "That's why I am here … I want to!"

4

I Was Afraid You Were Going to Ask

rue to his word, Anna Marie's father gave his blessing on our marriage and maintained his caveat that he would never provide any financial assistance. I liked it best that way. I even saw to it that we always paid for even the milk or eggs that came from the farm.

Down deep inside I knew that we could make it just fine. Anna Marie and I had both been blessed with a "can do" attitude and constitutions to match. I recalled from the boyhood success stories that Cecil Rhodes of African fame had detested the word "cannot" more than any other word in the English language.

My father had his own way of dealing with the "I can't" syndrome. Whenever he heard one, of his sons say this, he would make us sit down and figure out not one, but ten ways to do what we said we could not do. "You certainly would make it easier on yourself if you would simply figure out how to do it successfully the first time around," he would say.

It had never been difficult for the Jackson brothers—Bill, Dave, and me—to make money. Every year we became better at the entrepreneurial challenge of making other people "better off." I was able to pay all of Anna Marie's and my college expenses without ever taking out college loans.

I had declared my academic major as philosophy and religion. I never really felt a call to be a preacher; becoming a minister seemed more like a logical conclusion. From observation, I already knew how to "marry them and to bury them." I accumulated credits for twelve semester hours of Greek, and had fulfilled all the other requirements for ordination. I had successfully learned how to craft a sermon in homiletics class and had even won the annual Sermon Award Contest. And Anna Marie was already involved in the "shepherdess" program that instructed future pastors' wives how to act.

But there was always this gnawing feeling, *What if this is not what I am supposed to do?* Then I thought, *Lord, that doesn't make sense because I want to be totally dedicated to you and to help other people.* In terms of what I could imagine at the time, that meant I would need to be either a preacher, like my dad, or a missionary, like my uncles Bob or Chester. I had long decided I would rather be a preacher than a missionary.

I was holding down five different jobs simultaneously during our college days. My best paying job was one I held for six straight years. At four o'clock every morning I would pick up my bundles of the *Idaho Daily Statesman Newspaper*. Then, I would drive more than one hundred miles every morning delivering the papers in my Mercedes diesel car. I had to hurry in order to make it to my seven-thirty morning classes. When I slid into my class seat, I felt the satisfaction of knowing I had already earned more before breakfast than my professor would make all day.

Graduation approached and I was still unsure of my career path. I kept remembering how I had vowed since childhood to be a millionaire by the time I was twenty-five years old. To tell the truth, I felt more fulfilled making money than being a preacher boy.

I sought out my major professor and asked him for some objective advice. "How am I supposed to know if I have a 'call' to be a preacher?"

His answer startled me. "My advice to you is that if you can do anything else, and not go to hell, you had better do it."

What in the world did I just hear him say? I made a decision as I left the building: if there was a chance that I was not going to be a preacher, now would be the time to get qualified to do something else!

I went straight to the registrar's office. "What are the requirements," I asked, "to get a second major in secondary education, with teaching fields in English and history?"

I had to scramble! I had to complete the required methods classes, additional psychology classes, and queue up for a semester of supervised practice teaching. I managed this by attending three neighboring colleges simultaneously, then transferred all the credits and successfully graduated with my class having earned my double majors. While Anna Marie finished her degree, I enrolled in the nearby university and acquired a master's degree. Both of us received our teaching credentials from the State of Idaho.

All this didn't mean I knew what I was going to do.

Every four years our church denomination had a large convention called "General Assembly." That year it was held in Portland, Oregon, and Anna Marie and I attended. A distinguished gentleman, who had been a college chum of my dad's approached me. "I'm Dr. DePew, pastor of Denver First Church. Aren't you Jim Jackson?"

I shook his hand.

"I was hoping to see you here. What are you doing these days?" he asked.

I explained that I had finished my master's degree, and Anna Marie had completed her undergraduate work. "My English and speech professor wants me to go to Africa with the Peace Corps," I said. "My philosophy advisor wants me to go to seminary, and my education advisor is insisting that I enroll at the University of Oregon for a Ph.D. program."

"Let me solve your quandary and tell you what I think you ought to do," Dr. DePew said boldly. "I want you to come to Denver and be my minister of music. George and Esther are moving back to Des Moines. How soon could you come?"

"Let me pray about it and discuss it with Anna Marie and I will call you when I get home."

"Well," I said to Anna Marie as we drove back to Idaho, "We've been looking for a bolt from the sky. This seems to fit the criterion." We both felt that moving to Denver was the right thing to do.

I buttoned up all my little businesses and loaded all our belongings, including our energetic little two year old son, Douglas, into a GMC pickup. We even stuffed our Mercedes diesel full of clothes and hooked it on behind. Away we went to mysterious Colorado.

Our instructions were to locate the University of Denver campus, and, from there, to drive to 2000 South Milwaukee Street. We pulled our little convoy into the paved alley behind the church facility, walked to the pastor's study, and exuberantly shook hands with Dr. DePew. "Hi. We're here!"

"Uh, yes, yes ... please sit down, nice to have you here. Uh, we have a little problem ... the minister of music folks have decided not to move back to Des Moines ... nothing major ... I'm sure! You see ... another wonderful couple that serves as our ministers of youth and education, Wes and Vangie, will soon be leaving here and moving to Montana. If you don't mind switching hats, we will just move you right into that spot. I've checked out your qualifications and you are certainly qualified to do either. I knew it would be all right, so I didn't feel that I needed to talk to you until you got here."

I looked around the room, out the open door onto the patio area. I was nine hundred miles from home and wasn't in much of a bargaining position. "OK. Fine," I said, as my face grew hot and my pleasant expression kept buckling into a grimace.

"Oh, by the way," Dr. DePew added, "an elderly couple just moved out of our caretaker's quarters on the backside of the gymnasium. Why don't you, Anna Marie, and Douglas move your things into the apartment? It has only one small bedroom, but I'm sure you can make it work. It will be convenient and you can start locking and unlocking the facility. That way you can get acquainted with all the people in no time at all."

I reminded myself how my mother always said, "It's not the set of circumstances in which you find yourself, but how you respond that makes all the difference in the world."

That homey wisdom wasn't much help. This must have been how the boy Samuel felt getting dumped off at the temple. I wondered if Eli's place had an apartment and gymnasium attached?

Little Doug's crib wouldn't fit in the small bedroom with our bed. We took just the springs and mattress of his bed and placed them on a couple of cinder blocks. A least he couldn't hurt himself if he fell out of bed!

About six weeks later I was unlocking the church and ran into the pastor. "How is the plan coming along? I need to talk to you about the progress," I inquired.

"I was afraid you were going to ask. You see, our youth and education folks have decided not to move to Montana. Not until their kids graduate from Englewood High School. Sorry it didn't all work out better. You can stay in the caretaker's quarters for a while if you want to."

"OK … fine," I said. It was far from "fine," of course. I could hear Satan laughing at me. Why didn't the pastor tell me what was happening? Why no communication? Why had we felt so strongly that we were to move to Denver? Why did God bring us nine hundred miles away from home to dump us? Time had run out for us to apply for teaching jobs.

As the Colorado winter sky began to get dark and gray and heavy, so did my heart. For one of the first times in my life I began to question God, and certainly the integrity of His people.

With no income, I did what I needed to do. I sold my Mercedes and my GMC pickup. The "can do" training began to kick in, and I bought copies of *The Denver Post* and *Rocky Mountain News* newspapers, pulled out the "Classified" sections, and started trading—not rabbits this time but automobiles, right out of the alley behind the church.

Maybe, just maybe, God wanted me to move to Denver, but not necessarily to that church! I didn't know what to think, really, except that I had a responsibility to my family.

5

Hardball Banking

Before long my eldest brother Bill and my middle brother Dave moved to Denver as well. It was like taking the bookmark out of our story of working together and continuing the adventure. We soon decided to go into the automobile business as partners. We only had to obtain a license and a location, and we wasted no time doing so. We were all young and could afford to take risks because we had nothing financially to lose. We named our new venture, Denver Auto Mart, Inc., and our approach, if not unique, was gutsy.

We started buying cars from all over Colorado and the surrounding states—Nebraska, Wyoming, and Oklahoma. Then we brought them into our reconditioning facility. That required buying our own auto transport semitrailers and acquiring transportation permits. We equipped the business to take previously owned cars and make them look new: tires, upholstery, body, paint, and mechanics. Then we would transport these "cream puffs" to hungry retail dealers around the country.

I had met some nice people at the church before Anna Marie and I moved out of the dinky apartment. We decided to continue to attend there in spite of having what seemed to be a sharp stick poked in our eyes. We upped the church attendance through bringing along all the cousins and college kids we hired to help at Denver Auto Mart.

One day a Latino fellow named Jesse Marquez wandered in to buy a station wagon. He had three of his little kids with him. I thought of the story of Dwight L. Moody and asked the kids if they would ever to go to Sunday school with us. They were excited at the prospect!

The next Sunday we went to the government housing projects and picked them up. Jesse was all smiles and said there were other kids in the projects who wanted to go with us the next week. Then the guys at work wanted to get involved in helping take kids from the projects to Sunday school.

I went to Pastor DePew, and he loved the idea of bringing as many of the kids to the Sunday school as possible. "The denomination is presently putting pressure on all of us to show increases in our attendance. This will be good."

We started devoting our Saturdays to walking the streets and alleys of the projects, asking moms and dads for permission to pick up their children. Occasionally, I would have a quick flashback of my standing on a box singing in the Mexican labor camps in Idaho while my dad played his harmonica. Soon we had to chip in and rent a couple of buses. Our wives got busy helping out the Sunday school departments.

All was well for about nine months, and I knew Dwight L. Moody would have been proud of us. The pastor began to cool, though, because there was some grumbling in the ranks. "Things were a lot better and a lot easier the way they were before," said the head of the primary department. "I don't know why we have to assume the responsibility of other peoples' kids. This church has its hands full just getting our own kids to heaven."

The whispers became a brush fire and went out of control. "These project kids are using up all our materials and we don't even feel safe anymore sitting on the toilets. Can you even imagine all the diseases these new kids are exposing us to? We never want to see these project kids back here again!"

I completely lost respect for the pastor when he used the tragedy to enhance his own reputation. During a card game in the projects, at which there had been drinking, the uncle of some of our kids stood up, pulled a gun, and killed the kids' dad. The church completely failed to react—no compassion, no reaching out, nothing. Our pastor did respond, in a fashion. He had never stepped foot once inside the projects, but he managed to write a sterling article for the denominational Sunday school magazine describing the shooting and how the church was addressing the violent world of the projects. It described how good it was for him and the church to have reached out with great compassion and love to these people in the streets. The denomination loved it, but something broke inside my heart.

"I'm really wasting my time here," I said to Anna Marie. "These people are disconnected from *reality*. Keep Douglas and baby Jay in the church, but as for me, I'm going to spend my time working. That way, I can do a lot more for people *who actually care*."

Quickly—with astonishing speed, in fact—the further I went from the church the more I appreciated the "fringe benefits": the wealth I began to accumulate. That's not how I thought it was supposed to work. I had thought those who were pure in heart would be successful and wealthy with God's rich blessing. Now the more distance I put between religion and me the more successful I became. The old conflict between becoming a preacher and a millionaire completely disappeared. I didn't spend twenty seconds worrying about it.

I wondered to myself, *Is this why most people don't want to get mixed up in a church?* I thought that by bringing disadvantaged kids to Sunday school that everybody would be better off and everybody would be happy. But the church people obviously didn't feel better off because the new kids were using up the crayons and messing up the bathrooms. I didn't have to worry about all that anymore. I was going to concentrate on making money.

At last, I felt comfortable with a single purpose as I focused on accumulation. Our business was growing, and our assets were increasing. My energies were channeled, and we were creating new opportunities all the time—not just taking advantage of the obvious ones.

I had to laugh at myself, however, whenever I would pull out the checkbook and pay my tithe to an institutionalized organization that I didn't like. What was that all about? But that's what I felt I ought to do.

Was it really possible that I would be a millionaire by the time I was twenty-five? It looked like it!

One of the contracts we took on during the heady Denver Auto Mart days was with a man from Taiwan named Jimmy Chu. He paid us handsomely to dismantle some very large pieces of US military surplus at the Tooele Army Depot in Utah. We used our semitrailers to deliver the items to the docks in San Francisco. We were then instructed to ship the goods on separate boats to Taiwan.

I was the crane operator. On two different occasions sections of the crane's boom buckled and I was nearly killed. Shortly afterwards, we had an accident in one of the semitrailers and I narrowly escaped death. In my exuberance and independence I was caught short with a stern message from God. "Just a reminder: I can have your life anytime I want it!"

Was it time to do some more processing? Was that the "hound of heaven" chasing me?

My brothers and I were having a grand time as young, energetic entrepreneurs. However, there were a lot of things about business that we had not learned traipsing through the neighborhood with our red "Radio Flyer" wagon. One day we received a phone call from our banker. "I have a good opportunity for you to sell your five-acre facility and make a quick return, and I think you ought to take it."

He was not only the president of the bank, but was also the head of the Chamber of Commerce committee for business growth in our city.

Our curt answer was, "No, thanks. We like what we've got and we think we'll keep it."

His answer: "We'll see."

What we didn't know was that the city was trying to persuade Andersen Windows to set up a manufacturing facility in Colorado. On one of their trips to Colorado the Andersen people had spotted our industrial location, which was fenced, paved, and close to a rail spur. They mentioned to our bank president that if they could get that location they could probably be persuaded to make the move. The bank president told them that he was quite sure he could deliver the site. It would be a nice feather in his cap and mean a lot of new business for his bank.

Our bank president was aware that we had purchased our location from his bank out of a bankruptcy situation. He knew what we had paid for the property and that we were vulnerable, since he controlled our mortgage and all of the financing on our inventories and business. He followed his "we'll see" with a telegram informing us that our interest rates on all our financing had just doubled.

In our very best display of inexperience, youthful exuberance, and ignorance, we jumped into our car, drove to the bank, and informed him, "You can't do that to us!"

We had hardly re-entered our office when we received another telegram notifying us that our entire financing package had been "called" and was now due and payable. Everything was "frozen." Suddenly we realized that we could not buy or sell from our inventory because we could not get any collateral releases even if we owned the equity. They held the titles and controlled our accounts. We had no wiggle room.

Our expenses did not stop, of course, and we still had those sticky obligations like paying the salaries of our relatives and friends. Everyone else's life went on just fine, but we were eating cornmeal mush for dinner and fresh carrots for breakfast, because we believed the bosses always pay their help first. At one point I had mortgaged our personal furniture at three different places to continue to make payroll.

We made an appointment with an attorney to get some advice. He smiled at us from behind his desk and said, "This is the way you handle an act of arbitrary and capricious aggression like you have here. You simply take out bankruptcy. Since your automobiles—the bank's collateral—happen to be scattered all over the western United States, you simply let him have the experience of trying to find them and tote them home again to get his money."

Then he added with a smirk, "Or, you just might try suicide!"

We told him that we didn't like the suicide suggestion, and since we were going to be around Colorado for a long time we wouldn't be filing for bankruptcy. (After this meeting my brother Dave decided to go to law school at the University of Denver, pass the bar, and become the attorney for the family. We realized that if we were going to be in business we would need much better advice than what had been offered by that guy!)

We began selling and trading whatever we had that was not tied to a frozen loan. We had to keep floating. The banker was eagerly waiting to foreclose on us so that he could deliver our property to Andersen Windows. He was strangling us to death.

Before the plug could be pulled, we found a steel company who purchased our property right out from under the banker's nose, letting us make even more out of the deal than we could have expected. We were badly bruised but not dead. We were then free to sell the rest of our assets, and pay off all our debts without even a "slow" on our credit. We also took some of the proceeds and set our cousins and friends up in their own business so they were no longer dependent on us.

The three Jackson brothers had learned some big lessons in the hardball world of business. We could have rolled over and played dead, but we were still alive and kicking.

During this time we often gathered at a restaurant, close to our business, which still offered coffee for a dime a cup. We analyzed our situation and dreamt. The conversations were extraordinary. Maybe what had just happened to us was the best thing possible. Hadn't Edison used his defeats to make him more successful? Alexander Graham Bell constantly went over his failures so that he and Watson could at last find success.

Bill reminded us of the time our dad had told him to tie his tennis shoe. "I can't," said Bill. "I don't have a shoe lace." Thereupon, our dad had Bill sit down and figure out ten ways to tie his shoe instead of just one way.

Let's look at where we are, we thought. *Maybe it is not the wise thing to rebuild our automobile business. Maybe there is a better way.* We were becoming successful, but the profit on automobiles would always be limited. So, we thought, *Why aren't we involved in something like real estate development where, for the same effort, the margin of return is so much greater?*

6

Making Money

"Oh, my goodness," my brother Bill exclaimed. "The lieutenant governor is dizzy drunk!" So was "Topper," his brother-in-law.

It was Memorial Day and we had driven to a dude ranch in the Winter Park ski area of Colorado. During the Denver Auto Mart days, when our financial guns were still blazing, we had tried to purchase the ranch. But in the meantime, the lieutenant governor and Topper had purchased the property and had subdivided about a third of it. The ranch was strategically located on the Fraser River with a panoramic view of the ski slopes. They had accomplished the rezoning, platting, and building of the roads for a subdivision. But they had become financially overextended when they had hired Mile High Pipe Line to develop the water and sewer district and lay the pipes. Now the lieutenant governor and Topper were in foreclosure for nonpayment. We had heard that they were in trouble, so we drove up to talk to them about their project and tried to explain that we could help them.

The lieutenant governor could only slur out, "Come to my office at the State Capitol Building on Wednesday to talk."

The re-evaluation sessions my brothers and I had over cups of ten-cent coffee helped us decide to keep the corporate structure of the Denver Auto Mart, but not to rebuild the automobile business. We had decided to turn our entrepreneurial efforts to specializing in real estate development and sales in the recreational areas of the Colorado Rocky Mountains. In the mid 1960s the ski craze was just getting ready to explode in Colorado.

During the lucrative days of Denver Auto Mart we had managed to purchase the Virginia Villa Motel on US Highway 40 in the ski area of Winter Park. We could now begin in earnest to redevelop the property. We set out to win the authority to build the US Post Office on one corner of the property, thereby guaranteeing that our site would always be the center of the town.

We needed additional inventories of residential, condominium, and commercial sites to round out our package. So, following his drunken instructions, we showed up at the gold-domed Colorado State Capitol on Wednesday to talk to the lieutenant governor. He was sober and open to our suggestions. After convincing him and his partners that we could successfully market the development, we entered into an agreement that allowed us to pre-purchase sites in bulk, with a rolling option that allowed us the freedom to purchase the rest of the development at our own pace.

"Jackson Brothers Investments" had now begun in earnest! We were fully engaged in the recreational real estate business in exciting and majestic Colorado. Within two weeks we had sold enough lots to satisfy the foreclosure demands that had plagued our new partners. Everyone was better off!

Also about that time we got involved in another ski area near Denver, called Vail. We were at the right place at the right time to get involved. People were still wondering if this new Vail area would ever become successful, so we were able to buy property at about $127 an acre as sheep pasture. That same land cannot be purchased today at any price; it can only be leased on a long-term basis—it's that valuable.

We now had spectacular real estate inventories in Colorado. The vehicle that would take us to the bank still turned out to be "rabbit transit"— our expertise in bartering. In the next few years we developed a marketing niche that made us very wealthy in a relatively short period of time.

The US government had approved an inclusion in the Internal Revenue Tax Code referred to as the "1031 Exchange Clause." As long as you were trading up from a lower to a higher value in a commodity, such as investment real estate, you were allowed to postpone paying taxes on any gains in the value of the real estate until the capstone holding was cashed out, liquidated. Then you would have to declare value on the transaction and pay the tax.

In the 1960s and 1970s almost no one understood the provision. In fact, almost no one even knew the provision existed. But the power of trading a less valuable asset for a more valuable asset, without putting more cash into the new property, multiplied the investor's leverage incredibly. We would simply point out the provision to the client's tax advisors. Then we would tell them that we were not tax professionals, but they could look up the clause for themselves and see if their situation would fit within the parameters of the exemption.

Let me see if I can use a simple example to illustrate the process:

Let's say a group of doctors owned a large medical building together. They had a lot of equity in the building, and some of the partners wanted to sell. Others did not because of tax liabilities—they would end up paying the government more than they found acceptable. There would be friction between the partners, which would only grow worse. Soon even their wives wouldn't be seen at parties together.

Jackson Brothers Investments would seat the doctors around a table and tell them we could solve their problem. We were going to take the medical building off their hands. In return, the first doctor would receive for his equity stake two condominium sites overlooking the ski slopes, three residential sites in the back filing, and a 7-Eleven store in Denver. The next doctor would receive three condominium sites overlooking the ski slopes, one residential site in the back filing, and a vacant commercial building in Colorado Springs. On around the table we would go with each doctor.

When we were finished with the allocation process, we would tell them that upon closing the transaction they would be free to do anything they wanted to with the individual properties. If they wanted to cash out, they could do that at their discretion at any time and pay their tax on the sale of whatever portion of the package they had received. For those who wanted to continue to hold their position, they could do so, having postponed their tax consequence, plus they were now released from the inconvenience of their old partnership. They would walk away with freedom and some great assets, and we would walk away with a beautiful medical building—plus we would have sold a large group of multiple sites in our development, all in one transaction.

The novel problem-solving process quickly caught on. Soon we were accumulating office buildings, mobile home parks, warehouses, homes, apartment complexes, and retail shopping center properties. If we needed cash, we would simply go down and put a mortgage on one of the properties we had received and let the tenants pay off the loan over time.

It wasn't very long before our reputation became widely known. Estate attorneys began contacting us, as they often dealt with squabbling family members who owned properties jointly.

People asked, "Who are these creative Jackson Brothers who would solve problems by allowing people to take pristine development ground in Colorado's finest ski areas in exchange for their headaches?"

I could sense that the game we were pursuing had a dangerous side to it. I was a typical type-A personality and was becoming addicted to the game of accumulation. There was an incredible adrenalin rush to it. I was gaining a certain confidence that I could find a solution to almost any problem and that I could always get exactly what I needed to put a deal together. I pictured myself standing in a river with money flowing toward me like water. As a child I had determined that I would be a millionaire by age twenty-five. By age thirty I was sixteen times wealthier than I had ever hoped to be in my lifetime. And that was using the 1960s and 1970s value of money, when you could buy a three-bedroom brick bungalow with an attached garage for thirteen thousand dollars.

The troubling thing was that along the way I had not seen that just because I had the abilities to earn and accumulate wealth for myself, exercising those gifts on my own behalf—or even my family's—wouldn't necessarily make me a happy man.

I would be sitting in a nice restaurant over dinner, and my mind would go back to the stories of my childhood heroes introduced through the books my mother read to her sons. Those heroes seemed to be a happy lot because they "did well" in order to "do good." I was doing really well, but I wasn't necessarily doing good. In the deals I was putting together everybody was ending up better off—financially. But I wasn't helping them—or me, for that matter—to become better people. I was putting together wonderful financial packages for the type of rich young adults called "trust babies." They hadn't a care in the world, really, to begin with. What was I doing with my life?

We helped to develop a project in the Steamboat Springs ski area. In order to fly the county commissioners around to see the plan, we rented a helicopter at two thousand dollars an hour. I sat there and realized that our approval was going to be based on how it affected the adjoining property that, coincidently, belonged to a couple of the county commissioners. That style of business did not make me happy.

In our business dealings we ended up with a lot of high-energy, testosterone-driven moguls as partners. They were fun to be with, but the more I studied them the more I concluded that they were not happy people. If they were not conquering a million dollar deal, they were conquering their secretary or somebody else's wife. None of them had successful home lives.

I watched my brother Bill get caught up in the chase and eventually go through three divorces and other sad relationships. One of his affairs nearly landed all of us in jail.

My brother began dating a woman who became an agent in our real estate brokerage. She needed a place to live. We had a cute house in the Polo Club area, and she had been allowed to move in. Then she spotted a lovely home we had in Evergreen, and she was able to purchase the property, with Jackson Brothers Investments carrying back a significant second mortgage. Well, when the romantic relationship cooled, Bill's girlfriend expected to be paid off. She demanded the total forgiveness of the second mortgage.

Brother Dave, as our attorney, told her, "Go fly a kite."

The woman went to another attorney, with whom she had a previous relationship. In the process of "consoling her," he advised that by employing hardball tactics, and going to the local newspapers and television with a criminal complaint, he could bring the Jackson Brothers to their knees. He thought we would be happy to settle quickly for the forgiveness of the note out of court.

But we didn't. That's when things got sticky.

My brother knew that the woman was intelligent, but he had underestimated her "street smarts." The court took handwriting samples, and, believe it or not, her handwriting did not match the signatures on the note and deed of trust. It looked like her signature had been forged. With that they leveled the indictment. The prosecuting attorney went with a conspiracy-to-commit-forgery charge, which meant the state did not have to prove that any particular person had signed the documents. We could have been convicted of a felony.

My nights in bed were spent staring at the ceiling. A reputation is like a flask of water knocked over in the desert: a terrible thing to lose, almost impossible to recover. What kind of justice would it be if they could make this stick?

Before the Jackson brothers went to trial, I had a serious talk in our upstairs family room with my two preteen boys and Anna Marie. I had just been given papers by a court process server. Their uncle Bill had been involved with an attractive woman, and she was accusing the three Jackson brothers of felony conspiracy to commit forgery. I fumbled around trying to explain how a woman who is giving a man what he wants out of wedlock may eventually demand something in return. I told them I had not been involved in any wrongdoing, nor had I any knowledge of any wrongdoing, but they needed to know that I would have to go to prison if convicted. Their eyes were huge. My heart was in my throat.

They told me that there had been a suspicious white pickup truck driving slowly back and forth in front of our house recently. I couldn't think what that had to do with anything, but it was creepy. My protective advice was that they not talk to any strangers in our neighborhood.

The jury was seated, and the attorneys opened with their legal statements. The trial proceeded amid charts, graphs, magnified writing samples, and wild accusations by the prosecutors.

Finally, the time came for our defense. In his opening remarks our attorney provided information that Bill's former girlfriend was ambidextrous. He promised to offer proof, based on other documents from our brokerage files, that she usually wrote with her left hand, but occasionally she signed documents with her right hand. Her right hand signature would match those on the note and deed.

Before our defense attorney could get started presenting our case, the judge ordered a recess and summoned the defendants and all the attorneys into his chambers. He severely reprimanded the prosecutors and especially the former girlfriend's chummy attorney. "I have never before in my tenure directed the jury to an outcome. But this is cruel and an embarrassment to the court."

Thereupon, we all went back into the courtroom where he issued a rendering of acquittal, slammed down his gavel and dismissed the jury.

Our acquittal still cost us about two hundred and fifty thousand dollars in legal fees. The scandal also negatively affected our reputation. I would never forget how my parents had to hear of the criminal indictment and see newspapers with the headline, "Jackson Brothers Indicted." I was learning lessons about having wealth and a high profile. As the Africans would explain to me years later, "The higher the baboon climbs up in the tree, the more he exposes his rear end." What was this millionaire ambition all about, really?

I was painfully coming to the realization that I had been sold a false dream. Whatever it was that we were all chasing would never be caught. I would never be allowed to drink the water from the seductive mirage. I fought tooth and nail to keep from reaching that conclusion. All I needed to do was go out and put another, even bigger, deal together. That should solve that! In my quiet times, however, I had to admit such compulsive behavior made me an addict. I was addicted to the accumulation game. I was doing well, but I wasn't doing good!

Part of my salvation was that I was married to Anna Marie, my pretty cheerleader and best friend. I mentioned before that we had been born in the same hospital delivery room and had grown up knowing each other. I think I had fallen in love with her when she was in the second grade. She knew me better than anyone else and knew that I had become deeply unhappy. We would talk about what was happening and what we were feeling.

"I'm on this freeway," I'd say. "I don't think that I like where we are going, but we sure are getting there at a breakneck speed. I haven't seen an exit sign for the last one hundred miles."

"When were we happy?" Anna Marie asked, directly. After a soul-searching discussion we came to the conclusion that we were happy when we were young, doing exciting things, but had nothing. But we couldn't go back or couldn't start over again. What would guarantee that we would make any better choices the next time around?

Anna Marie had dutifully and consistently kept our two boys in the same church we had attended. I hadn't gone to church for a long time. And, quite frankly, I couldn't have cared less. It was simply too painful to think about the bad experiences there. One day Anna Marie mentioned that the old pastor was leaving and that the church had invited another man to come. "Would you like to come with the boys and me and have a listen?"

I agreed to go, but then considered it a bad decision. We were sitting on an outside aisle next to the stained glass windows. The new guy came across the front of the church—white suit, white tie, with the most bodacious and arrogant "seminary strut" I had ever seen. "Oh, Lord, save us from your followers," I muttered softly. The first visit back certainly didn't "take."

Throughout the next few weeks, I drove our Grand Mercedes 600 Limousine back and forth to the developments in the ski areas, I would catch myself trying to figure out what I truly wanted. *How much wealth is enough? Where should I be when I'm 50 years old?*

I couldn't avoid seeing any longer that I was addicted to accumulation. I thought about the possibilities of a cure. It would be worthless for me to say, "OK, next year I will cut back by 10 percent, and the next year I will cut back another 10 percent, and eventually I will be out of it." That would not work for me. This insight made me physically ill. I had this sensation behind my eyes and throat that almost made me throw up. I somehow knew that if there were to be any real changes I would probably have to go "cold turkey" just like any other addict.

One night, while staying in one of the condominium units at our Winter Park development, I got up after everyone else had gone to bed. The embers were still glowing in the fireplace. I told God that I was sorry for being such a selfish jerk. I prayed that if He would let me out of the squirrel cage and out of the accumulation game and just let me be a simple man again, I would never use my talents and abilities to accumulate wealth for myself. I would use my talents and abilities to help other people. I felt that He forgave me.

Upon waking, my first thought was to get with Anna Marie and share with her what had happened. I also knew that I needed to get with a neutral person, share with him, and ask him to help me be accountable. The arrogant new pastor came to my mind. I felt I should go see him. That about messed up the whole process before it even got started. I really didn't want to do that. Then I thought, *Maybe this process is being made difficult in order to see if I am really serious, or just playing a head game.*

I told my brother that I was going to Denver for a little while and would be back later. I got behind the driver's wheel and headed over Berthoud Pass to the church near the University of Denver. The pastor was, oh, so very happy to get linked up with the Jackson Brothers. Over a cup of coffee he began to tell me of his plans to build a really *big* church and wanted to know if I would help him.

Before long I was getting involved again in the church. It was kind of a strange thing. My brothers, who still didn't want anything to do with the institution, began to encourage me to spend time there, especially in the music program. Were they still interested in doing good as well?

As a curious serendipity, the new pastor had hired one of my high school and college chums from Idaho to be the minister of music. Ken Tippitt and I had started singing together in a quartet when I was in the eighth grade and Ken was in the seventh grade. Our quartet was good, and we performed around the state and even won competitions. Who would have thought we would be singing together again in our thirties? We added another guy to the group, and before long we had received a recording contract with a Capitol custom label and a recording date at the famous Whitney Recording Studio in California. Little did we know that the recording from that session would end up being pre-nominated for a coveted Grammy award—a new group called the Carpenters beat us out!

At a later time, in preparation for another recording date, our group was rehearsing nearly every night. It was about one o'clock in the morning when we finished practicing. I headed for our home in Evergreen, Colorado, which is in the mountains about forty-five minutes west of Denver, driving my huge Mercedes Grand 600 Limo Sedan.

The memory of that March 12, 1973 night will never become dim in my mind for as long as I live. I can still remember the smell of the rich leather of the car and the spectacular view as I turned onto the road over Indian Hills. The Colorado sky had just dumped more than two feet of snow before the fickle jet stream had snatched away the clouds and shuttled them to Chicago. The sky was perfectly clear. At our hometown's

8,000 foot elevation, I could see bright stars extending right down to the peaks of the fourteen thousand-foot mountains along the Continental Divide. The fresh snow on the blue spruce trees sparkled like prized Antwerp diamonds; the individual flakes reflected the rays of the full winter moon.

I reached over and turned off the radio and started talking to God and telling Him how grateful I was for what He was doing in my life and in the lives of Anna Marie and our boys, Doug and Jay. The whole car was filled with an awesome presence. I felt that if I dared glance over to the plush passenger's seat I would see God Himself sitting there. I didn't need to look because I felt him speaking to my soul, *Jim do you really love Me?*

"Of course, I love you, Lord," I said. "Don't You remember where I have been all night? Of course I love You, or I wouldn't be here."

Jim, would you love Me if I took everything that you have accumulated away from you?

By that time the warm tears were freely coursing down my face as I tried to keep that big car on the road. As I thought about the question, the assets on our financial statement began to scroll down: office buildings, mobile home parks, warehouses, apartments, development properties—the works.

Then the answer snapped into focus. "Sure, God, I'd love You the same even if You took them all away, because we started out with less than nothing, and now I know the formulas and know the right people, and I'm sure that I could get them all back again if given a little time."

That answer wasn't exactly the one He wanted to hear. It was real quiet for a while.

Son, if I took even your abilities to accumulate for yourself away from you, would you love Me the same as you love Me tonight?

My heart almost stopped beating. In a split second it dawned on me as to what was happening. God didn't want anything I had. He just wanted me! If He had me, He would have everything I would ever have. I was crushed that I had not seen what He was getting at before. I wept without reserve as I tried to keep the big Mercedes on the road. I prayed a lot more as I drove those last snow-packed miles to home.

I parked the car in the garage and stood for a long time overlooking the frozen lake. "God, if You really want to do business, I'm ready to do business with You."

I made my way into the beautiful living room of our home. I sat down and took out a piece of paper and a pen. "Please, God, be faithful to me. If there is anything that would alter or hinder or block the flow of Your life or Your ministry through me, please show it to me and I will write it down and take care of it…anything You want me to do."

Divesting myself from all my holdings would be my first priority. Second was to go to my brother Bill to explain my new direction in life. Third was to go to a bookstore and buy my attorney brother, David, a new Living Bible. Other resolutions on the list were to write personal letters to a number of my clients and friends, explaining to them what was happening in my life.

It was about three o'clock in the morning. I was physically and emotionally drained, but I slept well. The next morning I got up, and there on the dresser was that same crazy piece of paper with the eleven things that I had written on it a few hours before. In a flash I recalled the entire evening.

Satan was also there in the bedroom that morning. He was laughing like an idiot at me. *What do you think you are doing? You don't have to be this serious about this whole thing. Name me anyone else you know who has had to be this serious about his commitment to God. You can get by with a lot less, right? Who doesn't?*

Even as the taunting continued, I grabbed the paper, shoved it into my suit jacket pocket, and headed down to our offices at Jackson Brothers Investments. I somehow knew that what all had transpired was deadly serious business.

7

The Garden of Gethsemane

After I recommitted my life to Christ, I quickly integrated into church life and soon held a number of leadership positions. The story of this second attempt to be a good, conventional Christian would prove even more fraught with damaging consequences than my first brief flirtation with ministry. But, Anna Marie and I were serious about depending on God, rather than material possessions, for our happiness.

Soon after I had written my list of eleven things God wanted me to do, Anna Marie and I set into motion the process of giving away all our accumulated assets. I think my boys missed the Bentley automobiles the most. I was sensing a feeling of happiness and fulfillment I had never known before—an unspeakable feeling of freedom.

I recalled the classic story of Rees Howells when God had urged him to pay off a struggling friend's rent debt that had accumulated for two years. After Howells had obeyed and paid off the debt, he walked back to the friend's home with him, and when he left him it seemed that all the joy of heaven came down on Howells. He felt joy in waves that his soul could not contain. He claimed that the incident changed his life and his attitude toward the world, toward his friends, and toward his giving. From that time on he said he could not help but give to those in need. "I live to give" became his motto.

We began giving to our college alma mater, which was involved in raising money and erecting buildings on campus. We gave to missionaries, needy religious organizations, Jewish causes, care centers for the elderly, and all sorts of denominational pleas.

Then the new pastor—I'll simply call him the Rev. Dr. Dimsdale—came to call. He wanted someone to help him build his new megachurch. Over a series of lunches and coffees, and across the desk in our Jackson Brothers Investments office, he would explain how he wanted a new kind of music program, maybe a TV show, lots of programs for the families, and exciting singing trips for the teens.

Then he hit on a raw nerve of mine. "I want to hire a full-time pastor who would do nothing but go to the Mexican projects and bring the poor kids on buses to our Sunday school!"

He obviously hasn't talked to the department leaders of the Sunday school yet, I thought to myself. They won't appreciate having "all the crayons ruined and the toilets infected." But maybe this guy could pull it off. I remembered how I sure couldn't.

One of my brothers, caustic and unconvinced, complained that the good reverend was suffering from an "Edifice complex."

To his credit, Brother Dimsdale hired a full-time "bus pastor" and started hauling the kids in from the city projects to his church. *Maybe the guy is for real,* I thought, and felt bad that my first reactions had been shallow and unfair.

But, wow, was he ever sensitive when he saw us giving away our assets to other organizations! He was nearly in a panic that there would be none left for his megachurch.

It did ease the situation when he found 10.6 acres in the finest part of town for a new church site, and Anna Marie and I came up with more than a third of the money in cash for the property. I started getting more and more involved in the church. The same was true of my brothers, Bill and Dave. The more they started giving to the church, the more they became involved.

For a few years, while we were still in the old church facility, there was a real spirit of excitement, dedication, and growth. Attendance had been running from two hundred fifty to three hundred. Then it doubled, and on certain occasions the fire marshal would have to scold us because our crowds were too big for the facilities.

I even became the executive director of the television program.

Then I remembered the story of young Dwight L. Moody and how he had started his own Sunday school class that eventually grew to about one thousand six hundred—the beginning of his worldwide ministry.

Anna Marie and I started a young married couples class with six in attendance and watched it grow. The three Jackson brothers would sometimes air our mutual feeling that the Rev. Dr. Dimsdale was without doubt the most insecure person with whom we had ever dealt. Perhaps he needed men like us to support him, though, and then he wouldn't need to be so insecure.

Plans were made to build a new facility on the 10.6 acres with a sanctuary that would seat two thousand five hundred people, with educational facilities to match. The price tag was high, and no lending institution was going to lend a congregation of six hundred enough money to build. At a breakfast meeting with Rev. Dr. Dimsdale, the Jackson brothers agreed to make available anything left in our inventory of warehouses, office buildings, mobile home parks, houses, raw land, or whatever would be needed to build the facilities.

We soon saw some of our properties become a custom-made Allen organ designed with five computers and all the new technology that was available. We traded for literally acres of new carpet, stonework, custom-designed ceilings, stucco, custom-designed sound and recording systems, windows, wood, concrete, sod, trees, sprinkler systems, bushes, and flowers. I rejoiced along with the classic spiritual writer Oswald Chambers who proclaimed, "I am God's and He is carrying out His enterprises through me."[1]

Rev. Dr. Dimsdale told us he wanted to protect us by never letting anyone else know that we had given all the things to the building of the church, saying, "It just wouldn't be good." Instead, he would say, "I was able to get all this done and paid for. Isn't that marvelous?"

Pretty soon Anna Marie and I had run out of assets. We were common folk just like everyone else. We had told God that we would give it all away, and we did!

The only thing that we still had left was our home in the mountains. Anna Marie, the boys, and I had all agreed that we would be willing to part with the house and move into a rental if need be. We had tried to give the house away, but each time our efforts were somehow blocked. It was bewildering. Why couldn't we give away such a comfortable home? Maybe it was the mortgage. One night we had come home and parked the car in the garage. Douglas and his mother had walked ahead and into the house. Jay tagged along with me as we walked along the creek. I had my arm around him, and he looked up at me and said, "You know Dad, we are really lucky."

"Why do you say that, Jay?" I asked.

"Well, because God let us stay at our house one more week, didn't He?"

A change came about as soon as we moved from our old church facilities into the new megachurch. We began hearing sermons on the theme, "Love is not a sentiment. It is a strategy."

Well, soon everything started becoming a strategy. Rather than trying to figure how we could help the poor and needy, we were spending our energies and creativity on sharpening our image and perfecting worship services as entertainment, in order to attract more people into our magnificent facility. It was no longer convenient to run the buses into the projects and bring in the kids; we had an image to keep up.

One day Rev. Dr. Dimsdale grinned as he told me, "These people will always love me if I continue giving them big concerts, dinner dramas, TV exposure, and a beautiful facility for their identity." He was dead right.

The next great themes became unity and greatness. "God made greatness, therefore greatness can't be wrong," the preacher admonished us.

"Greatness is obtainable with unity. God says that with unity anything is possible. What price would you pay for unity?"

Quite a high price, evidently, as now the church was running one thousand five hundred in attendance and continuing to grow in numbers. It had become big enough, not only to be attractive, but also to hurt people. If you didn't believe in unity and greatness, you were not tolerated, but squeezed out. I watched the victims leave quietly out the back door.

Our ideas of getting close to Rev. Dr. Dimsdale, supporting him, and helping him achieve his dream had not cured his insecurities and arrogance at all. We had only been enablers and inflamed the problem. I struggled with that, but kept holding on to the hope that our influence would be strong enough to encourage the pastor to change.

I recalled listening to conversations about how nearly all organizations, especially churches, go through a process of "institutionalization." Usually there is a leader with a dream who is endowed with a measure of energy and sincere persuasion. He gets connected with a group of equally sincere and motivated people who are open to pursue something new and rewarding. The leader becomes a prophetic figure. He rallies the people and points them in the direction of the goal.

Very soon the people don't want to settle for just a prophet, they demand a king! The leader willingly complies and seeks to measure up to this expectation. Once the leader gets a taste of being king, he eventually feels entitled, with the support of the people, to graduate to the position of "messiah," the one with a direct line to God that removes him from the need for accountability. Now, the people become the messiah's disciples ready to carry out his dictates, seeing whatever he desires as righteous.

By helping Rev. Dr. Dimsdale build the largest, most extravagant edifice in the denomination, we had helped elevate the man from prophet to king to white-shod demigod.

Once we were in the new facilities, Rev. Dr. Dimsdale wasn't satisfied to have just the parishioners come to his temple and bow. He began charging tuition for other pastors and lay leaders to come and learn from him how he had accomplished such a great feat. He instructed the conferees in "theocracy." He would start out saying, "I have some dreams that so far exceed this little building that one day this will look like an outhouse. In ten years we could build once or twice more and I could be pastoring a church of twenty thousand. Democracy is not God's way. Theocracy is God's plan. The big things that have happened in Denver, Colorado, have not come from committees. God said to me one night while I was spending the entire night in prayer, 'When are you going to learn that the feet don't direct the head? You're going to have people vote against you. If Jesus ran this church, He would have even more people vote against him. Don't ever forget that.'"

About that time a gentleman came to me and gave me a note. "No matter how noble the objective of a religious institution, if it blurs decency and kindness, cheapens human worth, and breeds ill will and suspicion … it is nonetheless an evil institution."

After reading the note, I said, "I need to think about this."

"Please do," the man said. "I think you should separate yourself from this institution because I think it is going to hurt you. And remember, the church is the only institution that shoots its own wounded."

I folded the paper and put it into my pocket and audibly said to myself, "What have I gotten myself into? All I wanted to do was to help people and make this a better world!"

When Rev. Dr. Dimsdale and I were together he would often ask me, "Jimmy, your brother has confessed all about his affairs and the women. Are there things you need to talk to me about from your past? Perhaps if I knew the details it would help you in your own spiritual life."

By then, I knew what he was doing, compiling ammunition. "No, I don't need to confess anything to you. I asked God to forgive me one night up at Winter Park. I felt He did. As I understand it, when He forgave me, He removed all the transgressions from me as far as the east is from the west, and buried the whole thing in the sea of His forgetfulness. If He forgot, then so did I. Nothing to tell anymore."

The pastor used the information he extracted from others, including my brother, to manipulate them. A knowing chuckle or a wink of the eye struck fear into many, and issues that should have been the subject of debate suddenly evaporated, as the pastor's will prevailed. He signaled his ability to use this information by boasting to his training conferences, "Some of the best people I have in my church today have violated their vows and committed adultery, and may be violating them still. I'm not going to kick them out; I'm going to love them."

Following the adage, "like priest, like people," his messianic attitude with all its pride and arrogance of being above the law soon began to permeate the institution. We had an epidemic of extra-marital affairs and promiscuity that started with the staff and soon infected the congregation. A shadow culture came to reign in the church that outdid the skullduggery of my old business partners.

Then came the discovery of irregular financial dealings and deficit spending, and the proposal to sell more certificates to replace certificates where there was no means to repay them. Requests were made for an investigation and audit, but the requests were summarily dismissed.

In February, 1979, I went to the Holy Land with my new pastor and a group from my church. The church's travel brochure noted the sacred sites we would be visiting, and even promised a special recording session with the Tel Aviv Symphony while in Israel. The singers for the recording sessions were to be chosen from those traveling with the tour group, which inspired a number of musicians to sign up!

We spent February 21 through 26 visiting all the sites of Jerusalem, Bethlehem, and even the Dead Sea and Masada.

On Thursday, February 24, I visited the Holy Land's Church of All Nations and wrestled there with God in prayer. The Church of All Nations sits in the center of a grove of ancient olive trees in the Garden of Gethsemane, where Christ went to pray before his arrest. No windows have been built into the church in order to re-create the abject darkness of the night of Christ's betrayal by Judas in the garden. Small fires and candles provide the only illumination, and on the walls the paintings depict Christ at his agonizing prayers.

I went into a dark corner by a pillar and knelt to pray. I had learned disturbing information about our pastor, and there were other reports about misbehavior among his staff and key church leaders. God seemed to be asking that I confront the pastor about these matters directly. I prayed in the flickering firelight, and the increasing weight on my conscience bore down on my will. God was insisting that I confront an evil situation. I resisted, explaining to God why others might be more effective with the pastor. God's voice became ever more insistent, the burden I felt increasing. Finally, I submitted to God's will.

The moment I resolved to do so, I felt a chill and a rush of panic. I started to shake uncontrollably, and the chaos inside came out in tears. Satan was promising that I would die if I followed God's command. When I left that church I was never the same again, because I knew that not only God was real, but Satan was as well.

Two days after my own prayer of doubt and pain in Gethsemane, on February 26, we visited Megiddo and went on to Jesus' hometown, Nazareth. We proceeded through the Jezreel Valley, past Mount Tabor to where the Jordan River flows into the Sea of Galilee. At that point I was baptized in the Jordan River. That had been a dream of mine since my childhood Sunday school days.

That night we spent at the Kibbutz Ayelet Hashachar, not far from Nazareth. As providence directed, the Rev. Dr. Dimsdale and I were assigned to stay together in a small cottage at the kibbutz. Following dinner we returned to our cottage, and I told him that I needed to speak seriously to him.

I started out with the least serious matter on my mind. Some of the people who were on the trip had become angry when they found out there was not going to be a "recording session" with the Tel Aviv orchestra.

Some members of our party had paid to come in hopes that they would be chosen to sing for the recording. It now appeared that, despite the brochure's claims, there never had been a "recording session" planned. "I think that you need to do the right thing and offer to refund those peoples' money if you knew there was no session ever planned," I said.

He argued, but finally agreed.

Next, I brought up the subject of his trying to take away a church member's family music business for himself. That made him angry as he tried to explain his actions.

Next I asked him to help me understand why he needed to exaggerate the attendance numbers being reported at our church back home. Then I brought up the problem with the false reporting of the financial situations at the church and the monies that were missing. I knew this to be true because he had tried to pay the sum back with a check that wouldn't clear. At that point our talk became really uncomfortable. I was beginning to think that I should have brought a witness with me. I still harbored hopes, though, that we could get things straightened out quietly and get on with building the church family.

The next items proved to be too much. I talked to him about all the adulterous affairs that were taking place, or rumored to be taking place, among the staff and leaders. That issue he denied, even though the evidence was clear. Then I asked about his marital fidelity.

That was it! Everything went haywire. He would not answer, but unleashed a barrage of accusations against me. "You have proven your disloyalty to me," he said as he shook his finger in my face. "You have denied me, and you will pay for it!" The dye was in the water. His course was set.

For the rest of the trip he would not talk or even look at me. If I was in the front of the bus, he would march to the back. On the way home, we were scheduled to stay together again in Copenhagen. He saw to it that those plans were quickly changed.

And while, as we returned from the trip, it wasn't immediately clear what he planned to do with his anger toward me, a year later it became fully evident. Yes, it took one year of careful planning before he pulled the trigger. (Revenge is a meal best served cold, as the saying goes.) One horrible year! He had to kill the messenger before the messenger could speak. My intention had not been to speak, but to get the train back on the track so we could continue the adventure. His fear did not allow him to see this—it was driving him crazy!

As the plan took shape, he started preparing his wolf pack. My involvement in the church's music program was unceremoniously curtailed. As I had no more wealth to give, I was seen as having no more value to the institution.

On one occasion, Rev. Dr. Dimsdale and I were in the parking lot after having been at a luncheon together. While standing beside his car, he leaned over the top of his open door, shook his finger at me, as he had at the kibbutz, and proclaimed. "I have made you what you are. I have lauded you around the country, and now I am going to break you!" He was serious.

At another point he informed me that if I would go to the platform in the church and apologize for my "disloyalty" in front of everyone, condemn my brothers, and publicly embrace Rev. Dr. Dimsdale, I could be "restored." He said he "knew" that I would eventually come around because I was a "good man."

I declined the offer and recalled the old note I had received earlier: "No matter how noble the objective of a religious institution, if it blurs decency and kindness, cheapens human worth, and breeds ill will and suspicion … it is nonetheless an evil institution." I was finding it harder to disagree with the statement.

The next issue that struck fear in the heart of the pastor was the Sunday school class of young couples that Anna Marie and I taught. The class had grown in number from six to three hundred fifty on one occasion, and those involved believed that we would soon be running at five hundred in attendance. Rev. Dr. Dimsdale was overheard saying, "If Jimmy's influence is not stopped, that class could vote me out." His actions should have been expected, because at one of his training conferences for pastors he had said, "The pastor has the privilege of appointing or removing teachers. He may exercise that privilege for any reason."

So, on March 16, 1980, he walked into the class and announced in our absence, "It's my unpleasant task to announce to you the removal of your Sunday school teacher. I could have just let this filter out, but integrity—if I don't have that, I don't have anything—demands that I tell you exactly what I have done. I want to make it very clear that it is not a moral issue, like another woman or something, but given my role as pastor and its responsibilities, I cannot allow Jim Jackson to continue. It would neither be appropriate nor advisable to answer any questions here in a gathering like this. You are going to have to trust me for a while and maybe later on I'll share more. A week ago last Friday night God very clearly gave me direction, and that I have to follow."

I had learned in the business world that lying is not only a refusal to face reality—it's a type of insanity. A person who will lie will do anything if the circumstances are right.

Anna Marie and I were not only hurt without measure, but I began to fear for the safety of my family. The wolf pack had been poisoned with the idea that they would lose all the concerts, dinner dramas, programs, and their very relationships with the Lord if they should ever lose their pastor.

We decided to be brave and see how the whole mess might end. We didn't have to wait long. The Rev. Dr. Dimsdale arranged for a process server to deliver a document that said in part that the three Jackson brothers were to forthwith withdraw from the membership roll and cease attending all services and meetings. We were "obliged to separate ourselves from the body of believers." We had just been excommunicated, Brigham Young style. According to that, we were separated from all those going to heaven. At least we weren't dead!

It didn't take us long to put the trauma aside and begin to thank God that, once again, we had been shown a way out of a really bad situation.

Yes, it still hurt when we drove almost daily past the facility that we had poured so much of our life's blood into and realized that never again would we sit and listen to the beautiful melodies from the magnificent new church organ, or sit and enjoy the beautiful windows, or walk on the acres of plush carpet. But as we drove by, we could still enjoy watching the beautiful trees and shrubs grow and know that lots of other people would enjoy the amenities provided.

We huddled up our family of four and reviewed and embraced once again the insight from the writer Oswald Chambers that the things we are going through are either making us sweeter, better, nobler men and women, or they are making us more captious and fault-finding, more insistent on our way. The things that happen either make us fiends, or they make us saints; it depends entirely upon the relationship we have with God.

I became permanently leery, though, of large churches that attracted people by offering them pleasurable entertainment, rather than equipping them to look outward to the poor and suffering.

8

Closing the Gates and Opening the Word

What was I supposed to do? I no longer had an office at Jackson Brothers Investments to go back to. I had relinquished my lifestyle of personal accumulation, giving away millions of dollars. I no longer had a church into which to pour my life and energies. For a second time, coping with the institutionalized religious world had left me worn out physically and beaten up emotionally.

Satan had not been able to take my life away as he vowed he would if I followed through on the agreement I had made with God in the chapel outside Jerusalem. Still, I was vulnerable right then to temptations of bitterness and disgust. What bothered me even more was the possibility that I might become neutralized, or more accurately, spiritually neutered, like so many others. They might still be walking around, but they were already dead on the inside. The "curse God and die" option suggested to Job can be chosen thirty years before a person actually falls into the ground. I prayed that we wouldn't end up living that kind of miserable existence!

God saw my fragile condition. In fact, I'm sure He had been planning on how to use it all along. He wasn't finished with my post-graduate lessons in relinquishment yet. He impressed upon me an overwhelming sense of "Jehovah *Shammah*," the Presence of the Lord. He also became "Jehovah *Rohi*," the Lord our Shepherd, who cuddled me in His strong arms, pulled me close, and protected me.

I am with you and I am pleased with you, He assured me. *You have responded well with what I have been assigning to you.*

The Lord pointed out that He had kept us from giving away our home along with the other assets. Our home in the mountains would become our safe haven and retreat until the present storm had passed over. We gathered our little family of four together, keeping the boys fully apprised of what was happening.

Growth starts where blaming stops. We could use what had happened in the past as an excuse to get off the trolley car at the next station, or we could stay on and prepare ourselves for the most wonderful adventure that we could ever imagine on down the line. We all agreed to stay on the trolley car together and get ready for something good.

I remembered once before bailing out of church and the best part of my relationship with God when my ministerial dreams gave way to trading jalopies in the alley behind our church apartment. I did not want to make that mistake again. We may have been caught up in a spiritual hothouse on its way to cult status, but that did not mean Christ had not come to found His church. We would have to move on in time to another gathering place of the faithful, where Christ, rather than the Rev. Dr. Dimsdale, remained Lord.

At some time in the past I had written, "Those who are intent on doing God's will must rediscover the beauty of the Scriptures." I went down to the local bookstore and bought a new Bible translation, Ken Taylor's *The Living Bible*, a paraphrased version that helped the Scriptures come alive.

I drove back into our yard and closed and locked the gates. For a time I needed to shut out the outside world and be alone with God and His Word. I got started and couldn't lay the book down. As I began to read, my mind turned away from charlatans and their institutionalized malpractice. I began to recall the good times in business and how I loved the study of economics.

I decided to read my new Bible all the way through and see what it had to say about economic concepts and business principles. I knew my Jewish partners in commercial transactions were business savvy, and I wondered whether it was part of their DNA or came from their tradition, as it had been passed down from one generation to the next. To my delight I began discovering insights into business and economic principles from the holy mountaintops of Israel. I even had to laugh when I read about how shrewd Jacob had figured out how to build his personal flock of sheep at Laban's ranch through determining the genetic pattern of speckled and dark colored sheep. Graduate dissertations could be written on Solomon's advice on economics and business in Proverbs.

I decided to write a book on economic principles and titled it, *What'cha Gonna Do With What'cha Got?*[2] Was it possible that God had an economy from which He worked? I was so intrigued that I decided to go back to the university and take some more courses on economics to get my head back into the business and economics game. I knew that I was on the right track when I discovered that my major professor at the University of Colorado, Dr. Paul Ballantyne, was a wonderful Christian man and loved my idea of writing the book. He volunteered to proof my work.

While at the university I was also able to sit under the teaching of Dr. Timothy Tregarthen and another great Christian, Dr. Michael Novak, who had written more than twenty-five books, including, *The Spirit of Democratic Capitalism*.

I had thought that it would take me six weeks to six months to produce the book. It actually took me over two years to research, write, and see it published. I thoroughly enjoyed the experience, however.

The difference between free markets and institutional politics is that markets reward being right and punish being wrong, whereas I had almost allowed my life to be subsumed by ecclesiastical politics. Becoming a simple business man again was refreshing.

The book, *What'cha Gonna Do With What'cha Got?* was well received and won a "Gold Medallion" Book Award. By then the healing process had pretty much taken place, and I was feeling ready for the next challenge.

Readers of the book requested that we put together seminars across the country in personal financial management. At these seminars I instructed the attenders how to train their own constituents in the book's principles. I used straightforward language to teach concepts like scarcity, choice, and cost. I explained the Federal Reserve System's governance of our nation's money supply, the monetary reserves required in the banking industry, and investment strategies. And, of course, I taught the seminar members how commodities, like rabbits, could be used to barter exchanges.

Denominations and individual churches loved the program because there was a heavy emphasis on stewardship, and its principles came from the Bible. In all, my team and I trained more than ten thousand attenders who in turn went back to teach their own people.

If not for the relationship with our church blowing up, I would never have carved out the time to sort, process, and synthesize a lifetime of learning. God was preparing me for the "next step" even when I had no clue that there *was* a next step.

Reading the ancient Scriptures, I saw a silver thread of economic principles woven into the fabric. Even more astonishing was the discovery of a far more precious strand of pure gold that bound the whole tapestry together. That pure gold strand was the powerful theme of "kindness, justice, and righteousness."

9

The Turning Point

As a result of my economics book, *What'cha Gonna Do With What'cha Got?*, I was invited by several leaders of developing countries to consult with them regarding their economic situations. First, I went to Zimbabwe in southern Africa, then to Ecuador, Peru, Venezuela, and finally to Brazil to work with President José Sarney and his chief economist, Antonio Basilar. Brazil's economy was experiencing three thousand percent inflation, and they were having difficulty repaying their debts to US banks. I was really enjoying being back in the business world, I have to admit. Occasionally, I would catch myself wondering what God might have up His sleeve, as I traveled to intriguing, but unfamiliar, parts of the world and worked with important government and industrial leaders.

In Brazil, a young medical student named Lorena became my translator. She was from a medical family. They had moved to Brazil from Chile during the repressive Pinochet regime. Lorena's mother, Dr. Natalia, was one of the best known gynecologists in the whole São Paulo area. Her sister, Dr. Natasha, was a dentist, and Dr. Paulo, Lorena's fiancé, was already well-known for his outstanding work in infectious diseases.

Lorena's family was unbelievably hospitable. Regularly, they invited me to go to church with them and then insisted that I come to their home for Sunday dinner. Following dinner I was expected to accompany them on their hospital rounds. I received a real introduction to Brazil's health care system. I guess that I had just never given a thought to the health care system of a developing country. What I was seeing was shocking. How could Lorena's family successfully practice medicine with such archaic equipment? Didn't they have anything new or high-tech, as they did in the United States?

At times my new friends would insist that I join them as they performed free medical services among the poorest of the poor in the Brazilian *favelas* or shantytowns. It was so dangerous in some of the favelas that neither the police nor the military dared enter the perimeters.

When I displayed my shock at their willingness to go into such dangerous places, they responded by explaining how they also would fly in small planes every October into the remote villages of the Amazon region and perform free clinics for the indigenous people who had the opportunity to see a doctor only once a year. I truly began to admire the members of the family and all the acts of goodness in which they were involved.

One morning Lorena asked me if I would like to join them as they went into one of the very large favelas to offer their free clinics. "Are you sure a red-headed gringo would be safe walking through a lawless favela of over a million destitute people?" I asked.

"Stick with us, 'Gringo,' and you will be fine," Lorena and her fiancé, Paulo, quipped simultaneously.

Very few cars or trucks were driven into the favela. Some residents were fortunate enough to own a small horse. The carts pulled by the scrawny animals were usually made of junked auto parts slapped together and bound by wire or ropes. Open sewers ran in front of or behind the shanties, and the deeper we traveled into the favela, the more the odors became so noxious my eyes smarted.

I grabbed the arm of Lorena and pointed out some huge, ripe red tomatoes growing along the pathway. "Look at the size of those tomatoes, those are huge," I said.

"Well, of course, silly boy, you can grow huge tomatoes if you plant them right in the stream of the sewer," Lorena said. "But unless you crave a good case of cholera, I would not advise that you eat one."

The shanties were usually constructed with pieces of scrap wood, discarded concrete blocks, plastic sheets, or even bamboo shoots. Most roofs consisted of overlapping pieces of junk metal held down by big rocks. Water leaks were usually slowed down with layers of intertwined banana leaves.

In front of one of the shanties was a crude fence shutting it off from the other dwellings. Behind the fence, perched on a deeply stained box on the rickety porch, was a sign surrounded by some very strange items. I stopped to snap a photo. "That's strange, but interesting," I said to Paulo and Lorena, "What's it all about?"

"Here in Brazil, and especially in these cross-cultural favelas, we have a lot of voodoo and devil-worshiping cults," Lorena said. "That sign indicates that this is a place where they sacrifice human babies; let's keep moving."

A very animated and friendly Brazilian man came running up to us. Lorena and the man began chatting away in Portuguese. The man who was obviously blind in the left eye, had dropped his pushcart loaded with scraps of cardboard and collapsed boxes. While he was still talking to Lorena, he approached me and started curiously touching my camera.

I wasn't happy about that because I could see my expensive camera being snatched from me and disappearing down the dangerous paths and out of sight.

"He wants to take a picture of us with your camera," said Lorena.

Over my dead body, I thought.

Lorena read my anxiety. "Relax a bit, Jeeem," said Lorena, scolding. "This is my friend, he has been to our free clinic before."

I took the strap from around my neck, gave the camera to the man, and tried to show him where to look and what button to push.

As we positioned ourselves for the photo, I noticed that the man had his blind eye pushed up against the viewfinder and his good eye was looking over the top of the camera to line us up for the picture. The picture was a great shot of the Brazilian sky, but I had made my first friend in the terrible favelas.

I watched as Lorena, Paulo, and some of Lorena's friends from the university med school worked with those desperately poor people. Almost none of the residents had proper identification papers or medical records, so government health care was not available to them. They had migrated to the São Paulo areas from northern cities like Recife and Salvador because there was no work for them there.

As I looked around, I realized I was completely engulfed by abject poverty. Pathetically poor and ill people showed up in droves for help that morning. I felt a lump in my throat when I realized that these simple people had no one other than volunteer doctors to help them. No one else in the world was even taking notice of their fevers and pain. What amazed me was that Paulo and Lorena could do so much good with just the few things we had carried into the favela that day. They really had made a startling difference.

I was being kept very busy with my work in Brasília, the capital. I was involved in an economic program called "Debt for Equity Swaps." The Brazilian government owed banks in the US lots of money and couldn't pay it back. A global economic crisis was brewing. The World Bank, United Nations, and even the US government had put an enormous amount of pressure on the US banks to make loans to the poor, lesser-developed countries of the world.

When the loans became due, these countries often could not repay them. Because the Nixon administration had taken the US economy off the "gold standard" in the 1970s, the banks had been allowed to use such things as "sovereign debt instruments from foreign countries" as credits toward their "fractional reserve" requirements. This meant the US banks recorded the notes of foreign nations as if they were a form of cash on their balance sheets. The United Nations or World Bank would probably have simply written off the loans and forgiven the countries and charged it all back to the wealthiest nations. However, the US banks were tightly controlled by regulations. When the debts became "non-performing loans," the banks were forced to write them down and subtract them from their "fractional reserves." That turned their financial viability upside down!

By employing the international Debt for Equity Swaps concept, the bank could find a substitute entity (other investors) to validate the debt (literally buying the note and replacing it with new guarantees). Then, taking the foreign country's old promissory note in hand, they could go and swap physical assets of the country to satisfy the note. For example, a group of corporations or businessmen in Brazil could buy the note, then swap the Brazilian government for oil concessions, natural resources, ocean port access credits, or even tax credits for the future. The US banks could not have taken raw natural resources or assets of the country in hand to satisfy the foreign note, such a swap could be done with an intermediary step. It was simply a new wrinkle to the bunny rabbit swaps, only now the red wagon was being pushed through an international neighborhood.

One day an American missionary to Brazil caught up with me. "Aren't you the James Jackson who wrote the book, *What'cha Gonna Do With What'cha Got?*" he asked. "If I put a group of Brazilian pastors, businessmen, and government people together, would you come and train them in economics from a Christian perspective?"

I readily agreed and we held the seminar in Belo Horizonte. I had never tried to teach an economic seminar through a translator. Of course, I had to un-Americanize my jokes, my US examples, and currency references. Everything had to be adapted to Brazil's economy. The only common references that everybody understood were the biblical principles. It was easy to explain that God also had an economy and it worked according to certain principles.

As a result of the seminar, I was connected to an energetic Brazilian man named Dr. Heraldo Neves from Rio de Janeiro. He was extremely excited about his medical clinic, and insisted that I come and visit him in Rio.

Dr. Neves worked in a hospital in Rio but had become involved in traveling out to an area called Mesquite, where he and some of his friends had purchased an old house. They had remodeled the old house into a makeshift medical clinic and were trying to treat as many of the three hundred thousand people in Mesquite as possible. He was becoming good at begging his other doctor and nurse friends from Rio to join him in his volunteer efforts.

When I arrived I was startled at what I saw. Hundreds of people gathered in the hot sun crowding their way toward the front door of the old house. Mothers were holding crying babies, and old ladies were waiting their turn. People rested up against the building wherever they could find a splinter of shade from the hot Brazilian sun. Many people had been there since early morning waiting to see the doctor. He was their only hope for medical attention for their babies or for themselves. As I approached the front porch area of the old house, I saw an ancient dental chair and drilling apparatus that was run by foot pedals and frazzled cables. That was Dr. Neves's dental clinic.

Through the front door I looked to the right at a room that had once been the front bedroom. It was painted a light blue color and had a poster of a baby pinned to the wall. On the rickety old table there was an old rusty set of baby scales. That was Dr. Neves's pediatrics ward.

What had once been a kitchen was now the emergency room and procedures theater that consisted of a canvas cot, an empty canister of oxygen, and a small metal cabinet with a glass front. Inside the cabinet were old re-rolled grayish bandages and a small mishmash of half-filled bottles. That was it! That was Dr. Neves's health clinic.

"I don't get it, Dr. Neves," I said. "You have all those people outside in lines that stretch as far back as one can see. They have come here thinking that you can help them, but when I come inside I can see that you literally have nothing in here to help them! Doesn't anyone come to help you? Doesn't your government help you?"

Dr. Neves was a short man with a high energy level and dark, penetrating eyes. He looked straight at me and said, "Meester Jackson, you are economista, you should know that we are experiencing inflation that is running over three thousand percent. I have no money, but even if I did I could not buy anything from the USA, Great Britain, or Japan. We are not allowed to buy anything from outside Brazil, since our *cruseiros* currency would then flow out of our country and into the other country, causing even more hyperinflation. And the government infrastructure here is not strong enough to help us. *We have no one to help us. So, we are doing the best we can with what we have!*"

At that moment I was slammed by a wave of unexpected compassion. I had crossed over a line. No longer was I a foreign economic visitor observing at an arm's length distance. All the hurt and tragedy of what I had previously seen at the free clinics in the favelas with Lorena came crashing in. I saw not only the hurting people in front of me and heard the crying of the babies there inside Dr. Neves's sparse clinic, but I felt the hopelessness of the millions of people in Brazil who were ragged squatters; the people who lived in the squalor and poverty of shanties with open sewers and impure drinking water; who faced the daunting and discouraging task of eking out their survival on the streets of the Brazilian cities. I hadn't experienced the scorching flames of passion and empathy like that before. Nothing in the ego-centered churches of entertainment and comfort, where I had spent my life, had ever ignited the compassion I was feeling standing in that ramshackle house of a clinic in Brazil.

Dr. Neves had put it all right back in my economist's lap when he said, "We are doing the best we can with what we have!" Were not those my very own words: *What'cha Gonna Do With What'cha Got?*

It was my turn to step up to the plate. From that moment I was committed to bringing help and hope to the needy, people who had no other advocate and no contacts with the advantaged folks that should be helping. I could feel the dammed up reservoir of hot tears pushing to escape my eyes. I stood there not knowing really what was happening inside of me. I didn't know how to respond to the compassion that I was feeling.

Finally, I blurted out my confession, "Dr. Neves, I do not know what I am talking about when I say this to you. But I think I could go back to where I live in Colorado and get some medical supplies donated to help you. We can work together deciding what I should look for."

Then for a split second my businessman nature and the logical side of me jumped in and briefly took over. "But, Dr. Neves, if I were to send some things to your clinic, you would have to guarantee that the goods would not get into the black market. I have been here in Brazil long enough to know just how corrupt Brazil's government officials can be. And I also know what can happen to good humanitarian intentions when all the charlatans and the 'Lords of Poverty' greedily step in and steal good things for themselves. I don't want to be part of that. I want to be part of your solution, not part of Brazil's corruption problem."

The intensity of Dr. Neves's countenance softened as he quietly studied my face. Then he said with a little smirk, "Well, Meester Jackson, you are working directly in Brasilia with Mr. José Sarney, the president of Brazil. Why don't you get the guarantees directly from him?"

I blinked my eyes and said, "Oh, OK, that makes sense."

I got on the airplane and flew back to the capital. I took Lorena with me to do the translating so there would be no misunderstandings. There I began working with Dr. Mauro Corbellini, the minister of health on President Sarney's cabinet.

In our meetings he said to me, "If you will go back to USA and obtain donated medical goods for Brazil, I will see to it that you can import the things on a tax-exempt basis. And, furthermore, I will give you a large storage space on the University Medical School campus where Lorena attends in the city of Campinas. You will have the key to the storage area, and you can decide where the medical goods should go based on your assessments."

I told the minister of health, "Thank you. That's all the assurance I need."

We shook hands and we parted. When I got back on the airplane I slumped down in my seat and put my hands to my forehead and began muttering. "Oh, my goodness, what have I just done to my life? Here I have just made all these commitments and I don't even know where to get a Band-Aid."

10

Paradox and Reversal

"The perception of your obligation," runs an old saying, "will determine your behavior." From the time I stood in Dr. Neves's empty clinic outside of Rio no shadow of doubt ever dimmed my commitment; with God's grace and guidance I was going to help those needy people in Brazil. I sensed from the beginning that I had entered upon a new phase in my life.

I boarded an international flight in São Paulo and considered my new commitment. It was a long trip from Brazil to Miami and on to Denver. Most of the trip I spent staring at the seatback in front of me. What an adventure my life had already been from rabbit economics to international consulting. In my mind I could hear the sweet, but strong, voice of my mother as she finished reading the story of Andrew Carnegie. "Your true measure of greatness," she said, summarizing the story, "will always be determined by your care for others. Not by what you accumulate for yourself."

God's economics, the topic of the economic seminar at Belo Horizonte, applied to me more than ever. I could see how the principles I had listed were working themselves out in my life ever more fully.

God Has Given
God Is Looking For A People
God's Economy Is Not Based On Greed

God Always Repays, But I Don't Give To Get
God's Multiplication Begins With My Subtraction
God's Economic Success Will Cost Everything I Value More Than Him

God had given me a love for business and economic principles. He had also given me a tender heart and a deep desire to pursue "goodness." He knew I needed to be in Denver and saw to it that I got there from Idaho. He made it possible to ratchet up the business opportunities from Denver Auto Mart to Jackson Brothers Investments, and blessed our creativity and efforts with millions of dollars of profits. He loved me so much that He called me out of that dangerous lifestyle and back into the church. That transition had allowed me to understand the principle of complete relinquishment. He then called me out and away from an institution that could have spiritually ruined my family and me.

Some of those experiences were not easy on me or on my family. Paradox and reversal of fortune belonged to the process. When I thought I was being sent to countries like Zimbabwe and Brazil to lend my economic expertise, I was being sent more particularly to Dr. Neves's ramshackle medical clinic. Just as my aborted ministerial stint sent me to Denver, so my work as an economic advisor proved more important than anything else in putting me into contact with the poor and suffering. God had taught me about His economy and then He had sent me into a needy world to work for His Kingdom, which would involve carrying on diplomatic relations with the foreign leaders of this world.

On the other hand, how could I better help a lesser-developed country with its economic problems than to help make its sick people well? You cannot have a strong economy with a sick population. God was accomplishing both my ostensible mission and His underlying mission at once.

Before I got off that plane in Miami I bowed my head, closed my eyes, and vowed to God that I would give him the *best of my life for the rest of my life*, working on His enterprises.

As the plane departed Miami and headed toward the Rocky Mountains, my thinking switched from review and contemplation to the startling fright of reality. I had made serious vows before I left Brazil. I had promised Dr. Neves that I would help him by bringing donated medical goods to an outpost in Brazil. Then I had gone to Mr. Corbellini, the minister of health, and worked a deal, allowing me to bring medical goods into Brazil with the government's blessing. I really was committed and would remain so when my pious sentiments faded.

Where in the world was I going to find any medical goods to donate and ship to Brazil? I knew nothing about medical supplies. I had heard stories about other Americans who would go to needy places in the world and get all excited about helping and take a lot of pictures and make a lot of promises to the locals about how they would return and help. But they would never return, and they would soon get over the emotion and forget the promises. I certainly wasn't going to be a part of that kind of false hope! I had to get started immediately.

I had heard my dad say a hundred times in his speeches,

"On the plains of hesitation bleach the bones of countless thousands
Who when faced with success, hesitated, sat down to rest,
And in waiting ... wasted and died."

Whom did I know that could help me? When my sons were growing up I always told them that they were never more than eight telephone calls away from receiving any information they needed. If they were willing to start calling, the chances were very good that they would hit the jackpot within the first couple of calls. They had to be mentally prepared, though, to make eight calls. Now, I needed to take my own advice!

After I arrived home and unpacked, I got on the telephone and began calling my friends. I invited them to lunch at a restaurant in Littleton, a Denver suburb. As we gathered, I got right to the point. I told them the story of Brazil and my promise to Dr. Neves. I described as vividly as

I could what I had seen in his meagerly appointed clinic and the people standing in the hot sun waiting for someone to help them with their medical problems. I wanted them to see the metal cabinet with the glass front that was full of dirty, re-rolled bandages.

"I need your help," I confessed. "I don't know where to go from here, but someone knows. I am not afraid to work, and I am willing to run down the leads. But I need you to give me some phone numbers, some names, some ideas."

A man by the name of Greg was sitting directly across the table from me. He looked up from his water glass and said kindly to me, "Well, Jim, I can help you. My partner, Pete, and I own a medical marketing company. That's what we do for a living. We contract between the medical manufacturers and the end users, like hospitals and major clinics. Each year those contracts go up for bids. Sometimes we get the bids, sometimes we don't. But one thing is for certain: we always have to have overstock. That's part of the deal. Why don't you come by our warehouse on Quincy Street, and we will see what we can do to help with this."

I went to the warehouse and met Greg and Pete. We walked the aisles of the facility, and they began pulling stock right off the shelves. By the time we were finished they had pulled more than fifty thousand dollars worth of wholesale medical goods from their shelves, and instructed a man to stack the supplies on pallets by the overhead door. "Well, that's all yours," said Greg, with a quick grin. "Why don't you see how many lives you can save in Brazil with your first donation?"

I quickly drove up to our home in Evergreen and rejoiced with Anna Marie for what had just taken place. We jumped into our old Dodge pickup truck and headed back to the warehouse on Quincy Street to load and transport the donated medical treasures from Greg's place to our garage in Evergreen. I had a strange feeling of destiny as I herded the truck home. God had been way ahead of me in locating the needed "Band-Aids."

My friends, Greg and Pete, caught my enthusiasm as they watched me working hard at loading and unloading the medical supplies. They called the offices of Denver Medical Supply Company and U.S. Medical Supply Company, both located in a commercial area north of Denver. When Greg explained what this "Jackson fellow" was doing and what Greg's company had just done in way of donations, they, too, agreed to help. Soon my garage was bursting at the seams with donated medical goods.

One of my favorite memories was walking into my shop and garage area and seeing Anna Marie Jackson, Ph.D., who had become my very first volunteer, standing with a bulky *Physician's Desk Reference* open on a box in front of her. Her left index finger was pointing to something written on the book's page. In her right hand she was holding a small package from the box. "What is this?" she exclaimed. "I need to make an inventory and categorize all these things for shipment, but I don't have any idea what this is supposed to be!"

I stood there and laughed at what was happening. I got a quick glimpse at what God was up to! He had taken me right up and out of my comfort zone. I knew nothing about medical stuff. He knew that, and that was exactly how He wanted it. He had dumped me into an area where I had no expertise at all! What genius! Now I had to become totally dependent on God and dependent on other people around me. I was not in any way in control. I knew nothing, and that's just how He wanted it to be! Now, maybe He could use me.

Likewise, I didn't know anything about shipping goods to Brazil. In my days of self-indulgence I had imported Jaguars, BMWs, Mercedes Benz, and Rolls Royce automobiles from England and Germany. I had used DB Schenker international shipping to handle my freight forwarding of the cars. So, I jumped into my car and drove to the Montbello industrial area in Denver and asked them, "Do I need to buy one of those huge 40-foot long ocean cargo containers in order to ship some things to Brazil?"

The woman behind the counter told me, "No, honey, if you have some things to ship to Brazil, we will arrange to have one of those big containers where you can load it. Then we will arrange to have it picked up and put on a railroad car and sent from Denver to Houston. From there it gets shipped to Brazil. Once the ship arrives in Brazil we will arrange for a big truck to haul the big container to wherever you want it. All you have to do is pay us, baby!"

Within a matter of a little over thirty days I had been able to collect more than two hundred and fifty thousand dollars worth of donated medical goods. They were supplies of the highest quality. The value of the goods had been figured at wholesale; I had no idea what their retail value might be. I started imagining how many Brazilian children's lives would be changed, and their parents' as well. I could only imagine the encouragement and hope and thrill Dr. Neves would receive with the goods. Maybe we would have enough medical goods left over to help other clinics and hospitals. We were finding ways to exchange "tax receipt rabbits" for people's lives.

DB Schenkers charged Anna Marie and me a little over eight thousand dollars to arrange and handle the forwarding for each of the first loads into Santos Port in Brazil. We somehow came up with the money. Looking for a cheaper way to transport goods from Denver to Santos Port, I thought I could shave the costs by loading the goods into U-Haul trucks. Our oldest son, Douglas, and his buddy, Jim, were home from college, so they jumped into the trucks and drove the loads as far as Phoenix. I'm not certain that we saved a lot of money, but it was a thrill to see the boys getting involved.

There was something magical about the arrival of that first ocean-going container load into Brazil. As Lorena described it, "There was a certain level of excitement when you first came to the clinic and hospitals. The people started thinking that you just might return and bring help to them. But other people have come before and promised lots of things.

"When the people actually saw the big container arrive, it dawned on them that someone really cared about them and would his their promises. You could just feel the hope they were feeling that was making their hearts get bigger!"

As it turned out, there was no way that Dr. Neves's little clinic could have utilized all the contents of that huge container load. His clinic would have been absolutely inundated. It was providential that we had been given access to space were we could store the remainder of the goods until we determined where they could best be used.

By that time I had become very well-acquainted with the leadership of the university where Lorena attended medical school. They all wanted to meet this American fellow who was willing to send medical supplies.

Dr. Vilmar Trombeta was the head of all administration for the university at Campinas. He was a strong, burly Germanic-Italian type who could rule with only the look in his eye. He had played Brazilian football earlier in his career and had stayed in remarkable physical condition. He was in charge of governing all the financial affairs of the administration. The two of us became very good friends in no time at all.

Dr. Aquinelo Cunha held the position of the chairman of the entire medical school and also acted as the chief director of the training hospital.

Dr. Reis, who came to ski every year on the Colorado mountain slopes not far from our home in Evergreen, was head of the surgery department and was the leading professor at the school.

All of us bonded very quickly. Of course, they were intrigued that the minister of health in Brasília had given me permission to use a space on the campus for storing our medical shipments. These were sharp men from the aristocracy of Brazil, and over dinner they told me that they perceived me to be a "very intelligent and good" man. "Therefore," they said, reasoning aloud, "why is it that you would leave any of your medical goods locked up in an area of our campus when we are so desperately in need of everything you have sent? Wouldn't it be more fitting for you to assess the needs of our hospital and medical school, and allow us to be recipients of your goodness? *We need everything that came in that container.*"

I knew they loved their institution greatly. They had given their lives to it. I knew their passion to educate their students in the best way possible. I knew that they were seeing that the uses of the medical goods would be greatly enhanced and multiplied through being used by medical students, who could then go out and help more of the hurting people of Brazil. Dr. Vilmar Trombeta also knew that if this Jackson guy would donate some of the basics to the hospital and school, he would have more discretionary funds available for other needs.

I let them present their case in full. Then I stared into each of their eyes, one by one, and finally broke out in a laugh. "Now just why in the world wouldn't I be eager to help such noble and honorable men as you? Of course, I will help your hospital and your medical school. We will be partners, and we will do things together to make your great institution even greater!"

Then I looked over at Lorena, who had been translating all the while for Dr. Aquinelo Cunha. "Now, Dr. Lorena, does all this meet with your candid approval?" They all howled with laughter!

From that time until she finished her residency, Lorena was considered a princess around the university. I began to see what an incredible difference the donated medical supplies had made. It was too soon to judge the effect it would have on the hurting constituents of the country, but I could see what we had gotten hold of was dynamite. The energy level of the entire campus, as well as Dr. Neves's little clinic location, jumped to unbelievable heights. And we had just started.

In my quiet times I would reflect on what had happened since I had started the adventure of relinquishment. I was not lying awake at nights worrying what I would do if I made a miscalculation and ended up losing everything. I was not concerned any longer that my personal value might be tied to a show of wealth. I was amazed that I was no longer being driven by the addiction of personal accumulation. I didn't need to put together one more, yet bigger, deal. My motivations were being profoundly changed.

I could now see what I would be doing for the rest of my life. I would be taking the areas of my life where I had strong affinities and abilities, and spend my time using those to help other people who were less advantaged. I would not only give away my accumulation, but I would give away myself.

I also began to realize that in the process, God had been very kind to me. He had given me time and opportunity to research and write down the principles that I had determined to be true in *What'cha Gonna Do With What'cha Got?* He even let me reinforce those beliefs by going out and teaching others and verbalizing the ideas to see if they really made sense.

Then there came a time when He said, "OK, enough thinking, enough talking, let's go back out into the real world and put it all to work." I could see now why I had been set on a course that took me into lesser-developed countries. That would be my work venue for the future. And I could see now why I had been introduced to top leaders and influential people in North America, Africa, and South America. Those were the people I would be working with for a long time to come on behalf of the less fortunate. I couldn't see what was taking place as it was all happening. As soon as that first load was sent into Brazil the pieces of the mosaic started coming together, forming a dazzling, multi-faceted picture, that caught the light of eternity.

The first load was delivered into Brazil in 1987, which we mark as the official starting point of Project C.U.R.E. I began working on the appropriate legal structure prior to this as I considered the nature of what God was bringing into being. The phrase kept coming to me that I was putting together a "business of goodness."

While back in Denver, I played around with names for the organization and finally felt comfortable with Project C.U.R.E (Commission on Urgent Relief and Equipment). That described what we would be doing in the future—perhaps throughout the world.

I filed the name with the appropriate governmental agencies and made certain that my 501(c)(3) designation with the Internal Revenue

Service was valid and up to date. The tax contribution receipts that I would be able to deliver to the manufacturers of medical goods and other donors were essential to the barter that would make everyone better off.

For the next three years as I worked to launch the enterprise, I systematically let go of everything else I was doing in Brazil. Someone else could help with Brazil's economic programs. I needed to concentrate on building an organization in the United States and South America devoted to improving Brazil's health care system. With that new focus miraculous things began to happen.

11

Devils and Angels

My heart and mind had been captivated by the possibilities of bringing help and hope to the wonderful, but needy, people of Brazil. I felt as long as I stayed close to God I would have everything I would ever need to fulfill God's plan for Project C.U.R.E. He would not ask anything that was beyond my jurisdiction to give. God would expect me to devote all my insights, business experience, energy, and creativity on behalf of the Brazilian people.

I didn't have any money left to give, and I knew that acts of goodness were not necessarily accomplished by perfect people. I was going to need to recognize my own limitations, but at the same time push those limits. I still knew how to grow a business, and I was still familiar with basic economic principles that would allow me to develop a model for this new and fragile entity called Project C.U.R.E. I thought our work in Brazil might keep me busy for the rest of my life.

I recalled the little sign I used to have displayed on my desk: ENDEAVOR TO DO SOMETHING SO GREAT THAT UNLESS GOD INTERVENES YOU WILL FAIL. And, I took great confidence in remembering what my dad used to tell his parishioners, "God can do a lot with a little, if He has all there is of it." I was going to give to God "all there was of it."

My approach was to continue to stay involved in the free clinics located in the rural areas and the favelas that were staffed by medical students, and also the small clinics that we had already begun to help, like

Dr. Neves's clinic. But then, I wanted to start spending more time at the two medical universities in Campinas, and also begin to branch out and become involved with helping other hospitals, not only in Campinas, but throughout Brazil.

On each of my trips I would team up with more hospital directors and work more closely with the department heads of the institutions in order to fully understand their dreams and needs and plans for their futures. Together, we tried to figure out and agree upon projects that could be accomplished, and then set time lines for the work. We began experiencing great success with the Children's Cancer Hospital and the Corazon de Jesus (Heart of Jesus) Hospital where Lorena's mother was the head of the obstetrics/gynecology department.

Our most rewarding successes were being realized at the university medical school and hospital where our friends, Dr. Vilmar Trombeta, Dr. Aquinelo Cunha, and Dr. Reis were in charge. One day Dr. Trombeta took me aside and told me, "Jim, you have brought us millions of dollars worth of supplies and extraordinary pieces of high-tech medical equipment, but do you know what you have brought us that has made the most difference?"

"What's that?"

"One thing," Vilmar said, "you have brought us hope! Even our staff meetings are different now. We used to be so discouraged because we had nothing and could access nothing. The staff would just grumble and fight and the only thing we could agree on was that everything was impossible. But now they are saying, 'Look what Project C.U.R.E. is doing. If they believe in us that much then we can start doing good things too.' They started figuring out creative ways to meet challenges because they have hope!"

Dr. Vilmar Trombeta began to get brave and decided to build an addition onto his crowded hospital. He asked me to accompany him when he met with the city officials to obtain the permissions. When the facility was nearly ready we had lunch together. "Jim, I really need three hundred beds and other furnishings for the rooms, could you possibly get those things for me?"

My heart sank because I didn't have any beds or mattresses or tables in my warehouse at home! But I said, "Yes, Vilmar, we will furnish your new addition with three hundred new beds and mattresses."

I fretted and stewed all the way back to Denver. Where would I ever get three hundred beds for Vilmar's hospital?

When I returned home I told my son what I had done.

"When did you make that promise, Dad?" he asked. "I mean, *exactly*." We figured out the day and time I had made the promise. Then he told me, "On that very day the assisted care center in Morrison, Colorado called us and informed us that they were getting ready to redecorate their facilities and wanted Project C.U.R.E. to have all their beds and infection-proof mattresses and all the over-bed tables and night stands."

"How many?" I asked, breathless.

A big smile flashed across his face. "Three hundred beds!"

But other developments smacked more of demonic interference rather than divine intervention. I really needed people to step up and volunteer to help with the new adventure. Being out of the country so much hampered my ability to cultivate supporters and strategic partners, so I was also eager to hear about folks who might provide needed expertise.

One of the executives who had been donating a lot of medical goods to me brought along an older fellow who was unusually interested in what we were doing. He had been part of President Harry Truman's "Marshall Plan" team after World War II, sending donated American goods and cash to help rebuild Europe after the war. He had told one of my friends that he knew all about organizations like Project C.U.R.E., and how a whole lot of money could be "cranked out" of such efforts for people who were involved. "A lot of Americans became very rich off the Marshall Plan," the man said. The older man, whom we will call "Crawford," was an attorney as well. Before long he had brought along a few other men and their wives to help at Project C.U.R.E. One day he asked me to join him and his friends for lunch at the Denver Athletic Club.

When I arrived and lunch had been served, "Crawford" explained how much he and his friends liked Project C.U.R.E. and what we were doing. "And, also, that's really a great international name you've chosen," he said. He then announced that his group had decided to take over the organization and appoint themselves to the board.

"You've got a wonderful thing going, Jackson, but I don't believe you have any idea what you have a hold of," Crawford said, "You haven't made provisions for anybody to make the kind of money out of this venture that is capable of being made. You aren't even taking a salary for yourself, and everyone else is expected to volunteer.

"So, I checked into the corporate structure of your organization at the Colorado Secretary of State and found that you have not filed Project C.U.R.E. as a Colorado corporation. Therefore, I am going to file the appropriate papers today, and I will be president and my friends here will constitute the board. You can help us on a volunteer basis if you would like."

That made me angry. I was so repulsed that I couldn't figure out whether to hit him in the mouth or vomit. I had already put up with enough crooks, manipulators, and charlatans in my life to last an eternity!

I decided to calm my Scotch-Irish impulses and respond civilly to the man even though he didn't deserve it. "I'm disappointed in your abilities as a lawyer," I said, looking him in the eye. "A good attorney would have been more thorough in his research."

I then pulled out the paperwork that showed that we had properly filed Project C.U.R.E. under the Benevolent Brotherhood Foundation my brothers and I had started in 1973. Everything was perfectly legal and in order. Crawford was chagrined.

"Why don't you start your own organization?" I asked him. "The world needs the help, and I would welcome the competition. But, please don't bother us anymore." To this day I am proud that I said no more. What I wanted to say would have burned off Crawford's scraggly eyebrows.

Crawford and his buddies did start another organization that lasted for about six months, then crashed and burned.

About that time I was hit with another "shocker." A man who was involved in the wholesale medical supply business volunteered to let us use part of his warehouse space to store Project C.U.R.E. goods before shipping them to Brazil. The arrangement seemed to be working until I discovered that he had stealthily slipped over into the space we were using while we were not there and helped himself to some of our inventory. He had sold our goods for more than five thousand dollars and kept the money without saying a word.

When I confronted him, he actually said, "Well, those items were free to you, so what are you complaining about? You didn't lose anything, personally."

I grieved almost more over the man's lack of morals than I did for the loss of the medical goods. I explained that the items had been given to Project C.U.R.E. in order to save lives of hurting people in needy situations. How much did he think those lives were worth? Less than the five thousand dollars he had pocketed?

Needless to say, I rented a truck and quickly moved the remaining goods out of the facility to another donated space in the corner of another warehouse.

We had dedicated ourselves to building a business of goodness. But it was still a business and had to be run like a business or it would not succeed. It was going to take a lot of study and planning in order for us to excel in what we had set out to accomplish. We needed to figure out our model, set our goals and benchmarks and evaluation procedures.

The problem with most humanitarian or philanthropic organizations is that the well-intentioned people involved believe the organization will succeed because of their cause. Even a great cause cannot be sustained by flouting basic economic principles and neglecting standard business practices. I was beginning to see that we had bitten off an immense piece to chew and we had better get to chewing before we were in deep trouble.

The business concept or model that had taken shape in my mind regarding Project C.U.R.E. was one resembling a double franchise. There would be one franchise structure located within the US for the purposes of *collecting* donations. It would demand a fireproof legal structure; the ability to procure millions of dollars worth of donated medical goods; the knowledge and systems for soliciting donations of monies; the ability to attract and hold a great number of volunteers; an operations component that would rival any top corporation in America at handling inventory systems, making use of warehouses and transportation processing, and packing domestic and international shipments, arranging the logistics of these shipments and ensuring their safe delivery.

On the other side of the oceans there would be another structure with the primary objective of *distribution*, handling such components as the identification and qualification of future recipients of the medical goods or services, validation of imperative "needs," issues of delivery (e.g., ports and customs protocol), local forwarding to locations, and necessary set-up and installation; as well as accountability and follow-up.

I hoped both the collection and distribution components could be managed from one international headquarters located in Denver. To set up and implement that kind of international structure would be a huge assignment. We would try to bring into existence a humanitarian organization with all the excellence required of a "Fortune 500" company. I was eager to get started on the model, and a little frightened as well, I must admit. For the first time since my childhood I was starting with no money!

I knew from the standpoint of the supply and demand principle I was on solid ground. There was an almost bottomless pit of demand when it came to health care services in Brazil and other lesser-developed countries around the world. The monster of "death, dying, and sickness" was ravaging the world. In millions of cases those victims really did not need to die at all.

On the "supply" side of the principle, I was quickly discovering that there was an abundance of overstock medical goods in this country and companies were responding to our invitation to donate those items, allowing us to improve the bottom line of their company's financial statements. On a piece of paper it looked very simple: all that was needed was an efficient vehicle to collect the things in excess and deliver those items to places around the world where there was imperative need.

I believed that God had been preparing me throughout my entire life to help bring that vehicle into existence. On the other hand, there were media reports every day of international corruption, theft, kidnapping, hostage taking, and murder. And I was already dealing at home with the "Crawford" types who wanted to steal my corporation, and the warehouse guy who was stealing and selling my medical goods.

During a break in travel I began conducting research for our business model. I was intrigued by the organization "Second Harvest" (now known as Feeding America) headquartered in Chicago. They were in the business of effectively distributing surplus food all over America. They had arranged to take the overstock commodities of large food manufacturers and wholesalers around the United States and distribute them to regional and local warehouses in their system of "food banks." From these locations food would be distributed to needy families and individuals through a network of charitable organizations. They had absolutely nothing to do with the international scene, but I felt I needed to learn all I could about their philosophy, procedures, and logistics policies. I called and explained the mission statement of Project C.U.R.E. and asked if I might visit.

I was surprised to find that the chief executive officer of Second Harvest was a lovely Catholic nun. She was so gracious, and quickly invited me to come see her. She was an exceptionally bright lady and held an MBA degree. I bought my airline ticket and flew to Chicago to meet with Second Harvest. I was able to stay for several working days, and they were kind enough to allow me to have appointments with all their key department heads. The Second Harvest organization liked what Project C.U.R.E. wanted to do around the world, and assured me that they saw no element of competition whatsoever. Therefore, they were happy to mentor me and show me anything I wanted to know about their organization.

I wanted to know specifically how they ran their satellite operations in various cities. I also wanted to find out whether it would be possible to stay in business for a sustained period of time giving away medical commodities. From the beginning I had wanted to be able to structure the model so that we could take the donated medical supplies and pieces of equipment to the needy recipients and not charge anything. It seemed like everyone else on the international scene ultimately had to start charging for their goods in order to stay in existence.

In my quiet times, especially while traveling, Satan would slither up and blindside me with doubts. *You are stupid. Why did you give away all your wealth at the beginning? If you had been smart at all you would have kept hold of your wealth and now you would not always be scrambling because you don't have any money to do what you say you need to do. You could have been independent and financed all of your "good" ambitions! Sixteen million dollars would have gone a long way.*

My answer would be: *Yes, that's the whole point. I could have done it by myself—or thought so. God knew that and made sure I couldn't maintain that illusion. I needed to humble myself and learn to be dependent on God and on lots of other people around me.*

These mental conversations kept reminding me that I had been addicted to accumulation and needed to be freed of that addiction. It was not what I *had* but *what had me* that was the problem in the first place. Had I not given it all away and become free of the accumulation addiction, I would never have been in a position to completely trust God and depend on His friends and mine. I had to give it all away and start over with nothing, in order to give God glory and honor for what He was doing with Project C.U.R.E.

Without any working capital in the bank our assignment was a tough one, though. God would have to help us with an infusion of His creativity in order to get access to donated warehouse space, trucks, forklifts, and lots of volunteers. Our whole operation would be "volunteer intensive" because there was no money for a payroll. People who wanted to help Project C.U.R.E. would have to do so as an offering to God. Often this demanded professional abilities and highly-skilled labor. (Thousands of people have volunteered to help Project C.U.R.E. in the last twenty-five years, and the venture has long since become more theirs than mine.)

A case in point came about early on when I was able to acquire a complete Meddars cardiac catheterization laboratory for Dr. Vilmar Trombeta's medical school hospital. I needed to find an especially talented technician who would be willing to travel to Brazil, install and test the equipment, and train the doctors and nurses on the lifesaving heart machine. If we could successfully get the equipment installed and running, it would attract many needy patients and lots of lives would be saved. And the medical school's reputation would be heightened, particularly with potential students.

A friend of mine introduced me to Jeff Martin and his wife, Kathy. Jeff worked as a technical instructor for Siemens Medical. His job was to train hospital staff members and doctors in the use of advanced medical equipment like the cath lab. Kathy had a medical background and was a specialist in hand therapy. Kathy had been a Christian for several years and had gone to Africa previously, where she had gained experience treating Hansen's disease (leprosy). Jeff had become a Christian very recently.

You can only imagine how hard I prayed about the situation before I met with Jeff and Kathy and invited them to go to Brazil with me to install the cardiology equipment and train the medical people—without any compensation! I was so touched and encouraged by their positive response.

In the end Dr. Vilmar agreed to cover their expenses, and he even had Kathy teach sessions at the university on physical therapy and the disease of leprosy.

Dr. Vilmar Trombeta and Dr. Cunha met us, accompanied by an English-speaking technician from India and technical maintenance man from the hospital who would be assisting Jeff. I was proud and grateful as I watched Jeff and Kathy, realizing that here were top people in their fields who willingly used their vacation time to volunteer and brought help and hope to the needy people of Brazil.

I kept standing back, marveling at the growth that was taking place with Project C.U.R.E. I found it fascinating to be a part of something so unusual and world-changing. I would tell Anna Marie, "I am not really doing what is taking place."

She would look at me with a twinge of bewilderment in her blue eyes and say, "But I keep hearing you pray for wisdom and favor wherever you go. Why are you so surprised when God answers your prayers?"

We kept concentrating on building our business model in Brazil. We were learning how to become cultural entrepreneurs in South America, and we were certainly making a positive difference in Brazil's health care delivery system.

By the spring of 1991 the secret of Project C.U.R.E. was getting out. People from other South American and Central American countries began contacting me. "Why are you limiting your help to just Brazil?" they asked. "We also desperately need help!" Countries like Guatemala and Honduras had been devastated by tropical storms.

I really couldn't come up with a good answer to defend limiting our help to just Brazil. Perhaps it was time to roll this humanitarian health care model out to other countries.

12

Beyond Brazil

When requests flooded in for Project C.U.R.E. to deliver aid outside Brazil, we had to consider whether or not we could build an organization capable of meeting such challenges. In the five years that we had been working in Brazil, from 1987 through 1991, had we learned enough? Or had we learned too much, as we understood, perhaps too well, how the world's corruption causes most aid organizations to founder? Many of the largest agencies were so thoroughly poisoned that they actually had become part of the problem. The needs of the world were overwhelming, and I found myself quailing at the challenge.

As I thought through the wisdom of expansion, I was reminded of the episode someone had shared with me while I was traveling in Asia:

> Past the seeker as he prayed came the crippled and the beggar and the beaten. And seeing them, the holy one went down into deep prayer and cried, "Great God, how is it that a loving Creator can see such things and yet do nothing about them?" And out of the long silence, God said, "I did do something . . . I made you."

In the end, there was no way I could escape the mandate to help. Hadn't I been witness to the miracles that had taken place in Brazil? I had a deep confidence that if we would take up the challenge and move forward to meet additional inequities in global health care, God would send many people to help us. Still, it would take a lot of planning, research, and unbelievably hard work to overcome the inertia of nothingness and bring into existence a newly capable Project C.U.R.E.

God encouraged me by bringing to mind a story I had learned while I was young. Florence Nightingale nearly remade the British health care system single-handedly while serving in troop hospitals during the Crimean War. The sanitary conditions she insisted upon reduced the mortality rate by 75 percent. Once home, her own health permanently broken, she campaigned relentlessly via correspondence for further reforms of the British health care system. Britain embraced her as a hero. Florence Nightingale knew her part, but gave the greater credit to God.

> If I could give you information of my life, it would be to show how a woman of very ordinary ability has been led of God in strange and unaccustomed paths to do in His service what He has done in her. And if I could tell you, you would see how God has done it all and I nothing. I have worked hard, very hard. That is all: and I have never refused God anything.

I was willing to work hard, and I had pledged to give the best of my life for the rest of my life. Now God would need to go ahead of us and help us work through all the knotty problems of international benevolence.

Let me explain key concepts that came to the fore in Brazil and then influenced Project C.U.R.E.'s model. I have been using, and will be using, phrases throughout this writing like "change makers," "entrepreneurs," and even "social and cultural entrepreneurs." Let's tie down some basic concepts and phrases that we will examine. First, we need to understand what an entrepreneur is. I can do that best by going back to another one of my favorite stories learned during my childhood.

There once was a man who entered a shoemaker's shop and told the proprietor that he liked the pair of shoes on display and wanted to know how much the pair of new shoes would cost. The shopkeeper told him that the price of a new pair of shoes would be one hundred dollars. The man tried on the shoes, liked them, pulled out his money, and paid the shoemaker the required one hundred dollars. The customer was going to wear his new shoes right out of the shop.

The shopkeeper courteously wrapped his customer's old other shoes in a package of paper, and the man tucked them under his arm to leave. As he turned to exit the shoemaker's shop another man entered, walked to the counter, and indicated to the shopkeeper that he needed desperately to purchase a pair of shoes. "How much will you charge for the shoes?" the second man asked.

"My shoes cost one hundred dollars a pair," the shopkeeper answered.

"But I only have fifty dollars."

Thereupon, the man who had just purchased his shoes stepped forward and pulled from under his arm the package that contained his used shoes. "I have here a good pair of shoes that I would be willing to sell for fifty dollars. Try them on."

The second man tried on the shoes and found they fit very well indeed. "These will work just fine," he said. He gladly pulled out his fifty dollars and paid for his shoes.

Both men left the shoemaker's shop smiling. Both ended up better off. They shook hands and went their separate ways.

Now, both of the men bought a pair of shoes that day. Each had paid fifty dollars for his pair of shoes. The one man had ended up with a used pair of shoes for his fifty dollars. The other man had walked away with a new pair of shoes for his fifty dollars.

The story of the shoes had always intrigued me. As a boy I determined that if it were all the same to everyone, I would like to become the man who ended up with the brand new shoes for the fifty dollars. A second look at the simple story reveals that there are a lot of interesting principles involved, and one element in particular made me curious.

In order for the successful transaction to take place it seemed that there had to be a someone who was perceptive enough to see the need, quickly figure out a solution, and be able to move to rearrange the resources to everyone's benefit. There had to be an individual who would step forward and become a "change maker." In the story, the fellow who figured out a way for the second man to purchase a pair of shoes with the money he had available to him and offered to sell his other pair of shoes was handsomely rewarded for his creativity. Individuals who possess those problem-solving skills within an economic society are known as "entrepreneurs."

Within an economic system there needs to be other fundamental factors. These can be summarized as land, labor, and capital. In our story about the shoes everything could eventually be traced back to a connection with the land. In order for the cow to produce the hide for the leather shoes, it had to eat grass or hay grown from the land.

The second component necessary to an economic system is labor. Someone had to take the cow leather and make it into the shoes. The shoemaker's role in supplying the labor was absolutely mandatory. Even if he had a robot make the shoes, someone needed to program and oversee the labor of the robot.

The third component included in any economic system is capital. Capital, of one kind or another, is necessary to move the labor force forward in its activities related to the land. The tools of the shoemaker, or any other commodity or service fashioned by mankind with the intent to increase the productivity of the labor of the shoemaker, could be considered capital, as could the money that "capitalized" or set the shoemaker up in business.

Entrepreneurs are crucial, though, to the advancement of any economic system because they move other components out of the position of lower into a position of higher productivity and increased yields. There has to be someone who sees a need and realizes that he has tucked away in a package under his arm exactly what's necessary to make everyone in the situation better off.

A person who has entrepreneurial abilities can take something that would appear to be of little or lesser value in its present existence and organize it through skillful and creative efforts into a position of added value. Once that happens an enhanced final product or effort is created that can be duplicated by no other known method. When the entrepreneur successfully organizes and transforms what was once seen as a vision of possibility into a product or service of value, he is often rewarded in great measure. To take a recent example, sand has existed for ages, but it took a long time for entrepreneurs who learned how to turn sand (silicon) into microchips to come along and revolutionize the global economy.

Entrepreneurs are "change agents" in any economic system. Others in the economic system who want or need that new enhanced product or service will gladly exchange what resources they have in their possession in order to obtain the new commodity from the entrepreneur.

As I thought about what we were doing with Project C.U.R.E., I became intrigued with the close parallel between the "discipline of economics" and the "discipline of social structure." The role of the individual runs parallel in both. Change agents in an *economic system* look a lot like change agents in the *social structure*.

Much like the "discipline of economics," the "discipline of social structure" includes some very simple and understandable factors. Instead of the *land, labor, capital,* and *the entrepreneur,* as we examined in the discipline of economics, the discipline of social structure rests on the four pillars of *traditions, institutions,* the *family unit,* and the *individual.*

Traditions are the embodiment of those ideas that we hold to as necessary and true. They are the sacred concepts that we believe in and practice and transfer, often at great expense and effort, to future generations.

In order to preserve and promote chosen traditions, societies will often develop organizational vehicles known as institutions. Institutions such as tribal councils, schools, churches, or even government structures assist in the promoting and preserving of society's traditions.

There would be no long-lasting traditions or institutions without the family. It meets the needs of intimacy, procreation, development, and security.

The fourth pillar of any social structure is also the most fundamental component. Absolutely nothing would happen—there could be no traditions, institutions, or even the family—without the individual. That seems pretty straightforward.

We can overlay the discipline of economics with the discipline of the social structure and note intriguing similarities. In the social structure nothing changes or happens without the involvement of the individual. Likewise, the economy is helpless and useless without the entrepreneur injecting into the formula vision, energy, sustained focus, new solutions, initiative, and a hope for new beginnings. In this sense, it is fair to consider the fact that a new discipline, which we will call "cultural economics," should be explored.

Is it possible that the entrepreneur, working as a change agent in the arena of economics, could also transfer those talents and abilities to the discipline of the social structure, and likewise be a change agent in cultural economics? I personally believe that it is not only possible, but absolutely necessary, for the needed paradigm shifts of global transformation to take place. That paradigm shift is behind my admonition to thousands of people in more than one hundred and fifty countries to shift personally from success to significance in their own lives.

My constant theme runs as follows: take the skills that you have developed as an entrepreneur in the economic arena and apply them in the world of cultural economics. That's truly the path to changing the world for the better.

The reason why I am so passionate about this possibility is because it is exactly the paradigm shift that took place in my own life. I was blessed with talent, intuition, and insight. I was able to negotiate within the arena of economics and business and become very successful. As I said before, I was doing well, but I was not doing good.

I was driven to transfer the use of my gifts from the economic world to the cultural, humanitarian, and spiritual world. I needed to become the individual who stepped forward as a humanitarian change agent—who rearranged resources to everyone's benefit. I felt compelled to move humanitarian and cultural components from a position of lower into a position of higher productivity and increased yields. I personally needed to find a way to move from "success to significance."

I encountered lots of circumstances that I could have conveniently used as excuses to not pursue the shift from the world of personal asset accumulation to the world of cultural and humanitarian economics. The real rewards of satisfaction, fulfillment, and happiness have come as I have purposefully captivated those talents, insights and experiences and with laser focus dedicated them to the task of becoming a "compassionate cultural entrepreneur."

The concept of the entrepreneur embodies the notion of personal responsibility and accountability. Instead of looking around and asking why someone else or the government hasn't come up with a solution to the problem, an individual citizen steps up, accepts the responsibility as personal, and says, "Yes, I can do that. I can come up with a solution to that problem. I can fix that so that everyone else is better off."

In my travels around the world I observed on every hand that there were plenty of change agents dedicating their talents to destruction and evil. I saw the horrors of Pol Pot's Cambodia. I witnessed the ravaged societies of narcissistic leaders like Stalin, Kim Il Sung, Mao, and Nicolae Ceausescu.

But I have also met many individuals who are cultural heroes. And just as Project C.U.R.E. was encouraged into being by Dr. Neves, and Dr. Lorena and her family, so we would continue to find cultural entrepreneurs and change agents in other countries with whom we could engage in making positive cultural and spiritual changes.

I had now been traveling internationally since 1984, and I was not naive about the dangers, complexities, and pitfalls of dealing in the international community. Before Project C.U.R.E., during the period when I was serving as an international consultant on economics, I was invited by the World Bank and International Monetary Fund to participate in a "think tank" in Indianapolis to help develop model economies for lesser developed countries around the world.

During a coffee break, a tall, regal-looking woman approached me and said, "My name is Maxine Partee, and I am the personal representative of Robert Mugabe, president of the new country of Zimbabwe in Africa. As you probably know we just recently took over the government of Zimbabwe from the Ian Smith regime, and we have great hopes for the future of our country."

She went on, "As I was listening to you, I thought, 'He needs to come to Harare and help us.' Would you consider coming to Zimbabwe and working with President Mugabe and his cabinet?" The new president and his advisors, Maxine Partee went on to explain, had already discovered that they were woefully short in economic expertise.

After a lot of correspondence, and after President Mugabe had sent his nephew, Mr. Chickowore, one of the cabinet members, and an Indian economist to my home in Colorado, I returned with them to Harare and worked with them in developing some economic policies and procedures.

(After this, leaders in Ecuador, Peru, and Venezuela also invited me to their countries. This eventually led to my work in Brazil.)

I had great hopes at first that I could make a significant contribution to the newly-named Zimbabwe (formerly Rhodesia). Then I saw, first hand, how it was all likely to unravel, as it has, with disastrous consequences that have scandalized the world. At one of our dinner meetings in the capital, Harare, some of President Mugabe's military generals were pressing him for homes, autos, and financial "bonuses." In their boisterous laughing and drinking, the generals in no uncertain terms reminded the president that if it hadn't been for their "loyalty" he would not be in the position of president. It would certainly be dreadful if their requests for the "bonuses" were not met and they had to go find another "champion."

Although I kept perfectly silent, it was at that point that I decided that my help would be better invested elsewhere. Of course, in the ensuing years that scene morphed hideously into a monstrous government that has killed tens of thousands. The country that was Rhodesia, the "breadbasket" of Africa, has become a land of grown-over farms and broken systems.

The same pattern has occurred in African nation after African nation. A new "liberator" leads a rebellion and overthrows an existing corrupt regime, only to become more corrupt than his predecessor, as was the case of Laurent Kabila taking over Zaire from Mobutu Sese Seko in the story I related in chapter two.

So, how could a fledgling organization called Project C.U.R.E., located in Colorado, USA, bob and weave successfully through the systematic corruption of governments on needy continents and deliver help and hope to the sick?

Even if we were to find a way around the domestic dangers, how could we counter the inbred corruption of the international aid organizations woven into the fabric of established and well-funded groups of mercy?

I had picked up a copy of Graham Hancock's book, *The Lords of Poverty*,[3] and had read it on some of my long flight segments. The more of the book I read, the more disgusted I became. Hancock had done extensive research documenting the power, prestige, and corruption of the huge international aid and relief business. He cited how "Hunger Project" had collected nearly seven million dollars in Britain and the US for the starving in Sudan. Out of the seven million dollars, only two hundred ten thousand dollars had gotten to Sudan through dispensing grants to other organizations that actually became involved in Sudan's plight. The bulk of it had been spent on enrollment and committees, communication, information, education services, publications, management in general, and fundraising.

Another story the author followed was where eighteen million dollars had been raised by International Christian Aid for famine relief in Ethiopia, but the organization had failed to send a single cent to Ethiopia. Priority One International in one year had sent only eighteen cents of every dollar received for donations.

I felt the blood pressure behind my eyes increase as I read of the account of the United Nations High Commission for Refugees. Time and again UN monies raised from participating countries never even reached the countries hosting the refugees targeted to receive help, let alone the refugees themselves. Hancock cited one incident where an agency in East Africa received four hundred thousand dollars from the UN. The entire amount went for "relief staff support costs." The relief staff consisted of "recent graduates of Columbia University still wet behind the ears, none of whom had been in Africa before and they had no relevant experience."

Lords of Poverty does not dwell on individual charity organizations, but exposes the ineptitude and corruption associated with the large organizations connected to the United Nations and the World Bank. One incident he related told how Sidney Waldron, a construction engineer working for the UN, was one day summoned to take care of a "sanitary emergency" in a town in Somalia. Thinking the emergency probably had to do with the ever-present cholera problem that stalks the refugee camps, Waldron hastened from Mogadishu to the town of Belet Weyne. Before leaving he consulted with other engineers about the "basic slit-trench and pit construction, labor recruitment, payment plans, and tool availability," in order to be prepared to build sanitary facilities for two hundred thousand refugees. When he arrived he found that the regional UN chief needed a private toilet and shower installed.

By the time I had finished the book I was angry at the United Nations, the World Bank, and all the rest of the bloated international humanitarian organizations that had been created to meet the needs of the hurting and bind up the wounds of the broken. How was it that they had adopted practices of unchecked greed, corruption, and abuse that surpassed the failings of the nations they were supposed to be helping? They seemed to have no qualms about shoving their hands into the pockets of US taxpayers, and those of other wealthy nations, who had absolutely nothing to say about where their money was going?

I knew from Project C.U.R.E.'s work in Brazil that if we had not been able to receive the government's cooperation at the highest levels, and did not have the partners we did among Brazil's medical establishment, the aid Project C.U.R.E. had sent would have been subject to the same theft and inefficiencies that plagued other organizations.

So, if we had an opportunity to structure an international agency that would be capable of sharing sustainable help and hope to a needy world, just what would it look like? What would be the set of "unique distinctives" that would enable us to be effective where so many other large efforts had failed? Somehow I knew that we would be wasting our time if we settled for becoming another "big-scheme" humanitarian organization, with little integrity or accountability, poorly conceived goals, and methods and fraudulent administrative behavior.

The door was wide open, though, for smaller, leaner organizations that would be self-disciplined enough to concentrate on one aspect of the larger problem, becoming the best in a particular niche. Small agencies by themselves could not end world poverty or resurrect broken health care systems, but they could be very powerful and effective instruments in meeting the desperate needs of the poor and sick, providing hope and new opportunities.

It was then that I realized how invaluable the "laboratory" of Brazil had been. Project C.U.R.E. had providentially discovered a set of ideas that, taken together, amounted to an entirely new way of delivering medical relief. The challenges of expansion brought these ideas to the forefront in a way that made me realize just how different our "business model" was. Without quite knowing it, we had been building our charitable boat into a larger, ocean-going ship even while sailing.

I also began discovering something else around this time—something personal. I was beginning to sense a deep feeling of joy and fulfillment. As I began to see the pieces of the desired puzzle coming together I experienced a strange new energy and creativity. I told Anna Marie that I was becoming the "happiest man in the world."

13

Up Close and Personal—Always

Project C.U.R.E. began the day I stood in a poor Brazilian clinic, looked at its pathetic supply of old bandages, and promised to bring Dr. Neves what he needed. From the beginning our organization was grounded in a direct response to situations I knew firsthand. This became the hallmark of Project C.U.R.E.—we never delivered supplies anywhere before assessing the needs in person.

Many and varied sorts of people have tried to deflect Project C.U.R.E. from this first principle. One day I received a phone call from a Baptist preacher in Texas. "Hello," he said, "I understand you've received some warehouses full of very good donated medical items, is that true? Do I have the right Dr. James W. Jackson?"

I said he did.

"Am I glad to reach you! I'm connected with some missions projects in Mexico and also the old Soviet Union. I am going to give to you their addresses, and I'd like you to ship them what they need. I will be sending you the exact list. They need these medical supplies right away. Both places are in crisis."

"I understand, but that's not how this works. If you'd like, you can fill out an application for Project C.U.R.E. to come to your missions and perform individual 'needs assessments.'"

"What in God's name are 'needs assessments?'" asked the preacher.

"You don't need to assess anything. *I'm* telling you what these hurting people in Mexico and Russia need. I've already done the assessing!"

I took a deep breath and explained that if the situation seemed right I would travel to the locations and perform a complete assessment of the facility. That was the only way we could proceed. "Our assessment study consists of about ten pages of questions. We try to determine not only the appropriate medical supplies and pieces of medical equipment needed, but also the level of expertise of the staff members, the availability of water, electricity, potential numbers of patients from the local area, the political feasibility of working within the country, potential theft and black market problems involved, the nearest port cities, etc. To do this work right requires a lot of information."

My preacher friend remained unconvinced. "Maybe we have a bad connection, here, Dr. Jackson. Or you aren't listening. I already know good and well what I need you to ship. What you want to do seems to be a needless expense, and who's going to pay for it? Is this thing a racket or what?"

I kept my cool. "You, or whoever would be the sponsor of the project, would be expected to pick up the cost of the travel and to host the person doing the assessment while he is there," I answered. "It's important to have the sponsor be financially invested in the project from the beginning."

"Let me ask you one more question," said the pastor, "Did God give to you all the things you have in your warehouses?"

"You could say that, since God owns everything in the universe. I'm sure we agree on that."

"That's exactly what I am saying to you, friend. You don't own those medical goods in those warehouses. God gave those things to you to give to me."

"I thought we were giving them to people in Mexico and Russia?"

"To me for them! You know what I meant."

"There's some expense involved, pastor. Project C.U.R.E. donates all the medical supplies and pieces of medical equipment, but your sponsoring organization would be responsible for the shipping and handling costs of the ocean-going container loads needed to deliver the medical goods."

Click, the phone went dead.

We were very serious about our stewardship responsibilities at Project C.U.R.E., and one of the first policies set into place was that we would never send anything anywhere unless we had been willing to go personally to that venue first and meet the people involved and evaluate the situation. Very rarely did we ever discontinue the relationship after we had once visited the proposed recipient. That was because we tried earnestly to qualify the request before it got to that point.

We found that whatever was considered "*free*" was somewhere along the process considered "*without value.*" If the sponsors or recipients did not have a worthy "buy-in," then you could not expect them to collect the goods from the port or go through any other aspect of the project that demanded honest effort. If it cost them nothing, it was too great a temptation to say, "Oh, well, if we lose this shipment, Project C.U.R.E. will give us some more since it was free anyway." It was our responsibility to insist on integrity and help the recipients perform as qualified partners.

I had been shown statistics suggesting that up to forty percent of all relief goods and aid flowing out of our country never made it to where the contributions were supposed to go. Most of the problems could be laid at the feet of the donors who were willing to simply ship things to recipients without becoming personally involved in the administration and accountability of the project.

As of this writing Project C.U.R.E. has never lost a container.

I can best convey the seriousness with which we approach "needs assessment" by telling a story from Vietnam. Believe me, traveling to such places is not a pleasure cruise, much less a "racket." (In fact, in terms of personal cost, it was the travel that would finally catch up with me.)

We had become involved in Vietnam in 1996, donating medical goods to the southern region of the country, including Ho Chi Minh City (old Saigon). Our successful endeavors there catapulted us to the northern seven provinces between the capital, Hanoi, and the China border. Our work in furnishing the new three-hundred-and-fifty-bed hospital in Viet Tri caught the attention of the Vietnamese Charity Association as well as the leadership of the Vietnamese People's Party that still ran the politics and economy of the country. By 1998 Project C.U.R.E. had effectively placed close to $6 million into the health care system of Vietnam.

One day Dr. Vinh Ngoc Le, a gentleman who lived in Aurora, Colorado, called my office. Dr. Vinh had complied with all our paperwork requirements to request assistance from Project C.U.R.E. for Vietnam. He wanted to persuade me to visit, as soon as possible, locations in the central and coastal areas of Vietnam around Da Nang and Quang Nam with him.

Dr. Vinh Ngoc Le had tagged his effort as "The Nehemiah Medical Project for Vietnam." His primary institutional target for the assessment was the Dien Ban District Hospital in Quang Nam, located about twenty-four kilometers from Da Nang. His friends and he had already raised enough money to pay for the shipping and handling costs and would pay for my airfare and hotel expenses in Da Nang. He stuck to the facts, saying little about his motivation. In due course I found out that he had once practiced medicine at this hospital before becoming the communist government's political prisoner. Despite a harrowing escape and long years in which his family was separated, he never lost the desire to return and help his people. Dr. Vinh Ngoc Le indicated that should this first venture with the hospital in Quang Nam be successful, he would like the option to continue working with Project C.U.R.E. as a long-term partner in Vietnam.

Our travel took us from Denver to Los Angeles, then to Bangkok via Japan, then to Hanoi and on to Da Nang.

It had been raining hard in Bangkok when we departed—a storm that covered nearly the whole of Southeast Asia. The flight was punctuated by a whole lot of turbulent weather. We landed on a rain-drenched runway in Hanoi. It continued to rain very hard in Hanoi, and if possible it was even more turbulent and stormy when we landed in Da Nang.

Dr. Vinh Ngoc Le and a couple of his buddies met my flight. Our van made its way through waves of rain and deep water on our way to the hotel. Many of the intersections of the city had water running above the sidewalks. A spectacular lightning display lit up the dark Vietnamese sky as the storm continued.

I checked into the Hoa Sen Hotel, a typical Vietnamese side-street hotel of about ten rooms. I immediately memorized the address, 103-105 Hong Vuong, in case I should get into a jam during my stay and need a rickshaw to deliver me back to the hotel. It was about nine o'clock at night, but my new friend, Dr. Vinh Ngoc Le, insisted that we eat some hot noodles before going to bed.

Back in my room I looked out the hotel window before getting into bed. The rain fell so fast and hard that I couldn't see to the other side of the narrow street.

Saturday morning I woke up singing a little song that my mother taught me when I was a little boy. She used to sing the lead and I would sing the harmony. I hadn't thought about the song for so many years that I was surprised to remember the chorus.

It's just like Jesus to roll the clouds away
It's just like Jesus to keep me day by day
It's just like Jesus all along the way
It's just like his great love

I thought, *Now where did that come from?* My mind must have been working all night on the problems the rain might present and the challenges Project C.U.R.E. was facing back in Denver. The song was a gift and an answer.

"Thank you, God, I accept those conclusions!" I said right out loud in the hotel room. "It has always been your love that has pulled me through everything else ... so, too, it will be now!"

Then, amazingly, I started to sing the words to the verse I had never memorized, or had long since forgotten.

Oh, I could sing forever of Jesus' love divine
Of all his care and tenderness for this poor life of mine
His love is in and over all, and wind and waves obey
When Jesus whispers, "Peace be still"
The storm clouds roll away.

On my way from my bed to the shower I sneaked a look out of my hotel room window to the streets of Da Nang. It was still raining. But I smiled and thought, *Yup, it's raining out there ... and out there are lots of logistical problems, but it's not raining inside of me today and that is what counts.* Inside of me I had heard, *Peace, be still,* and that settled my mind as to God being in control.

The heavy rain continued all day Saturday. Dr. Vinh Ngoc Le telephoned the director of the hospital we were to assess in Quang Nam. The floodwaters in Quang Nam had risen so much that it was no longer possible to drive to the hospital from Da Nang by automobile. The director suggested we wait a while until the water receded. So, I found some plastic sheeting, wrapped myself up in it, and went for a walk in the rain.

In Da Nang the average worker made about the equivalent of fifty dollars US per month. The dream most often expressed by the people I talked to in Da Nang was to somehow acquire a motorbike. They wanted to stop riding in rickshaws or riding their old bicycles, and get modern, new motorbikes. The most common motorcycle I viewed in Da Nang was the Honda 90cc. The families that had been able to purchase one would haul the entire family on the small motorbike. As I walked, I watched the families navigating the rain-swollen streets. They simply wrapped themselves in sheets of plastic and sputtered on, trailing puffs of blue smoke.

I walked back to the little hotel. The storm had begun to intensify even more. I closed my eyes and listened to the sound of the rain beating a fierce rhythm on the sheet metal of the window ledge.

On Sunday morning I attended church with Dr. Vinh. Before the pastor delivered his message he made an announcement. The flood waters had risen so dramatically in the Quang Nam area that twenty-five people climbed into an old "long boat" to escape the flood. The water was so swift that the boat had capsized and all twenty-five had died in the swirling water. That was the area where Dr. Vinh Ngoc Le and I were planning to do the assessment on the Dien Ban District Hospital. As we left the Vietnamese church the rain was still coming down in torrents.

At two o'clock that afternoon I received a telephone call in my hotel room. It was from a Vietnamese man who spoke broken, if understandable, English. He explained that he was from the ministry of health, and he was trying to figure out a way to get Dr. Vinh Ngoc Le and me out to the hospital in Quang Nam. The roads were impassable and the constant rain had flooded the hospital. The storm might persist for the next couple of days, if not longer. He said he and another medical officer would like to come and visit us at our hotel at three o'clock and discuss the situation farther.

At three our visitors arrived at the Hoa Sen Hotel riding on motorcycles and wrapped up in plastic like Christmas presents. Once inside the hotel we ordered hot tea and sat and talked. They informed us that we might get through to Quang Nam on motorcycles, but only if the rain stopped soon.

I explained to them that it was very necessary to get to the hospital as soon as possible because my departure to the United States was scheduled for Tuesday and I could not delay those arrangements. I also explained that I had made a commitment to Dr. Vinh Ngoc Le that I would go with him and assess the hospital so that we could send the greatly needed medical supplies to them. Now that the flood had inundated the facility, it was more important than ever that we make it to the hospital. "If I don't get to the hospital before I leave, then I cannot send any donations there. I am willing to do whatever it takes to go to the hospital with you."

They said the water level inside the hospital was presently over six feet and rising. They looked at me and then at each other as if searching for a way to explain the unlikelihood of the trip to the American.

I went right on assuring them that if they would find a way to get us there we would still be willing to go out to Quang Nam. They could not believe that an American would care enough about them to go out in the storm and help one of the flooded hospitals. They agreed to make whatever arrangements could be managed—probably two more motorcycles and lots more plastic sheets. But we didn't hear from the health ministry people the rest of the day.

I awoke Monday morning to find that the rain had stopped during the night. As I looked out the window of my hotel room, I realized for the first time since I had arrived in Da Nang there were mountains to the west of the city. And the Hoa Sen Hotel was only three blocks away from the previously unseen sea.

I met up with Vinh Le for our regular bread, cheese, and mud-black coffee breakfast. While we were eating, two men approached our table and introduced themselves to us. One man worked for the health services in Quang Nam, and the other was a driver. They had secured a very large truck and had come to take us as far as we could get on the road to Dien Ban hospital.

There were lots of motorcycles back on the streets of Da Nang as we drove out of the city. The two men told us that in the past thirty years there had not been a storm like the one we experienced. There was minor flooding all along the road toward Quang Nam. The river was running far out of its banks and was almost up to the bottom girders of the main bridge as we crossed. After about fifteen to twenty kilometers we could see where the water was high enough to run into the houses alongside the road. Several times groups of people who had gathered along the roadside yelled at us and waved their arms to warn us. But the driver kept moving on. At times we drove through water that was deeper than the tires on the big truck.

Down the road a couple hundred yards I could see a crowd of people gathered, blocking the entire roadway. The truck driver worked our vehicle through the crowd as far as possible, then he squeezed over to the side of the road and shut off the engine. We would be walking from there. I grabbed my camera bag and my leather notebook and followed along. Suddenly the roadway dropped off into about three feet of water. The people were gathered at the water's edge. Ancient fishing boats had docked at the end of the washed-out road and were being employed as rescue vessels.

The health ministry had arranged for a boat to ferry us the next six miles of what was now open water to Dien Ban District Hospital. Men on the boat hollered and waved for us to join them. To get to the boat we had to walk up six different slippery planks onto the deck of another boat and then climb from that boat into our wooden relic.

The boatmen used long poles to push us into the deeper water. We floated down what used to be the streets of Quang Nam. On either side of these "Venetian canals" were homes and shops inundated with reddish-brown floodwater. The water reached the rooftops of the older homes, while those built on higher ground had water freely running in and out of the windows and doors.

The water kept deepening as we went. Our boat was about eighteen feet long and constructed of worm-eaten, spongy wood—it started out waterlogged and felt ready to break up beneath us. The hull was about three feet deep and half-filled with water. A removable plank deck kept us seated above the stew. Near the middle of the boat was a hand-cranked, one-cylinder engine. The operator of the boat signaled one of his helpers to crank up the engine as we moved from the building-lined "streets" out into open water. The cast iron exhaust pipe rose off the engine's manifold about fifteen inches and belched black oily smoke on everyone as we accelerated.

The operator had a heavy string of nylon fish leader attached to the engine's spring-loaded throttle mechanism on the carburetor. The nylon string went around a wooden pole on the deck and back to where the operator sat controlling the boat's rudder. When it took both hands of the pilot to guide the rudder, he simply put the throttle string around his big toe.

We had moved into water deep enough that it was running just beneath the electrical lines that attached to the power poles. We had to be extraordinarily careful just in case any of the two hundred forty-volt power lines were still "hot." We warned each other when to duck.

It took quite a while to travel out to Dien Ban District adjacent to the city of Quang Nam.

As we approached the "city limits," we once again had to work our way down tree-lined streets and along houses and shops. The hospital was located in an immediate population area of about one hundred thousand people. There were more than six hundred thousand people in the Dien Ban District as a whole.

Other small boats and rafts were actively involved in trying to rescue the people from their homes. People were on their roofs. I saw chickens and ducks in the trees, and dogs, and even a pig, floating on pieces of broken buildings.

At one "intersection" we met up with the director of the hospital, who was in another boat. He had come to welcome us and lead us to his very wet institution. As we crossed the town's Main Street, the water current sped up, causing clothes, utensils, furniture, plastic bags, and cups to come rushing at us. The rushing water was caused by the rapid backflow of the water headed out to sea. The "high-water marks" on the trees and buildings showed that the water had already gone down a good three feet. I thought of all the people who must have drowned, and the discovery of their bodies when the waters finally receded.

With the throttle string still wrapped around his toe, our boat operator guided our vessel in through the high-fenced entrance of the hospital compound. Our docking point was the stairwell of the second floor of the main hospital building. Everything on the main level remained under water: medical supplies and equipment, the ground floor wards, the hospital's administration files, everything.

The doctors and nurses had carried patients, charts, and a few other moveable items up to the second and third floor levels. They were without fresh water, electricity, sewer facilities, or sterile medical goods. They were dangerously low on food. No one could move to or from the hospital without a boat. They had placed two or three patients to a bed in some rooms. All the pediatrics, obstetrics, gynecology, and ambulatory patients had been crammed into the dark, smelly hallways where the floor was their bed.

Dr. Vinh Ngoc Le and I climbed out of our boat and went to the director's office to begin completion of the needs assessment forms. I quickly admit that it was tough to perform the assessment—the situation was so tragic. The doctors and administrators had gathered in the room with Dr. Le and me. I shall never forget the pleading, and almost desperate, looks in their eyes. The doctors had just completed two emergency surgeries before we had arrived. Those were surgeries performed without anything but "turn-of-century," "battlefield" conditions and procedures, including an old dilapidated anesthesia machine. Attached to the ancient machine was a crude apparatus that looked like an antique set of fireplace bellows. That contraption had been utilized for respiration.

I needed to know for the future what the hospital needed, but I felt insensitive asking. Obviously, they needed everything! Family members of the patients, who happened to be at the hospital, had no other choice but to stay there. They had made beds in the hallways, along with many of the patients, or out on the walkways.

In order to see all the departments, we had to get back into our boat and pole our way from building to building on the hospital campus. As we talked at the hospital, the conversation was mostly centered on the hardships of the past several days. We spoke of the hospital's need to replace its x-ray machines, emergency department equipment, operating room equipment, as well as all of the new supplies it would need.

In the immediate future the hospital would be faced with emergency issues, including no electricity, no clean water, no sterilization, no laundry, no kitchen, and contaminated materials. There would be a second flood, one of viral disease among the population, and they would have to deal with this flood without even the medical equivalent of old, wooden boats, if Project C.U.R.E. could not rush supplies to them just as fast as possible.

As I would never forget those moments of agony and survival that gray day in Dien Ban District Hospital, neither would I forget the spirit of appreciation of the medical people and the community in general. As Dr. Vinh Ngoc Le had pointed out, "Nobody, but nobody, has come to help these people." We were the first on the scene. And we were there only by providence. The people were overwhelmed by the sight of an American being there, at the tall American red-head who was out in a boat, out walking the halls, holding hands with the patients and families. When the people of Quang Nam would spot me from another rescue boat, or from their houses or rooftops, their faces would light up, and hundreds along the way would wave and holler "hello" or "hello, American" and wave or give me the international "thumbs up" sign, The people of Quang Nam, who really didn't have much to begin with, had lost practically everything.

As Dr. Le and I left the hospital, I gave the doctors a set of Dr. Frank Netter's classic books, *Atlas of the Human Anatomy,* and three new stethoscopes that I had toted along with me.

On our way back to the makeshift "dock" and our truck, it turned quite chilly and the wind came up, making white caps on the brown sea. At one point the boat operator asked if I could swim. "Yes, I can," I answered him. "But I don't care to, thank you!" I never saw a life jacket of any kind during our entire adventure.

Dr. Vinh Ngoc Le had been a great trooper. On our return trip in the big-wheeled truck back to the hotel, Dr. Vinh Ngoc Le and I began to talk about our adventure. The timing and the circumstances seemed so providential. We had changed the dates of the trip from December to November. Dr. Vinh Ngoc Le had picked the Dien Ban District Hospital to help way back in February 1998. Vinh Le had been able to travel with me and host me in an area where he had grown up. He already had all the necessary contacts. It would have taken me forever to arrange for the contacts and to work out the logistics. God had kept us safely holed up in our hotel in Da Nang while the storm raged. God calmed the storm just like He said He would.

The water had started to recede on Monday. That was the only day we could have traveled to Quang Nam. Our tickets and visas were for us to begin our return to Denver starting Tuesday. Had the rain not stopped exactly when it did, the water would not have receded far enough for us to float under the electric wires. Had we started our trip to Quang Nam later, or had the rain stopped any earlier or receded more quickly, the old homemade motorboats would have hung up on everything because the water would have been too shallow.

Dr. Vinh Ngoc Le and I agreed that God's timing had once again been incredibly and undeniably—in fact, absolutely—perfect. God giving me such clear assurance that He was in control of the storm was a very special re-enforcement to my faith.

Project C.U.R.E. had been willing to engage in a "risk-taking" position in order to fulfill its commitment to perform the needs assessment for Dr. Vinh Ngoc Le and maintain the integrity of the established protocol. Our needs assessment studies are always crucial, and in this case the study directed our attention to the one spot in the world that may have needed our help more than any other.

Following up with another report after the medical goods had been delivered to the recipient completed our assessment policy. We wanted to make certain that what we had sent from our warehouses had been received and utilized properly by the recipient hospital or clinic. Sometimes that follow-up would be achieved through e-mail reports and photographs. Sometimes we scheduled Project C.U.R.E. medical teams to go to the same venue and perform free clinics in conjunction with the hospital. Occasionally, we returned personally and did an on-site report.

In the case of the Dien Ban District Hospital outside Quang Nam, Anna Marie and I returned eighteen months later to view the flooded hospital. As we drove through the gated entrance to the hospital, we were met by excited and grateful doctors and nurses. They could hardly wait to express their thanks for Project C.U.R.E. coming to their aid and sending nearly a million dollars worth of medical supplies and pieces of equipment in the months following their flood.

After we were directed to the hospital administration conference room, the staff graciously presented huge bouquets of flowers to Anna Marie, Vinh Ngoc Le, and me. I was nearly overwhelmed at the difference Project C.U.R.E. had made through the supplying of medical goods to the people at the Dien Ban hospital after their flood experience.

As soon as our formal dialogue was finished in the conference room, the doctors were eager to show us all the things that Project C.U.R.E. had sent. The first thing they wanted us to see was the huge x-ray machine that had been installed in the room labeled Radiology. The last time I had seen the room, everything was under the floodwaters. The doctors were ecstatic as they showed us the new installation, how everything worked, and that the x-ray table was even movable and adjustable. Then they led us into the x-ray developing room where they proudly showed us the beautiful automatic x-ray developer. All the other hospitals were still developing their x-ray negatives by dipping them from one pan of solution to another and hanging them from wire hangers until they were dried. They proudly showed us the wall-mounted light boxes that we had sent them for viewing the finished x-ray pictures.

As we walked down the long hallways, we stopped in room after room filled with fresh, new medical supplies of needles, syringes, sutures, and latex gloves. These rooms also had the new adjustable hospital beds that we sent. We were shown new dental chairs, wheelchairs, examination tables, birthing tables, stainless steel carts, IV poles, shelving, and even new gurneys. I realized that the medical equipment would be there saving thousands of lives each year, long after I was dead and gone.

I was handling the emotion of the occasion pretty well until we headed into the Surgery Department. I remembered that old anesthesia machine with its fireplace bellows. That picture flashed back into my mind as I followed the surgeons and doctors into the new operating room. They were almost jumping up and down as they showed me the anesthesia machine that Project C.U.R.E. had sent. They took off the protective plastic cover and plugged the cord into the wall socket. The anesthesia unit began to beep, and lights began to flash, and level meters began to bob up and down. The doctor then turned on the automatic respirator function and just stood there and watched it "breathe" by itself. As it pumped and wheezed and expanded and contracted by itself, the doctors laughed and talked excitedly in racing Vietnamese. What pleasure they took in this machine because they knew it would save lives! The operating room also included Project C.U.R.E. lights, tables, suction pumps, and electric cauterizers. I could only guess how many lives they had already been able to save, having been empowered and enabled by the new supplies and machines. By that point tears were in my eyes and I was having a difficult time seeing through my camera viewfinder to take pictures. All those items had once been in one of our Project C.U.R.E. warehouses in the United States.

"After the terrible flood, no one but Project C.U.R.E. came to help us," the director told us. "What you sent to us was exactly what we needed! Not even our own government could do for us what Project C.U.R.E. did for us," said Dr. Tran Cong An, as he thanked us again and again.

14

The Challenge of Neutrality

By the year 1993 our "business model" included "distinctive qualities" that were becoming the established identity and mission of Project C.U.R.E. We were now insisting that we perform an "on-location needs assessment" to qualify the targeted medical facilities and the people they served.

As with our insistence on performing the needs assessments, other distinctive qualities were shaping the character of Project C.U.R.E.

Because of our experience gained in Brazil, we were learning to avoid the black market depredations, that plague so much relief work, by having contacts at the highest levels of government. The principle of partnership extended through various levels of in-country contacts, and at home as well, especially in terms of the partners who directed our attention to different places in the world. The partners could provide shipping and assessment financing, and many times had the medical skills necessary to put the resources we provided to good use.

These distinctive characteristics might make it seem that Project C.U.R.E. was "choosy" or highly selective about where we went and the people with whom we were willing to become partners. Paradoxically, we adopted one distinctive principle that seemed to run against the cautionary approach suggested by these other principles. Project C.U.R.E. committed itself to political neutrality, and went anywhere in the world, without regard to politics. We insisted on dealing with the top leaders in a nation only for the sake of ensuring that our medical supplies would reach the common people. We had no requirements as to the politics of these leaders. We put "love your enemies" into practice.

By the year 1995, we were working in hostile places such as Russia, Uzbekistan, China, Cuba, and the "hermit kingdom," North Korea.

Sometimes I would receive comments from folks like those in the Cuban-American community in Miami, who asked, "Why are you helping the people in the villages of Cuba? You should leave them alone. If enough of the people die because Castro isn't taking care of them, then they will rise up and revolt and overthrow Castro. Helping them just prolongs the situation and keeps us from getting to go back to Cuba."

This may be political realism, but it isn't necessarily what Christ called us to. Christian mission possesses a higher logic than the world can understand: an understanding of cause and effect that counts on divine intervention.

In October, 1992, Anna Marie and I traveled to Seoul, South Korea, where we were hosted by the pastor of the nation's second largest church. During our stay we were invited to travel north to the historic Panmunjom armistice center located squarely atop the 38th latitudinal parallel. Not many folks get to visit that site. Because of the governmental and military contacts of our host, we were allowed to sign our lives away—indemnifying the government against any loss should we be injured, shot, or captured—and were placed in an armored military vehicle. We drove over the land-mine-surrounded roads of the DMZ (demilitarized zone).

Inside the armistice building was located a green-topped table strategically placed—one side on the north side of the 38th and the other half on the south side. Through the windows on the south side, United Nations soldiers peered at us, and on the north side, DPRK (Democratic People's Republic of Korea) soldiers, glared. We were instructed not to make eye contact with the DPRK soldiers, and to avoid absolutely any possible incident.

Technically, the Korean War has never ended. Only an armistice was signed in 1953 allowing the fighting to stop. Peace was never declared.

After our visit to the armistice building itself, several of us gathered outside at a small flag plaza where sixteen flags fly representing the countries that were involved in the Korean Conflict. There we listened to the huge outdoor speakers from the DPRK side blaring out their propaganda message, condemning the puppets of South Korea.

With tears in his eyes our host pastor talked of how his heart was broken over the plight of the people in the DPRK. Members of his church faithfully gathered every morning at four o'clock, even after forty years, to pray for their loved ones locked away inside North Korea. "I will never be able to go to the North and take the message of hope to our people who were so quickly separated from us," he said.

He looked at me squarely. "Jackson, you, with all your medical donations and diplomacy, have the neutral position to get your foot in the door of DPRK. Would you go inside DPRK?"

"I don't have any contacts," I said, stammering, "but my answer is 'yes' I would go."

As the reader has learned, I try to keep my promises, however quickly considered. Through various diplomatic channels within the South Korean military, and interested parties in the United States, we managed to contact a DPRK official who was willing to meet with us in New York City.

We met at a hotel coffee shop in midtown Manhattan. Our strategic contact, Ambassador Ho Jong, brought with him another DPRK colleague, Dong Kyong Chol.

The first part of our meeting was devoted to Ho Jong lambasting the United States over everything from the Francis Gary Powers U2 spyplane episode to the present embargo pressures. Because of Great Leader Kim Il Sung's great *Juche* ideals—which teach that man is the master of everything, and the Korean people are the masters of Korea's revolution—the DPRK needed nothing. His country was self-sufficient in every way.

Nonetheless, I described what Project C.U.R.E. was all about and our desire to work with North Korea's health care delivery system.

As we lined up to get lunch from the buffet table, the ambassador went first, I went second and the ambassador's colleague, Mr. Dong Kyong Chol, followed me. Standing in line I felt a tugging on my coattail. Mr. Dong spoke quietly to me in very good English, "Mr. Jackson, I am very impressed with what you do all around the world with your medical goods. I must tell you," he said very softly, "in the DPRK, we need everything!"

I learned a lesson in diplomacy that day: Listen patiently to the first story, and very carefully for the second message.

As a result of that meeting in New York City, we were officially invited to visit Pyongyang to participate in Great Leader Kim Il Sung's eighty-first birthday celebration. We would team up with a group called North Star that would provide a musical-cultural presentation for the occasion as well.

When we contacted the Korea Desk at the State Department in Washington, DC, regarding obtaining visas into North Korea, the curt reply was, "Mr. Jackson, you are not traveling to North Korea." In so many words the officials told me that they were there to keep fools like me from causing international incidents.

The State Department also warned that they had reason to believe the DPRK government might hold me as a hostage.

A visa into the DPRK can only be obtained from one place, and that is from the North Korean Embassy in Beijing. The State Department thought that once I arrived there my paperwork might turn up suspiciously missing and I would have wasted a trip to China. Others had told the State Department they had been invited to the DPRK's capital, Pyongyang, but when they arrived at the DPRK Embassy in Beijing they could not obtain a visa.

The State Department seemed to believe that I must be lying when I claimed that I had an official invitation to Pyongyang to celebrate Kim Il Sung's birthday!

Eventually, the State Department found out that the invitation was for real, and they started softening their stance when they realized that perhaps an American would actually be allowed to enter the hermit kingdom.

Finally, the State Department told me, "We still have reason to believe that they intend to hold you, and if they do there is no one there to intercede for you. None of the free world countries has operatives there. You'll be on your own as soon as you leave Beijing.

"We'll allow you to go only on the condition that you return via 'Foggy Bottom' (the CIA's headquarters) for a debriefing on your way home."

"This is a humanitarian effort," I said. "In my work I remain politically neutral. If I am to be debriefed upon my return, I will simply go to the DPRK, and the first thing I will tell my hosts will be, 'Do not show me anything I should not see, do not tell me anything I should not hear, and do not introduce me to anyone I should not meet! I'm required to give a report on everything regarding this trip to my government upon my return.'"

When I reached Beijing in April, I was pleasantly surprised to find all my paperwork in order and my airline ticket to Pyongyang waiting at the impressive marble and stone North Korean Embassy. I requested that they not permanently place their visa into my passport, which had been a prerequisite of my government to travel to DPRK.

I was then informed that there were only two flights per week from Beijing to Pyongyang. Tuesdays and Saturdays were the designated flight days, and since it was Tuesday, April 6, I would need to proceed immediately to the Beijing airport and be prepared to board the Air Koryo flight to Pyongyang at two thirty that afternoon.

The old former Russian Aeroflot plane was packed with passengers of every description. Representatives from every non-aligned communist country in the world had been invited to the festival celebrating the birthday of Great Leader Kim Il Sung. DPRK touted their regime as the "purest form of agrarian communism," and people came to observe and be part of the experiment. Many of the representatives from Libya, Venezuela,

Cambodia, and the old Soviet glared at me, wondering what an American was doing on the airplane.

As we circled the Pyongyang airstrip and approached for the landing, I could see long columns of uniformed military personnel lined up on the tarmac. The plane came to a stop, the pilots shut down the engines, and a stairway was pushed up to the door. A man in a black suit and black tie mounted the stairway accompanied by two military men with automatic weapons. Upon entering the cabin, the suited man called out, "Mister Jackson, step forward!"

I was in the second row from the front, and my heart stopped. With my shoulders and scalp tingling, I thought, *Oy! It didn't take me very long to land in jail.* The conversation with the State Department replayed in my mind: "We have reason to believe that they will hold you hostage." A couple of other names were called out after mine.

The chosen few followed the men down the stairway and into a waiting military vehicle that headed to the front of the long column of soldiers. The uniformed men and women began singing and shouting and waving fresh-cut azalea plants in our honor. It was a hero's welcome. Never before had Americans come to Pyongyang for the leader's celebration. Even though there was still danger aplenty in what I was doing, I was now breathing a little easier.

After the wild reception at the airport, the guests were taken to their rooms. There were very few automobiles on the streets of Pyongyang. Most folks were taken by old buses to the main downtown area of the city. Kim Il Sung had spent forty years building Pyongyang as a monument to himself and his Juche philosophy. There were grand statues of the leader everywhere, impressive buildings, manicured parks, and dazzling performing arts theaters, including Kim Il Sung Stadium, seating one hundred thousand spectators, and the great May Day Stadium that would comfortably hold more than one hundred and fifty thousand.

My home for the next two weeks would be in a guest compound nestled within a well-appointed villa with chefs and housekeepers. There were five maroon Mercedes autos in the country, and one had been assigned to shuttle me from appointment to appointment. As soon as I was unpacked there was a meeting planned to introduce my personal hosts, Mr. Chon Yong Gap and Mrs. Rim Gyong Hi, who were senior intelligence officers. They asked if there were any special meetings I wanted set up while I was in Pyongyang.

"Yes, I would like to have meetings with the minister of foreign affairs, the minister of health, the minister of finance and trade, and the ambassador at large. I would also like to view the Kim Man Yu Hospital, the General Hospital here in Pyongyang, the Maternity Hospital at the university, and have a personal meeting with Great Leader Kim Il Sung."

At the mention of Great Leader Kim Il Sung, Mr. Chon Yong Gap almost swallowed his entire rice cake in one gulp. The other meetings he promised to set up. Then I made one more request, as I would each of the eight times I visited Democratic People's Republic of Korea in the years that followed. "On Sunday I would like to attend the Pongsu Protestant Church that was built here in Pyongyang by the Great Leader in memory and honor of his mother, who was a devout Christian."

"We will see what we can do about that request," said Mr. Chon. As he left the villa, Mr. Chon added, "Do you realize that no other American has ever placed foot inside this guest compound before … ever?"

To their credit, our hosts kept their word and arranged for every meeting I had requested—well, sort of. Regarding the meeting with Kim Il Sung, I had to settle on that trip for a group meeting and a photo.

I loved it when we went to the church because our atheist hosts had to sit right next to me and interpret every word of the services!

I was a little surprised at how open the leaders were in the meetings that had been arranged. In some cases it was as if they had been waiting to talk to someone from the West regarding the economic principles of free markets: supply and demand, encouraging production through personal incentives instead of forced quotas, and new methods of food production and processing. The minister of health and I quickly became good friends. When he realized North Korea might receive long-needed medical supplies, a modern anesthesia machine, delivery tables and instruments for their birthing rooms, and dental equipment for the clinics in the type of small towns in which he grew up, he was like a little boy with a new schoolyard chum.

I was even invited to a meeting where the ambassador at large and the minister of foreign affairs and other top advisors to the president were discussing a newly-passed piece of legislation regarding the Ten Principles of Reunification, which were to become the guidelines for talks with South Korea.

At the birthday festival there were five different venues running night and day, with performers rotating from one theater, or concert, or circus venue to another. I marveled at how Kim Il Sung could stage such a spectacular public relations event for his own birthday, until I realized that every citizen in the country works full-time for the government precisely to make such events possible.

On Friday, April 16, the day before I returned to Beijing, I received a message at the guest villa stating that the ambassador at large and the minister of foreign affairs requested my company at dinner that night. We were to dine at the People's Palace of Culture. Intuitively, I felt that the meeting would be of special significance, and was excited about the invitation.

The dinner was an absolute delight, with far more waiters lined up around the table than dinner guests. Our sumptuously appointed table was singularly placed in the middle of a very large, darkened banquet hall. We had not gotten very far into the eight-course dinner when the ambassador at large, Mr. Choi U Jin, picked up the conversation that we had begun at his office two days before. "What message do you bring for us from your president?" asked the Ambassador.

He then explained again how they could send no further messages to the United States until the United States had responded to their last statement. "The ball is diplomatically in the US court, but they have not responded. We only hear of possibility of further damaging sanctions!"

I smiled as graciously as possible at the ambassador at large and the minister of foreign affairs, and explained, "I'm sorry, I carry no message to you from the president. I am a humanitarian, and I am here because I love the common people of the DPRK and want to pursue the possibilities of helping to bring them needed health care items. Maybe that spirit of philanthropy can set the stage for some new talks coming out of this festival."

What I said seemed to have gone unheard as the two North Korean leaders plunged into a discourse on spent nuclear materials and their desperate need for certain products and services. Finally the ambassador placed his chopsticks on the porcelain dragon plate. "You are going to take a report back to your government, Mr. Jackson. What is it that you have seen while being in Pyongyang for over ten days?"

I thought I could easily talk my way past that question: "I never dreamed that the DPRK would be such an outstandingly beautiful country. The rugged mountains, the pristine rivers, the deep green forests, the gentleness of the people, the …."

The ambassador held up his hand and stopped me. "No," he said softly, but sternly, "I want to know what you have seen while being here in DPRK!"

I instantly knew that I could not just continue to blather. I had to fish or cut bait. I decided to fish. "You really want me to tell you what I have observed while in Pyongyang?"

"Yes, Mr. Jackson!"

"OK, I will tell you then, When I arrived, and we were driven to the guest compound, I was impressed by the wide and lovely roads—every bit as wide and beautiful as those in Seoul. But there were almost no automobiles on the roads. You have five maroon Mercedes Benz autos for guests, and a handful of older Volvos given to you by Sweden. You have a few older Mercedes but they are not in good repair. You have only a few older buses for public transportation. When your people need to be transported in the mornings and evenings to their work assignments, they are picked up in the back of open dump trucks. That tells me you do not have enough capital to purchase autos and trucks, and do not have trading partners for vehicles. Most of the vehicles using your wide and beautiful roads are old military vehicles left over, either from the 1950s Korean Conflict, or even from World War II. The other morning I saw some of your soldiers. Their personnel carrier was stopped in the middle of an intersection. The transmission had broken, and the soldiers had taken off their shirts and had removed the transmission and dismantled it and were repairing it in the street. That told me that you don't have access to spare parts for even your military vehicles. All the time I have been here I have not seen one good tire on any vehicle. They have no tread and they are dangerous. You do not have trading partners where you can procure tires."

Everyone at the table had put down his needle-thin silver chopsticks and was staring at me with open mouth. "Should I go on, Mr. Ambassador?" I asked quietly.

"Oh, yes, oh, yes."

"You were kind enough to me to grant every meeting I requested during my stay, and this allowed me to observe other signs of your economic health. When we would drive up in front of a large building for an appointment, I would see pretty Korean ladies running around turning on lights before we arrived. Every building was cold and the people were wearing coats when we entered. Leaving, I'd glance back and the ladies would be running around turning off all the lights. That told me that you do not have enough fuel to heat even your main buildings and not enough electricity to light your workplaces consistently. You do not have any trading partners to help supply your energy needs."

Once again the ambassador's hand came up. "Mr. Jackson, you are a very keen and observant man. You have described to me things that I had not even noticed. And you are totally right." He then motioned to one of the attendants who took the whispered orders and scurried away. "I want to show to you something that no other Western eyes have seen." He then cleared part of the table and spread out some paper plans and maps and motioned for us to gather around him. "This is how we are going to solve our trading partner problem," he said. Then he pointed out on the maps an area in the very northeastern region of the country where the nations of China, Russia, and the DPRK join at the place the great Tuman River empties into the East Sea. "We call this our 'Golden Triangle,' where three of the earth's greatest powers converge, the port of Rajin-Sonbong. The closest Russian port, Vladivostok, freezes over every year. Rajin-Sonbong never freezes. Warm currents and the peninsula guard the great port so that the waters are always calm. We are presently developing the port's truck and train transportation, and will be able to handle 100 million tons of freight a year there. It will be a free economic trade zone for the world. We can offer millions of qualified laborers to perform value-added amenities to tax-free goods and commodities. Rajin-Sonbong will be the world's next Hong Kong!"

I was stunned at being taken into the confidence of such high-ranking leaders. They had openly discussed such matters as nuclear issues, future trade plans, and considerations for the future reunification of North Korea and South Korea. By that time the dinner had lasted over four hours. The ambassador and minister of foreign affairs personally walked me out of the magnificent People's Palace of Culture building to where my car was waiting. The ambassador took both of my hands in his, peered unflinchingly into my eyes, and said, "Mr. Jackson, you are a traveled and experienced businessman. Come back to Pyongyang and we will develop Rajin-Sonbong together."

When I returned to Washington, DC, and had lunch with those who were to debrief me, I related the happenings of the two weeks and answered every question as best I could. When I got to the part about telling the North Korean leaders bluntly of my observations of the DPRK, the intelligence officials' mouths dropped open and their eyes popped out. "No one would have talked to them that way. A trained diplomat would have told an Asian leader exactly what he wanted and expected to hear. But that is why they respected you and took you into their confidence. They admired you for having the personal freedom to say exactly what you wanted to say and to talk to them honestly."

That trip initiated a long and productive relationship with the North Koreans that included having three sets of high-ranking leaders come at different times to stay in our home in Colorado. Project C.U.R.E. began shipping millions of dollars of donated medical goods into the extremely needy hospitals and clinics throughout the country. We were issued the first shipping license from the Department of Commerce to ship directly into the hermit kingdom of the DPRK.

On one occasion my son and I were actually in Pyongyang when the huge dam broke on the Yalu River. At the time, two of our huge ocean-going containers were off-loading in Hong Kong onto North Korean ships. Ours were the first and only donations of aid to DPRK during the tragedy. Their question to me then was, "How did you know that our cities would be flooded out and our people would be in need of your supplies ... how did you know?"

On my fourth trip back into the DPRK, I had a very rewarding experience. The different leaders enjoyed taking turns hosting me upon my return to Pyongyang. I had become good friends with the minister of health, Dr. Choi Chang Sik, and it was his turn to have me come to his department and welcome me. His offices were formal and elegant with plush chairs, hand-woven carpets and delicate lace furniture coverings. We sat at separate, low-profile, hand-carved tables, being served insam, or ginseng tea. Several attendants in the room transcribed every word that was spoken during the meeting.

We joked and laughed together at the beginning before formal protocol took over. The host always speaks formally first, then the guest is given time for a brief response; the discourse continues back and forth. Minister Choi Chang Sik cleared his throat, and I knew it was time for the formalities to begin.

"Mister Jackson," he said, "three more of your very large ocean-going cargo containers have recently been received at our Nampo port and I have personally overseen the distribution of the medical goods to the hospitals and clinics where they were needed most. Great Leader Kim Il Sung, Dear Leader Kim Jong Il, and all the people of the DPRK personally thank you for your kindness. But you are a mystery to us, and we are somewhat confused. We have recorded every word you have said while in the DPRK, and have filed those words in our Grand Building of Education. You have given millions of dollars worth of needed medical supplies and equipment to our people. We cannot figure out what it is that you want. We have reviewed your words and you never give away what it is that you want from us. *Mister Jackson, What is it that you want?"*

I leaned back against the ornate lace on the chair and chuckled. "Dr. Choi," I said, smiling, "you have asked me a very direct question. I will answer you with a very direct answer. Had you not asked me directly, I would not have answered you directly. Do you have time for a very small story?"

"Of course, I have time. Please go on."

"When I was a little boy I determined that I would be a millionaire by the time I was twenty-five years old. You understand what it means to be a millionaire?"

"Oh, yes" he said.

"My brothers and I worked very hard and we tried to learn as much as possible about becoming rich. By the time I was thirty years old I had become sixteen times wealthier than I ever dreamed I would be in my entire life. But no one had told me that accumulating wealth wouldn't necessarily make me a happy man. I was not a happy man. My wife and I talked about it and asked each other the question, 'Just when were we most happy in our life?' We agreed that it was during the time when we had no money, but only had love and good health and a dream. So we decided to give all our wealth away and start over again. I asked God to forgive me for being such a selfish man, and promised that from that time forward I would spend all my energy and time helping other people. God answered my prayer and changed the mainspring of the ticking clock of my life. I became a different person than before. You now ask directly what I want from you. The answer is that *I want nothing in return from you* for any good thing that I ever do for you. I have given these medical supplies to you and your people because I love you, and I will never ask anything from you in return."

The minister of health was totally stunned as he sat looking at me. He then lowered his cup of tea down to the ornately carved table and stood up. When he stood up, I stood up. I was culturally aware enough to know that Asians do not touch others in public—they just don't! But Dr. Choi came to where I was standing. He approached me, opened his arms and hugged me with a big bear hug!

"All my life I was trained to hate you, and even kill you," he said. "But you are my brother! I love you!"

Project C.U.R.E.'s stance of political neutrality does not mean that we do not recognize tyrants when we meet them—and I've met dozens in every corner of the globe. It means that we enact Jesus' command to love not only our neighbors, but our enemies as well. The power of this love is the only thing greater than the force and violence that tyrants, dictators, and corrupt politicians employ. My witness to the North Koreans that day—and since, as our work there continues—was only *possible*, much less credible, because we were willing to act toward the North Koreans in the light of the Scriptures' teaching that even their government officials are made in the image and likeness of God. We could never have reached the common people of North Korea in their suffering—for which the whole world has sympathy—if we were unwilling to take the often uncomfortable stand of political neutrality. There's a reason Christ describes His kingdom as "not of this world," and that reason allowed for the invasion of the hermit kingdom by love.

15

Avoiding the Pitfalls— and the Thugs

The journey I have been on over these past twenty-five years with Project C.U.R.E. is too long and complex for a chronological accounting. Just mentioning the various circumstances that opened up more than one hundred and twenty-five countries to Project C.U.R.E. would become too long a read. I can best describe the process through which I became the "happiest man in the world," and discovered what I believe to be a new model of cultural transformation. Through enhancing the entrepreneur's ability to mix the principles of secular and biblical economics and business, and applying those principles to real needs in developing countries, we had discovered a creative method to accomplish "cultural transformation." By bringing real answers to medical needs in poor countries we were becoming effective also in delivering economic and cultural change.

Certainly little of what I've been a part of would have been possible if God had not given us access to national leaders around the globe. Otherwise, corruption at lower levels most certainly would have had its way.

At 11:40 a.m., December 7, 1988, an unprecedented earthquake nearly destroyed the country of Armenia. In a few shattering moments, eighty thousand of the three hundred and fifty thousand residents were killed in just the city of Gyumri. All the buildings of the city were flattened; the gas lines, sewer lines, and water lines collapsed, and what was left burned to ash.

The Soviets, who controlled the country, at first agreed to send aid to the people of Armenia, and promised to repair the country. Russia's own economy was already in chaos, though, and the Soviet Union would collapse in a matter of months. The Soviet forces, after surveying the damage in Armenia, pulled up stakes and went home.

Thirteen years later, in 2001, Armenia was still in ruins. I was asked to travel to Armenia to assess the situation by a couple of wealthy Americans, George Fermanian and Steve Lazarian, who had deep familial ties there.

My flight arrived in the capital city of Yerevan at the spooky hour of three thirty in the morning. I made it through passport control and customs, and walked down the long, damp corridor where the darkness was poorly dispelled by light bulbs dangling from raw wires. I was greatly relieved when out of the darkness stepped Dr. Petros Malakyan, a 40-year-old Armenian fellow who would be my host during my stay.

Dr. Malakyan had put together an assessment agenda that was going to be nearly impossible to accomplish. The days were crammed full. Early during my visit we stopped at what had been a district hospital. The earthquake had reduced the facility to rubble, but different organizations had stepped in and were in the process of rebuilding the old structure. Old people who had survived the quake, but lost their homes, had also moved into the skeletal building. These old people shuffled here and there and appeared to be practicing being dead.

While we were assessing the situation, Dr. Malakyan had sent someone to fetch the two nurses that remained. Soon, two old Armenian women, dressed in tattered and soiled white lab coats, pulled over worn-out sweaters, layered over dresses that had seen better days, greeted us through smiles of broken teeth. They led us to a room they shared that also served as the clinic. The older of the two knelt down beside her narrow cot and pulled from beneath it three small cardboard boxes. Those three boxes contained the sum total of all their hoarded medical goods. One very old needle and syringe lay in one of the boxes along with some bits of soiled cotton, salvaged strips of tape, and one thermometer. The other two boxes were filled with dusty stuff I didn't even recognize. With Dr. Malakyan interpreting, the two old women asked if I could possibly help bring them some things, since they had a lot of old friends living there who were sick, but they had no supplies or medications to help. I assured Dr. Malakyan, and through him the two nurses, that Project C.U.R.E. would be interested in working with their program to help the elderly in Gyumri as part of our plans to help Armenia. As we left the dilapidated former hospital, the elderly people shuffled out to see us get in the car and wave goodbye.

"This city of rubble and ruin was my home," Dr. Malakyan said with feeling. "This is where I was born. People here in Gyumri built temporary shacks to live in to get out of the cold of winter. That's all that's here today. The people still live in those temporary shacks."

Our next stop was at the Catholic Mission Center. Inside the compound we met with Sister Montiel Rosenthal, who was in charge of the Catholic work in Gyumri. She had originally come from Kentucky and gave us some pertinent insights from her position as a medical doctor in Armenia. She warned us, discreetly, about Rouben G. Khatchatryan, the man in charge of all health affairs in the northeast region of Armenia. "Because of men like him, this area doesn't really stand much of a chance to work its way out of its problems. You'll see when you meet him; he hasn't missed too many good meals."

Our final appointment that day happened to be with this very man, Rouben G. Khatchatryan. The man was really a work of art—the living, breathing epitome of the old Soviet bureaucrat under corrupt communist rule. Rouben G. Khatchatryan was a large man whose brown wool suit coat did not come close to stretching around his gigantic stomach. He had a prominent overbite. When he laughed the light reflected off his gold teeth and bounced around the room as if from a disco ball.

"You need to send money to me here at this address so I can optimize my region," he said straightaway. "As you can see everything was ruined during the earthquake. There is a law that says that the rich countries have to send money to the poor ones, so I need to have you send money to me here."

I explained how Project C.U.R.E. was now involved in eighty-three different countries around the world and how we operated.

He quickly answered, "I don't need anything you have like supplies. You can just send the money to me … I will optimize my region." He was persistent and powerful enough in his approach to convince me that he had intimidated many well-intentioned visitors from the United States and elsewhere into doing what he requested. It was also plain to see that any money sent to Rouben G. Khatchatryan never made it further than his back pocket.

Rouben sensed that I was not buying his story. So, he resorted to a creative approach.

"Come here and sit down and I will show you a great lesson. Once I agreed to let a group in America help me with medical supplies. Before it was all over I learned the real reason they wanted to help me. It was not for me, but for them. If they could find someone in a poor country to dump their bad goods on, they could make millions of dollars from the US government giving them tax money returns."

While Rouben was telling me his story, he was pulling out from a bottom desk drawer some pieces of glass. He began polishing them with his shirt-sleeve. Eventually he handed me a couple of the glass pieces to hold. "The people from America told me they were going to send eye glasses for all the children in my region who could not see well. I signed the receipt when the shipment arrived marked 'glasses.' The shipping man then took the receipt and delivered it back to America, and people there got their millions from the USA tax. But, what you are holding—these 'glasses' are no more than bottoms of bottles cut and packaged and sent to me. So we don't take donated items here anymore, only US cash money. No one is to fool us like that again. So that's why I say you can just send the US dollars to me and I will take care of everything. I will optimize my region."

It probably was not the most diplomatically correct thing to do, but I couldn't help it. I laughed right out loud at Rouben's incredible scam. "I have seen the shameful way you have 'optimized your region,' sir," I said. "Your greed is standing in the way of the healing of your people."

I stood up and announced that Project C.U.R.E. would never work with him. Then, I'm not sure why, but I had the temerity to ask him to pose with me for a photograph. I never wanted to forget him; I would share his picture with the people back at my office.

Truly knowing no shame, he proudly stepped over next to me as I handed Petros the camera, and he took our picture together. As I was leaving his office, his greed led him to try one more time. He took me by the arm and pulled me toward his desk, close enough to grab a crumpled-up photograph. "Wait," he said, "I have a program to train some nurses here in Gyumri. Look at these lovely Armenian nurses! Could you send me maybe fifty thousand dollars cash to help me fund this project?"

I laughed again and said good-bye to Rouben.

"Isn't that a shame?" Dr. Malakyan asked as we got back into his car, "That's what we have to put up with out here in Gyumri, my very own hometown."

The next day was Tuesday, April 12. After a quick breakfast of bread and cheese, we scurried through the sparse traffic of Yerevan to the Neurological and Neurosurgery Hospital. Dr. S. C. Zohrabian, the head of the hospital, and also the president of the Armenian Neurological Association, described to us the tremendous needs of the hospital, and nearly begged Project C.U.R.E. to help them by sending the necessary supplies and pieces of needed equipment. He said they needed everything, and I saw for myself that, indeed, they did.

I shall never forget what happened at the next two appointments. Consistent with another of Project C.U.R.E.'s cardinal distinctive characteristics, "work with the top decision-makers in order to get the goods to the people," we decided to go directly to Armenia's minister of health, and also to the head of the official Humanitarian Assistance Committee. We had to leap frog over the top of the greedy gatekeeper, Rouben G Khatchatryan, and ensure safe passage of our donated goods into Armenia.

I was able to get an audience with the minister of health, Dr. Jeynalian, who providentially was joined by Haik Gregorian, the head of public relations for Nagorno-Karabakh, the small neighboring country that Project C.U.R.E. had previously helped during a genocide conducted by Russia, Turkey, and Azerbaijan. Dr. Jeynalian, who had lost one of his legs (I believe in a land mine accident), watched me very closely all the time I was talking about Project C.U.R.E. and our work around the world. As he made comments or asked questions, and listened to my replies, he never took his eyes off of me. I showed the officials pictures of our work in Nagorno-Karabakh.

Toward the end of our meeting, Dr. Jeynalian said, "I study people and I have about a 99.5 percent accuracy record in judging character. I wish everyone who comes to Armenia would do business like you do business. Most come but do not want to take the time and effort to work correctly. Today, you have come here to make sure everything is correct from the top. That is the way it should happen. I am compelled to trust you totally, and I will give you my word that I will work with you on any of your projects. Anything you want to do in Armenia is hereby approved."

Dr. Malakyan was so flabbergasted that we had to nearly pick him off the floor. As we went out he remarked, "Did you hear what the minister of health said? That is unprecedented! I've never seen anything like that."

We then went directly from the health minister's office to the office of Ara S. Simoyan, president of the Humanitarian and Assistance Committee of Armenia. That committee ruled on all issues of humanitarian work in the country.

On the way to the office, Dr. Malakyan confessed that his organization had found the committee very difficult to work with and the organization had not been granted approval for some of its projects. "These people are really tough," Petros told me. "I don't really know what to expect from them today. We'll just have to see." To add to the anxiety, we were late leaving the health minister's office, which put us a bit late for our appointment at Mr. Simoyan's office.

We received a very cool reception by Mr. Simoyan and his assistant when we walked in. When he found out we had just visited Dr. Jeynalian, he let us know that even the health minister sat in on *his* Humanitarian and Assistance Committee, of which he was president. I began to wonder just how our meeting was going to turn out. Then, as we began to talk, something incredible began to happen. I noticed Mr. Simoyan began to watch me very closely, studying my eyes and my expressions as well as listening to my voice. (These Armenian officials must have been schooled in body language as a means of character assessment.) He began to soften up. The tone of his voice changed, and he even injected some humor into our conversation.

I told him how we worked in other countries; how we went first to the individual hospitals and clinics and performed an "on-the-spot needs assessment"; how we walked the hospital hallways and met the department heads and asked them individually what they needed so that we knew we would be sending the appropriate things. I explained how, while in the country, I tried to make appointments and personally meet the main decision-makers to let them know who we were and what we were doing in their country. "If at all possible, I try to meet the president or prime minister when I am there. Then, when I return home to my office, I communicate to my people what I have learned, and we determine what we have in our warehouse that would be appropriate for that country. Using the computer listing of what we have, we form a 'pick list' appropriate for that country and its hospitals and clinics. Then, we send that customized inventory list to the intended recipient in advance. The recipient has thirty days to study the list. Anything that would not be desired or appropriate can be stricken from the list by either the health minister or customs official, or, in the case of Armenia, by the president of the Humanitarian and Assistance Committee. Whereupon, when Project C.U.R.E.

receives the approved list back at our headquarters, we then actually pull the inventory from our warehouse and load out the forty-foot container and send it on its way."

When I finished explaining our procedure I sat back in my chair and relaxed. The committee president sat silently studying me for a while longer in silence. Then he said, "There is something inside you which compels me to totally trust you. I am fascinated. I want to work with you on any projects you have. As far as this committee is concerned you have all 'green lights' for your work in Armenia. We will be here to aid and assist you in your endeavors. I promise it will not take thirty days to get your list back. It will get full priority from Yerevan. Thank you for honoring us and being here."

As we walked the long hallway and back down the marble steps of the government building, Dr. Malakyan said, half-stuttering, "That man said almost the exact same thing the health ministry man said. They accepted you so completely, and in such a short time. I think as you talked to them they saw a good Spirit coming through you, and they were responding to it. More was accomplished through you in a short period of time than many months or years of working through the bureaucracy. That was a most amazing thing to experience."

What if we had not taken the time to see the right people at the top?

16

Partners and Networks

As I explained to the Baptist pastor from Texas who said "God gave you those supplies to give to me," the sponsoring organizations or individuals with whom we collaborated were critical to Project C.U.R.E.'s success. We would only go into countries where we were invited, and we would never start anything from scratch, preferring to collaborate with existing endeavors. That way we could remain focused and multiply our efforts by helping people who were already engaged.

The ways in which individuals and sponsoring organizations have discovered Project C.U.R.E. have been various, surprising, and often poignant. Expatriate communities in the United States frequently bring the needs of their home countries to our attention, as in the case of Vietnam's Dr. Vinh Ngoc Le. It's a testimony to the human spirit that immigrants do not forget those they leave behind, even when they have been exploited and abused by their countrymen. There's a profound impulse to return and help. Unimaginable evils often inspire the most heroic redemptive efforts, and these efforts have a way of establishing networks of association that cross every type of barrier.

An African named Ohmar Dja had immigrated to Denver from a village in the country of Senegal in West Africa. He worked the swing shift at the big Hyatt Regency Hotel in downtown Denver, and would finish work a little after midnight, then catch a city transit bus to where he lived. Ohmar had come to America to try to earn money for his impoverished family. His family depended on Ohmar's paycheck to get by in the village of Diorbivol along the Senegalese River at the country's border with Mauritania.

One night Ohmar Dja walked out of the hotel to the bus stop where he was senselessly gunned down—a crime that had no warrant or explanation.

Many people wanted to respond and help. John Schafer, general manager of the Hyatt Regency Hotel, the Denver Mayor's office, and the *Denver Post* newspaper contacted Project C.U.R.E. to see if we could provide assistance.

I was introduced to Mohamadou Cisse, who was the president of Denver's Senegalese expatriate community. He would be my contact person.

The citizens of Denver mourned Ohmar Dja, and raised enough money for Mohamadou Cisse to accompany the body back to Senegal, where his family could give him a proper burial. Denver's citizens also purchased a twenty-three-thousand dollar water pump for Diorbivol, as a memorial to Ohmar Dja, so the village farmers could lift water from the Senegalese River onto their parched crops. A small fund was also established to guarantee the education of Ohmar's children.

I agreed to accompany Mohamadou Cisse in October to assess the medical situation, not only in Ohmar's village, but also in Dakar, Senegal's capital. While there, we would also assess the medical institutions in the surrounding cities of Diamniadio, Bargny, and Rufisque.

During the October trip we determined Project C.U.R.E. would honor the life and family of Ohmar Dja by taking our C.U.R.E. Clinics medical team directly to the village of Diorbivol, where they would provide free medical services to all the people of the remote area. We would also take with us about twenty thousand dollars worth of wholesale medical supplies and simple pieces of equipment in order to reopen and fully equip the local clinic in Diorbivol that had been closed since 1993. Then we would work with the minister of health in the capital city of Dakar and let him know that Project C.U.R.E. would invest another $1 million in medical supplies and equipment in Senegal's health care delivery system in Dakar and the surrounding cities. Based on that infusion of aid to the general health system we could bargain for the health minister to keep the Diorbivol medical clinic open as an ongoing memorial to Ohmar Dja.

In May of the following year, longtime supporter and friend of Project C.U.R.E., Dr. Merle Jacobsen, and Laurie Tucker, his head office nurse, led the C.U.R.E. Clinic medical team from Denver into Senegal. Mohamadou Cisse's brother, Dr. Cheikh Cisse, who was a Senegalese physician, joined them in Dakar. Mohamadou and I traveled with the team as well.

We had done our homework by preparing all the required Letters of Donation and Authorization for Entrance documents. Fortunately, we were able to slide through customs with our twenty thousand dollars worth of medical goods without a hitch or a demand for a payoff.

We had not taken a break in our flight schedule, but had flown straight through from Denver to Africa. When our host took us to the small Tabara Hotel, the entire team was so exhausted we would not have known whether we were in Mexico City or Missoula, Montana. The next day we were in for an eleven-hour drive from Dakar to the village of Diorbivol.

Senegal is about the size of South Dakota, with a population of more than 10 million, with 2 million crowded in Dakar, the most important West African seaport. Seventy-five percent of the people were subsistence farmers. Average per capita annual income ranged between six hundred dollars and one thousand five hundred dollars. That's a lot of poverty. The French introduced the growing of peanuts into Senegal during the colonial days. The *ground nuts* still accounted for 40 percent of the country's cash crop. French is still the official language of Senegal, but a number of tribal dialects flourished. Only about 30 percent of the population could read and write. Despite the French Catholic influence, today more than 90 percent of the people are Muslim.

As our van headed north out of Dakar along the coastline, the ocean breeze coming into the left side windows of our van kept the temperature relatively bearable. There was no such thing as air conditioning.

By four thirty that afternoon we had reached the city of Saint Louis, where we had a greasy lunch of rice, sautéed onions, peppers, and other spices mixed with chunks of fish. You could also order a variation called *Poulet yassa* that substituted the fish with chicken chunks.

From Saint Louis we turned east. The farther we traveled away from the sea the hotter it became as we made our way into the Sahara Desert. I was grateful that we were traveling through that part of the country in the late afternoon.

The Senegalese River divided Mauritania from Senegal. As we moved closer to the river the landscape changed. Crops had been planted adjacent to the river where they could be irrigated by the crudest means. Soon we spotted small fields of onions, cabbage, rice, beans, tomatoes, and even groves of heavily laden mango trees.

As it became dark we pulled into a town called Richard Toll amid fields of sugar cane. On the edge of town was an old sugar-processing factory left over from the colonial days. About eight thousand workers were still employed there. I could immediately see the economic difference the factory made. The other small towns and villages along the way had nothing like Richard Toll's shops of wood and canvas, and its many vendors with their goods spread out on the ground beside the road.

As we continued along the river, darkness fell quickly as it does close to the equator. The night soon became pitch black, almost extinguishing the van's headlights. There was no other traffic on the road. The African night was hot and sticky and foreboding.

We could smell the burning charcoal and cooking fires through the windows well before the villages hidden away in the darkness could be seen. As we moved closer, the cooking fires looked like they were dancing on the desert floor. They dotted the African horizon with eerie orange accents.

About eleven o'clock that night, our driver suddenly pulled off the road at an unmarked intersection. He announced in his native dialect that it was time for him to eat his dinner. He would go no further until he did. He then proceeded to saunter over to a village cooking fire and negotiate for some food.

It was good to get off the thinly covered wooden seats of the van and stretch my legs and neck. I breathed in the hot, desert-night-air and looked up into the African sky. The stars were shining as brightly as they did in the high altitude of Colorado. Mohamadou Cisse slipped alongside me and told me that we would be in the village of Diorbivol by a little past midnight.

Having finished his supper, the driver turned our van onto a sandy track that led away from the main road. From that point, the driver simply had to know the goat trails and cattle trails that would take us to the village. At one point we were following along the bottom of a dry riverbed. Mohamadou explained that during August and September, when the rains came, the swollen Senegalese River would back-flood that area, leaving the village of Diorbivol an island accessible only by boat.

Suddenly, we cut up the steep sandy embankment to the top of the bluff. The driver announced that we were approaching Ohmar Dja's village. We made a turn around a big scraggly bush and the van's headlights picked up the reflection of some white patches of cloth. Then, the headlights caught the whites of teeth and eyes of smiling black faces in the darkness. Along the goat trail were fifty or more villagers who had come out to meet us—in the middle of the night. I was impressed. We honked and waved out the windows of our van, and drove on in the darkness toward the village gate, while the welcoming party clapped and shouted.

At the entrance to the village the entire population had gathered to form a massive welcoming committee. They were singing, clapping their hands, and shouting. As we drove past, they used the sides of the van as a drum, and pounded out their welcome in time with their singing. "They've given us a royal welcome," I said, aloud.

After we climbed out of the van, we were engulfed in a sea of welcome and love. Everyone wanted to shake our hands, hug us, or clap us on the back. They were pushing and laughing and singing as we were led through the gates of the compound where Ohmar Dja's sister and her extended family lived.

A large cooking fire still smoldered toward the back fence with large black, cooking cauldrons still steaming. The entire village was far beyond the reach of any electric power line, so darkness prevailed in every direction, except on the front of the main building in the compound where one small, thin, light tube, of maybe five watts, fluoresced like a glow worm. That building and one other in the village was equipped with automobile batteries that powered its bluish light tubes. During the day, the batteries were slowly recharged by a rooftop photoelectric cell.

In front of the concrete block building had been poured a cement slab that was about ten inches higher than ground level. The slab had been covered with a layer of thin foam rubber matting like cheap carpet pad. We were directed to sit down on the mat and relax. The crowd motioned for us to lie down and take off our shoes. The people pushed closer and closer in their excitement. At one point, some of the village warriors had to beat the ground with branches and sticks in front of the pressing natives in order to push them back about ten feet from the edge of the slab. I worried that someone might be harboring a grudge against the Americans who had taken their kinsman's life.

Some of the women had brought metal dishpans with them. They laid them upside down on the dirt and began beating them with their hands as drums. The drumbeat unified the movements of the people and real dancing began. Two of our group got up and joined in. The warriors would not allow anyone inside the circle to dance with our people, except two very energetic young girls. These two young girl dancers made up for everyone who wished to be front and center. Emotions were running pretty high.

Finally, there were some welcoming speeches. Mohamadou interpreted for me. Then our group was led through a hallway in the center of the concrete building back into an enclosed courtyard in the back. As soon as we disappeared, the crowd began to break up.

Our visiting party was split up to sleep in two different locations. I was assigned, along with a couple of our nurses, Helen Brown and Laurie Tucker, and Mohamadou Cisse, along with two men from the health ministry, to stay and sleep in the back courtyard. Our host's thinking was that we would be more comfortable sleeping close to the facilities. The facilities consisted of two closets slapped up alongside the back of the concrete building. To the right of the entryway into the courtyard was a hastily constructed lean-to with a drain hole running out under the outside wall. That would be our dirt floor bathhouse. The closet constructed on the left side of the entryway was the new toilet room. I unlatched the hand-pounded metal lock and opened the roughhewn wooden door. I pointed my little flashlight into the closet and spotted about ten huge cockroaches. To use the toilet you climbed two steps up and placed your feet on slabs on either side of a six-inch hole in the dirt.

The village women moved the thin rubber mat from the front of the building to the dirt in the back. They first put down a thin straw mat on the ground, then laid out the rubber mat to make a big square area for all of us to sleep. They were able to cover part of the mat with a cotton sheet. That was the communal guest bedroom. Before we could lay our heads down on the thin mat, the African ladies brought in large dishes of seasoned rice, stewed onions, potato roots, and goat meat. We sat cross-legged on the mats and ate, or tried to, in our exhaustion. It was one thirty in the morning.

The ladies then brought in small pans of hot charcoal with small teapots nestled down in the glowing coals. It was time for the sweet, foamy espresso-tea concoction typical of West Africa. Watching the ritual of the ladies taking the quaint teapots out of the live coals, and pouring the tea back and forth to create the foam, was as unique and pleasurable an experience as drinking the tea.

No one took off his or her clothes. The custom was to just lie down and go to sleep under the stars. It was so hot that even a sheet over the top would have been unbearable. Laurie Tucker was kind enough to lend me a small wool travel pillow.

At precisely five o'clock the next morning, I was jolted awake by the wailing Muslim call to prayer. Our compound was directly across from the mosque. High in the domed tower were two giant loudspeakers. In most Arab countries where I traveled the call was recorded. Not so in Diorbivol village. That was a real cleric giving it his all. The roosters of the village chimed in with vigor, mimicking the sound with hilarious perfection. It was just too good. It was terrible!

There was a welcome cool breeze blowing across the dirt courtyard. I stirred on my bed and realized that my clothes, the back of my neck, my hair, and mat were all caked with gritty sand from the Sahara desert. By then the wailing from the high tower across the trail was over. I relaxed back down on my straw mat. I was in the southern belt of the Sahara Desert, sleeping outside on the ground, in a remote, Senegalese village, covered from head to foot with dirt. Wouldn't my old investment buddies cackle if they could see me now?

I wandered over to the cockroach-infested latrine. As I came out, a young village woman handed me a bucket of murky river water and a smaller dipping bucket. She motioned me to the bath closet with the dirt floor. Once inside, I closed the wooden door and got out of my clothes. There were no hooks on the walls or on the door where I could hang my clothes to keep them out of the dirt and water. I needed to be creative. In order to hang them, I wedged them in the crack between the door's top and its jamb. Then I got serious about washing, lifting out one dipper full of water at a time, lathering up with soap, and then rinsing with another dipper full. The real trick came when trying to put my clothes back on with mud-caked feet.

For breakfast, the young women came into our sleeping area with teapots of boiling water, a jar of Nescafé coffee, a few unrefined sugar clumps, and a dented can of dehydrated milk. They also handed us some long, skinny bread rolls that had been baked in homemade ovens over the cook-fires out in front of our building. They had no cups in the village, so we made our coffee in some drinking glasses.

After I drank my strong coffee, I grabbed my camera and headed down toward the river. Between the months of October and May, the twenty-three-thousand dollar water pump, that was a gift from the people of Denver, had been delivered to the village. The pump was not hard to find. I spotted it positioned on a wooden barge anchored to the shoreline and *floating* on the river. They had taken great care to build a metal canopy over the engine and pump to protect the unit from the weather. There had been a sign placed on the barge: A gift with love to the people of Diorbivol village from the people of Denver, Colorado, in honor of Ohmar Dja. Fishermen had already been out on the river in their homemade dugout boats catching fish to take to the village market. Several younger boys were giving baths to their small ponies and donkeys.

I was eager to get to the clinic site and see what needed to be done. The health ministry had run out of money, so no one had opened the clinic since 1993. The people had either gone without health care, or, in an emergency, they had traveled by horse cart clear back to Richard Toll or another distant town. The clinic had been located out at the very edge of the village a half mile from where we were staying. Beyond the clinic stood only rolling dunes of sand and scattered scrub bush.

On the front of the brown mud-and-concrete building was a faded red cross. That caught my attention and curiosity right away. Muslims use a red crescent, not a cross, as a symbol of medical relief. Were we continuing the ministry of someone who had once prayed for a successor? Directly in front of the clinic the village leaders had erected an arbor of wooden poles and brush to provide shade for those who would be gathering at our clinic. The arbor was about twenty-five feet in length and fifteen feet in width, and had rough wooden benches beneath the stick and brush roof.

My Senegalese contact, Dr. Mohamadou Cisse, had promised that the village people would clean up the clinic before we arrived. If, in fact, they had done any cleaning, I would have hated to see it beforehand. Dr. Merle Jacobson and the C.U.R.E. Clinic medical team got busy. We began throwing things out as fast as we could. All the supplies were outdated by at least six years, and everything was crusty and covered with layers of brown dirt and sand. The van driver summoned some of the village men to help him unload and carry into the building the twenty thousand dollars worth of medical supplies and small pieces of equipment that we had brought.

Before long, several hundred people had gathered outside the clinic waiting for us to open the wooden plank doors. We kept them closed and the windows shuttered until we completed our two imperative tasks. First, to unpack and put on the shelves all the supplies and medications from our C.U.R.E. Kits. And second, to complete the opening ceremonies planned by our hosts.

The crowd was growing by the minute. Off on the horizon I could see scores of people, some walking and some in donkey carts, coming across the hot sand. Some people were even coming in boats from other villages on the river.

At the welcoming ceremonies I spoke and Mohamadou again translated for me. I spoke of building bridges that reached all the way from Colorado to Diorbivol ... bridges of friendship. I expressed our desire to get to know them and promised that we would make ourselves available and open so that they could learn to know us. But we were also there to honor the life and memory of one of their brave tribesmen who had gone so far across the water and away from the village. Ohmar Dja had a dream to go away so that he could send needed help back to the village. "I am here to tell you that Ohmar's dream has come true. He was able to provide for his people not only money that he earned from his job at the hotel, but also now a pump to be used by all the village people.

"And today, another part of Ohmar's dream will have come true. Doctors and nurses with medicine and medical knowledge have come to your village to help the sick and wounded and bring healing to your hurting villagers. And there is now hope that other good things will follow in the future. Yes, Ohmar went away so that he could bring good things to you. None of us knew what a high price would be paid to deliver that help and hope to your village. But today you can be proud of your people, your village, and the brave and fruitful life of Ohmar Dja."

The large crowd broke into applause many times during the short speech, and especially as I presented Ohmar Dja's old, white-haired father with a warm hug and a big picture book of Colorado.

When the doors of the clinic were opened, we realized that crowd control was going to be a huge challenge. Everyone wanted to get in all at once, and parents were even trying to hand their sick kids in through the open windows. We had set up four patient stations. I would be in charge of counting out and dispensing the medications based on the doctors' orders. Mohamadou guarded the back door, and an orderly ushered in the patients. Three village warriors manned the front door. Careful records were kept on all our new patients.

As the sun began to bear down on the sheet metal roof of the clinic, we began to cook inside at one hundred and thirty-five degrees Fahrenheit. Laurie and Helen were having a difficult time getting their thermometers to cool off sufficiently between uses to get any accurate reading on body temperatures. We went through our bottled water in no time.

Dr. Jacobson started on the minor surgeries. One man had a ghastly looking tumor growing out of his head, almost as large as the head itself. Dr. Jacobson carefully removed the growth and excess skin and artfully reconfigured the balance of the skin and sutured it all back together like new. The man was so pleased and overwhelmed when they let him look at himself in a mirror that he just sat there and wept aloud.

An old lady with a large cyst on her inner right thigh came to see the C.U.R.E. Clinic doctors. She had previously traveled to the town of Richard Toll where the doctors told her they could do nothing. The cyst had become so large that it was almost impossible for her to walk. When Dr. Jacobson lanced the cyst, the pressurized puss shot clear across the room. She thanked the doctor profusely, and explained that now it would be much easier for her to walk the long distances demanded as she herded her goats.

I lost track of how many mothers wanted the doctors to professionally circumcise their boys. Usually that task was left to the tribal leaders who were notably clumsy and a bit brutish.

By one o'clock that afternoon we simply could not take the heat any longer. The people crowded around the building so closely that even if there had been a breeze it could not have come through the doors and windows. The more patients we ran through the clinic, the more seemed to show up. Word had gotten out, and people were even coming across the river from the country of Mauritania. At two o'clock we told the people to go find some shade and we would be back at four o'clock and see patients until dark.

The half-mile walk from the clinic back to our compound was miserable. My camera was almost too hot to hold.

I went inside the compound where we were staying and took off my shirt and laid down on the rubber pad. The water poured off me and soaked into the sponge rubber.

About three o'clock the village women brought in two big steaming platters of cooked onions, cabbage, rice, and meat, and set one each on the rubber mat that Dr. Jacobsen and I shared. I just looked at the food and smiled at the woman and said, *"Merci."* There was no way that I was going to eat hot food. I did, however, ask if they could brew up some of the espresso tea with the foam on top. The liquid might keep me from dehydrating, and the jolt from the sugar and caffeine was definitely needed about then. Even as hot as it was, the tea tasted great!

At four o'clock we went back into the microwave clinic. I took a quick inventory of the remaining medical supplies. I was so proud of the quality and variety of supplies that our Project C.U.R.E. people back home had placed in those large C.U.R.E. Kit boxes. As the doctors got back to seeing the mass of patients, I busily counted out pills and stuck them into little yellow envelopes and wrote the contents and directions for taking the pills on the front:

- Nine Motrin, one tablet two times per day with food.
- Twelve Tylenol, one tablet three times per day.
- Fourteen penicillin, one tablet three times per day until gone.

I would rotate from one patient station to another just to listen to the translators relate the symptoms to our medical people. One skinny woman told us she was ten months pregnant, but her husband had been dead for over a year. She thought if she didn't have a period, she was pregnant.

We saw lots of upper respiratory problems and congestion. The river was too much of a temptation for the kids, even though it was loaded with parasites. The parasites would get in the skin on the kids' heads, and their hair would fall out because of the sores. Their legs were raw where the parasites had eaten into the flesh. Parasites burrowed inside between their toes, under their arms, in their crotches—everywhere! We gave these patients antibiotics and topical ointment and told them to stay out of the river—the same river water I used that morning in our bath closet.

One dignified young mother brought her very sick baby to see the visiting doctors. Dr. Mohamadou Cisse, sensing the urgent need, ushered the mother right in to one of the four stations. The baby was about six months old, had diarrhea, and had been severely dehydrated for about a week and a half. Two days prior to the clinic's opening, the baby had stopped breast-feeding and would take nothing. By the time the mother brought the little one to us he was just barely breathing and his little eyes were glossed over with a thick white film. Dr. Cisse tried to insert a needle to administer some IV fluids. The mother's look of desperation told us that she knew her child was beyond hope.

My mind went back to a little girl brought into our free clinic out in the Serengeti in Tanzania. We couldn't get a pulse. She was in a coma and we couldn't detect breathing. But, miraculously, with IVs and antibiotics flowing down the tubes and into her little limp body, something happened. David White, president of Columbia HCA East Coast, had his face down close to the little girl's head, saying to her quietly, "Wake up, little girl, Jesus loves you, wake up." Within about forty-five minutes the girl opened her eyes, looked around the rough old building, and spotted her mother. By the next afternoon she was able to get up and walk with her mother back across the Serengeti to their village.

I sat down beside the mother and took the baby's hands in my hands. The dark-skinned arms and little pink hands were limp. I silently prayed for the mother and the baby and for another miracle to take place like the one in Tanzania. The mother asked for the translator to tell me, "I must be doing something wrong. This is my fourth baby that has died. I don't know what I am doing wrong."

The baby boy did not respond positively. He rallied just enough to cry a little whimper and then died. It stunned all of us. We couldn't slow down to mourn, but our hearts were broken as we watched the dignified mother carry her child out through the clinic door and across the lot to another lady's house. Together, with the mother carrying the baby and the friend carrying a broad-blade hoe, they walked out a ways into the desert. The friend dug a hole in the sand, and the mother laid the baby in the hole and they covered it up.

Early death in West Africa is common. Seventy-five percent of child deaths are due to diarrhea and dehydration. Most of these children can be saved simply with IV fluids administered at the right time. Once the child became sick and started dehydrating, his little body's systems would just start to shut down. Drinking contaminated water killed more children than any other cause; malaria ran a distant second. I kept thinking, *Perhaps if we could have been there a day or two sooner we could have helped save the baby's life.*

When the sun fell about six o'clock that evening it became too dark inside the clinic to see what we were doing. We told all the waiting people to come back at seven o'clock the next morning. Some camped out by the clinic door so that they would not run the risk of missing out again the next day. We had seen hundreds of patients, and we were all dead tired, dirty, sweaty, and sticky.

When we arrived at the compound, after our half-mile walk from the clinic, I asked for a village woman to bring a bucket of my favorite contaminated river water. She understood, and brought the water and a dipper and a towel, and I headed for the bath closet with the dirt floor.

The village cooking fires were soon blazing and the large black iron caldrons steaming. We ate about ten-thirty that night. The tasty food hit the spot. The meat wasn't chicken, so I presumed that it was goat. (I had learned never to think past my first presumption!) The village people did not own anything that they would not have gladly given to us. They were so appreciative and still in a state of awe that we had come to their village.

Tired as I was, my mind kept going back to that dignified young mother whose small baby boy had died just hours before in the clinic. I could still feel the soft little hands that were so limp. I kept hearing the little gasp that had been his last breath. My mind kept replaying the scene of the woman's friend digging the hole with the big hoe and the mother gently placing the baby in the hole and covering it with the sand. I wondered if I could have done more. Perhaps, we could have packed some Pedialyte in the C.U.R.E. Kit to replace the baby's electrolytes more quickly, or, better yet, we could have been there a day sooner ...

It was back to bed that night on the ground under the African stars. A slight breeze stirred, a welcome relief. Just as I was dozing off, I felt something crawling on my hand and up my arm. I quickly reached up with my other hand to give it a swat. In the darkness my hand latched onto one of the giant cockroaches from the moist latrine closet—probably in search of some variety in its menu. My fingers closed like lightening around the kicking invader. I threw the uninvited pest as hard as I could against the concrete wall. I would not have to deal with him again, but I had no guarantee that his brother or sister wouldn't follow shortly.

At five o'clock the next morning the Muslim mosque loudspeaker began to blare again with a call to prayer. Oh, yes, and the village roosters once again raised their own hilarious joyful noise. It was time for another scary river water bath, time to brush my teeth with toothpaste and saliva, and time to down another cup of super-strong Nescafé coffee with a chunk of raw sugar and goat's milk. I experimented by soaking the hard bread in the coffee. It worked a lot better.

We all hurried to the clinic to straighten things and prepare for the next onslaught of patients. As the people saw us walking the half mile toward the clinic, they all started pressing around us. They knew that it would be the last day of the clinic.

As we opened up and Dr. Jacobson and Laurie Tucker began their minor surgeries, the crowds began to grow outside. People were now coming from twenty-five to thirty kilometers away. The desert sun once more began to beat down on the sheet metal roof of our microwave clinic. I was sweating so profusely I could not keep my glasses on the bridge of my nose or see out of the sweat-stained lenses. By two o'clock that afternoon we were forced to get out of the building once again and postpone the clinic until four o'clock.

The C.U.R.E. Clinic medical team returned at four o'clock, but our faithful door guards and translators decided to stay out of the sun. We made a decision that we would go ahead and proceed without the door guards—a bad choice. When we opened the doors, the crowds pushed right in behind us. Suddenly, there was standing room only and more desperate people kept pressing in. We tried to tell them to go out and queue up, but they all just looked at us and started rubbing where they hurt. We were pinned and couldn't move.

Finally, Dr. Jacobson hollered to close the medicine cupboards and get out. We squeezed our way to the doors and walked out and sat down under the brush canopy out front. We motioned for the people to clear out of the clinic or we would not go back in. Since this didn't help, we decided to smile, relax, and wait for our translators and door guards to arrive; they finally showed up an hour later.

By seven o'clock that evening we told the door people that we could only see those who had already been allowed to enter the building. That announcement didn't go over very well. Dr. Cisse explained that in the future the clinic would remain open on certain days, staffed by the Senegal Health Ministry. Project C.U.R.E. had restocked the clinic with the necessary medical goods for them to get help in the future. By the time we straightened up and cleaned the clinic it was too dark to see your hand in front of your face.

All day long Mohamadou Cisse and his brother, Dr. Cheikh Cisse, kept repeating, "History was made today: nothing has ever happened like this before in Senegal villages."

When the translators and medical record keepers had finished their tallies, it showed that we had met the needs of *more than one thousand five hundred village patients*. Truly, that was historic. I was so very proud of our medical team and all of our people back home in Colorado who had poured their unselfish efforts into the project to help the village people and honor Ohmar Dja.

That night around the blazing fires the leaders of the village presented each member of the team with a complete Senegal tribal costume as a show of their appreciation. What took the cake, though, was when the leaders gave us the most precious gift they could imagine—the village's prize goat. To refuse such generosity would be a grave insult. We quickly put our heads together and decided that we would take the goat as far as the town of Rufisque, where Mohamadou's extended family lived. We would have his mother's household prepare a feast for us the night after we had returned to Dakar.

As our C.U.R.E. Clinics team drove out of Diorbivol village the next morning, the twenty thousand dollars worth of medical goods we had carried in on top of the van had been replaced by one frisky goat, who was bleating and tapping out his displeasure with his hoofs. Ohmar Dja's wife and a few members of their extended family also piled into the already crowded van for the trip back to Dakar. We had gone where we were needed and had been invited, and we had enabled work that had already been established in Senegal.

Back in the capital city, Denver's Mayor Wellington Webb and his wife, Wilma, met with Ohmar Dja's family and the Project C.U.R.E. team. US Ambassador to Senegal, the Honorable Mr. Dane Smith, had invited us to his personal residence in Dakar to celebrate the occasion.

My very good friend, Dr. James Terbush, medical liaison with the US State Department, also caught up with us in Dakar. Thanks to his contacts, Nan Mattingly, first secretary of the US Embassy in Senegal, Dr. Jesse Monestersky and Barbara Brooks from the embassy met with us to discuss Project C.U.R.E.'s medical activities throughout West Africa.

(Before I left Dakar, Nan Mattingly and Dr. Monestersky contacted the US Embassy in Nouakchott, Mauritania, and arranged for US Ambassador Timberlake Foster to introduce me to the president of Mauritania. I was to be traveling to Nouakchott upon my departure from Senegal.)

All of these officials were impressed with what Project C.U.R.E. was accomplishing throughout the continent of Africa. "Dr. Jackson," they said, "you do more for the positive image of the United States than all the junkets and programs we try to put together."

I relied heavily on well-positioned authorities to give me personal insights and suggestions into how Project C.U.R.E. could be even more effective in our global work. I counted even more on the networking that results when an organization is willing to collaborate with reliable partners for the benefit of others.

17

A Short Course in Changing the World

By 1997, Project C.U.R.E. was shipping desperately needed medical goods into well more than fifty countries around the world and lots of places within those countries. It had been ten years since our inception.

My commitment to visit and assess every recipient hospital or clinic before we shipped anything seemed reasonable in the beginning. But every time we delivered a million dollars worth of supplies and pieces of medical equipment, ten more requests came in from health ministers, local hospital directors, humanitarian groups, or church organizations. My schedule for 1998 included trips to twenty-three new countries. Every time I returned home, the organization had leadership needs that had been left in abeyance during my absence. I was feeling the pressure!

I needed to roll off leadership and responsibilities onto the shoulders of young, high-energy, creative, and dedicated people who could move Project C.U.R.E. into the next phase. I could not allow the organization to be limited by the twenty-four hours in my personal day.

I was on a Kenyan Airways flight from Nairobi back to the United States when I presented my case to God and asked for help. When I was home in Denver, I was spending my time recruiting volunteers; talking medical manufacturers and distributors into giving me medical goods; begging for trucks, pallet jacks, and forklifts; opening warehouses in

Phoenix and Los Angeles; and trying to raise lots of money to finance the whole operation. How could I continue to do all that and travel as well?

God already had put a plan in motion even before I had asked, and it was to exceed my wildest dreams. Our older son, Dr. Douglas Jackson, an attorney with an additional PhD in econometrics and business, had watched what we were doing and realized the incredible opportunity Project C.U.R.E. presented. God began to work on his heart and fanned the flames of compassion in his soul. He turned down an offer to be the president of a fine university in the United States, and agreed to come on as president and CEO of Project C.U.R.E. He would build the organization within the United States and I would devote my time, as founder and chairman of the board, to the international side of the rapidly expanding operation. Now, we could really move ahead. Having another economist on board, one who was even smarter than his dad, was going to make an eternal difference.

As Project C.U.R.E. matured, I observed that the principles we were implementing had implications for the entire enterprise of world relief. Most humanitarians and their organizations worked from their heart alone and, for the most part, completely ignored or violated the basic economic principles that were at the root of poverty and counterproductive governance. Our successful business model depended not only upon the premises that allowed Project C.U.R.E. to navigate past the shoals where others foundered, but on underlying economic realities that applied globally. We were at the forefront of what was becoming known as social entrepreneurship.

Perhaps, the best-known social entrepreneurs are Bill and Melinda Gates, the founder of Microsoft, and his wife. The Bill and Melinda Gates Foundation funds many worthwhile causes, particularly in the fields of disease prevention and education. Social entrepreneurship became popular after the boom years of the 1990s, when the founders of technology companies, venture capitalists, and investment bankers made fortunes at relatively young ages.

The Gates generation decided to use the expertise they had gained from the business world in addressing the world's most intractable problems: poverty, disease, inadequate education, and corruption in government. They had learned the principles and effectiveness of economic globalization. Goods and services could be invented in the intellectual capitals of the world. The raw materials of these goods could be drawn from many nations, manufactured in others, and shipped around the world. The whole process could be tracked with uncanny precision by software that could put factories in Macao into overdrive when inventory ran low in Dubuque. Marketing studies based on data mining or focus groups improved the development of goods and services, making the marketplace ever more responsive to peoples' needs. The new media sold these same goods and services with a minimum of labor or even human contact.

Why not apply the principles that made the global marketplace so efficient to the world's most difficult problems? Instead of the temporary fix of most humanitarian programs, why not use the tools of technology and global commerce to mitigate, or even solve, age-old problems.

The essence of social entrepreneurship—as with all entrepreneurship—lay in the reallocation of resources so that everyone would be better off. Our business model, for example, used overstock medical supplies, that might otherwise have been plowed into landfills, to improve the health of developing nations, while simultaneously improving the brand of medical supply companies and other partners through good will and tax deductions. Our collection, shipping, and distribution operations were prime examples of how to use economic globalization for good.

The wave of social entrepreneurship that came out of the 1990s was a wonderful development. It re-established in the public imagination that a person could do well in business in order to do good deeds in the world. The new social entrepreneurs made real contributions as well; those associated with the Carter Center virtually eliminated from the face of the earth the scourge of guinea worm—a frequently deadly parasite. Habitat for Humanity and Doctors Without Borders are two more well-known examples of social entrepreneurial organizations.

In fact, social entrepreneurship has become so popular as a way of addressing the world's ills that Christianity as a means of social and cultural transformation has seemed out of date, superfluous, beside the point. Social entrepreneurship, pursued in the light of what Christianity teaches, gains immeasurably, though. There can be no long-lasting change in society and culture that's not based on the truth of who we are as men and women, and our position before God.

This works itself out in the most practical of ways in the fields of economics, social mores (what I'll call cultural economics), and the commitment necessary to change the world when the world resists change at every step, often violently.

Project C.U.R.E., as a social entrepreneurial venture guided by Christian principles, was determined to strike at the heart of sickness, poverty, hunger, and the political corruption that's often responsible for perpetuating those conditions. The immediate avenue we had chosen to gain access was health and wellness. No country would be able to rise to its full economic potential if its citizens were sick and unable to sustain a healthy economy.

At the same time, Project C.U.R.E. looked for ways to use its economic expertise to help developing nations, particularly as this expertise related to health care.

Traveling around the world, I was often invited to lecture at universities, which gave me a chance to speak about social entrepreneurship guided by Christian principles. My hope was always that the students would take Project C.U.R.E. as a model and engage in social entrepreneurship in their own fields. I usually gave a talk titled, "The Economics of Compassion," as I did, for example, in Tbilisi, Georgia, at the large campus of Tbilisi State University, where I appeared as guest lecturer and tutor. Tbilisi is located a short distance from Gori, the birthplace of Joseph Stalin.

"All your life," I told the students, "you have heard about capitalists. I stand before you today and tell you that I am a capitalist, a very successful capitalist." (That would usually get the full attention of all the students, as well as the staff and professors). "But today I want to explain to you that I am a capitalist so that I can be a more successful humanitarian. You have no doubt been told that capitalism is bad because it is selfish and greedy. Come, and let's explore today some comparisons and some results. I am a lifelong observer, and I want to share with you what I have observed."

Then I went on to explain to the audience some of the history of economics. In the mid-1700s Adam Smith, a Scottish economist, proposed economic theories based on free markets, personal decision-making, divisions of labor, and minimal government intervention.

About one hundred years later Karl Marx proposed that Adam Smith was wrong. In order for a society to be successful Marx held that the economy needed to be controlled at the top by intelligent people who knew what was best for the society. Otherwise, class struggle would continue between the *haves* and the *have-nots*. The only fair thing, according to Marx, was to take away from those who have and redistribute to those who have not. Then there would be peace and equality. It was a case presented to the world of "freewill, creative compassion" vs. "planned, controlled compassion."

Now we have gone nearly another one hundred and fifty years and the experiments have had an opportunity to run their course. Today we can observe as history the results of both ideas.

The economic experiment of Lenin, Marx, Trotsky, and Stalin was plagued with at least two basic flaws from the outset. First, it was touted that the element of compassion was at the center of the philosophy. "We will overthrow the czars, appropriate their wealth, and equally divide it among the people." But the driving force behind the philosophy was not compassion, but control. The political elite—usually in a governing body called the Politburo—would be in control and decide on the meaning of equality for people in different circumstances. Another subtle flaw was that the operative word in the whole scheme was *take*. "Take from those who have and distribute to those who have not." The fundamental and emotional basis for the word take is a world apart from that of give. There certainly was no compassion in the word take. The operative word became the lodestar of the experiment. "Take, take, and take." That produced an economic culture on the flip side that was characterized by the notion of "give me, give me" and "what have you done for me lately?"

Somewhere in the experiment the noble ideas of give, share, and compassion were lost. They became foreign ideas. The entire conceptualizing and engineering of the experiment presumed that you could redistribute forever. Without an economic component of production and creative growth, though, greed and the entitlement mentality would eventually strip the coffers clean. And it did.

In comparing the two historic economic experiments it can be seen that Marxist-Leninist communism produced bankruptcy, poverty, and misery. Adam Smith's free market ideas enabled Western societies to draw on the wellsprings of their resources to cure not only many of their own national ills, but to reach out and be more compassionate than any other civilization in history.

The results have taken place in our own lifetime and we can observe and draw our own conclusions. You see, ideas have consequences. Theories and their results find their way into the pages of irrefutable history. We can judge for ourselves.

I am a capitalist today because it enables me to be successfully compassionate. I have the opportunity to employ theories and principles that can make the lives of others better.

Then I recounted how just a week earlier I had been in India assessing the results of some natural disasters. In the State of Gujarat, an earthquake registering 7.7 on the Richter scale had killed about thirty thousand people in approximately three minutes. Everything was left in devastation. I also traveled to the eastern part of India to Orissa state, where some twenty thousand people had been swept into the Bay of Bengal by a super cyclone.

"Who went to meet the needs of the disaster victims?" I asked the students. "Did the many nations of Africa rally around and take aid to the victims? No. Did the government of France jump right in and help? No. Did anyone from the Muslim or Hindu world rush to the aid of the victims? No. Did the Communists of China, Russia, Vietnam, or North Korea have the ability to go and do anything to help? No. Could India even help its own people? No. Did anyone from your country of Georgia take aid to the helpless victims in India? No.

"Who went to meet the needs of the disaster victims? It was the compassionate capitalists, and not the bankrupt communists or socialists or the economic fascists, who rushed in to meet the terrible needs. The system of capitalism and free market enterprise enabled them to be successfully compassionate."

Students the world over started opening their eyes, most particularly in those countries where the legacies of communism, socialism, and an overzealous welfare state worked to limit their prospects or had been succeeded, as in the cases of many old Soviet republics, by new forms of bureaucracy and often mafia control.

As I've stated, our philosophical goal at Project C.U.R.E. had become to strike at the heart of sickness, poverty, hunger, and the political corruption that's often responsible for perpetuating those things. Our dedication to social entrepreneurship positioned us to become agents of change in the most effective ways possible.

We wondered whether some day it would be possible for Project C.U.R.E. to help developing nations improve their broken health care systems through making available tutors and information that would allow them to revamp their failed medical philosophies and systems. We were presented such an opportunity in Ukraine.

Our reputation for supplying medical assistance had reached many levels in the Ukraine. We had shipped millions of dollars worth of goods there, including eighteen tons of medical books to the Pirogov Memorial Medical University in Vinnitsa, establishing the finest English-language medical library in all of Eastern Europe. Team members from our Nashville office had been particularly active in the country. Dr. Brian McMurray of

Nashville helped Pirogov University set up a complete dialysis department at the university hospital. Dr. Mark Johnson, a specialist in urology, joined Dr. McMurray and me on a visit to Vinnitsa where we were delivering seven hundred and fifty thousand dollars worth of medical goods. With his own funds Dr. Johnson purchased state-of-the-art surgical equipment, and recently developed medications that he gave to the university's urology department.

Edward Gluschenko, our English-speaking liaison, accompanied Dr. Johnson and me to the Kiev airport for our flight home. While at the airport, we asked Edward Gluschenko if there was anything else we could do for our friends in Ukraine.

Edward explained how the Ukrainian Legislature was in the process of determining the direction of the health care industry in their new republic. In the past, Ukrainian medical policies and practices, as was the case in all the other republics, had been sternly dictated by the Soviet designers in Moscow. Ukraine's health care delivery system was rigidly centralized. Doctors and other medical personnel were simply workers of the state. There was no room for creativity and no tolerance for deviation from mandated procedures and policies.

The Ukrainian health care system, as we well knew, had become a shambles. In 1985 the Ukrainian budget had devoted the equivalent of one hundred and eighty dollars per person annually to health care. Ten years later only sixteen dollars per person per year could be allocated. And now the system was completely bankrupt with *no* money for health care for the citizens.

At the same time, any doctor who contracted privately with someone for health care could be arrested and put in prison. Ukrainian citizens could not pay for health care even if they had the means—at least as a matter of law. The structure of the health care system was a toxic remnant of the old Soviet regime.

The country had eliminated more than sixty thousand beds from its hospital system, and the doctors had not received their government paychecks (the equivalent of only fifty US dollars per month) for four or five months. The situation had made criminals of Ukrainian doctors, since they were forced to treat patients privately and secretly in order to generate a livelihood. The situation presented the whole country with a huge moral problem. The state had no idea how it would come up with the necessary $1.8 billion in the coming year to provide medical care to its people.

With the collapse of the Soviet regime, Ukraine had an historic opportunity for change. Now was the time to change the philosophical direction of health care. Edward explained their desire to build cornerstones of free-market, non-centralized medicine into the system. The new laws were to be presented and voted on by parliament in late January or early February. Those new laws would set the direction for the future of the medical profession in Ukraine.

No one in Ukraine knew enough about free markets, though, to formulate the concepts. No one could articulate to the legislature free-market strategies and draw up a plan based on these principles that could be voted into law. Edward asked if we knew of anyone who could help at this critical juncture.

As social entrepreneurs providing medical relief around the world for the past fifteen years, we had learned what worked and what didn't. Among our people and networks of contacts we possessed the expertise to help Ukraine institute sustainable health care reforms. Could we assemble the necessary team and meet with the right Ukrainian officials fast enough, though?

As soon as we returned to our homes in the United States, Dr. Mark Johnson called me and we began to talk seriously. Who could help us? Just what would it take to help meet the huge need? How would we get everyone together? Where would we get the money necessary to bring all the people together for such a training occasion? Where would we all meet, the US or Ukraine? It was nearly Christmas, and the Ukrainian Legislature would be voting in January or February. Everything would have to be accomplished in about thirty days! Would it be feasible to bring a group of top Ukrainian leaders to the United States for a symposium? We would need to put on a crash course for them in basic democratic, free-market enterprise, and make sure that they understood the concepts well enough to present and debate the ideas on the floor of Parliament. A majority of the members would have to understand, and buy into, a brand-new paradigm of economic thinking. It was one thing to talk about freedom and another to change cultural institutions that had been established for so many years. No other republic of the old Soviet system had ever been so bold. Ukraine would automatically become a leader with such an economic and health care model. It had to be done correctly!

As Mark and I continued to talk, we began to get excited about the historic possibilities. We found ourselves saying, "Let's go for it!" If we could help implement free-market changes into Ukrainian medical law, then perhaps we could use the model to influence other former Soviet republics. I had personally met many of the ministers of health from the other Eastern European and Central Asian countries. Maybe we could just roll an adopted Ukrainian medical law package right over into the other republics.

Dr. Johnson got busy working with Edward Gluschenko in Kiev on choosing the appropriate Ukrainian leaders to bring to the United States. There was a National Board of Directors meeting of the Association of American Physicians and Surgeons (AAPS) being held in Atlanta in mid-January. The board offered to let us utilize some of their conference space at the Sheraton Gateway Hotel near the airport in Atlanta free of charge.

I got busy lining up the roster of economists. We really needed to have one heavy hitter with world-class economic credentials. Immediately, a person came to my mind, Dr. Paul Ballantyne, head of the economics department at the University of Colorado. He had been my favorite economics professors during my economics graduate work at CU. I had found him to be a wonderfully devoted Christian gentleman, and we had developed a warm friendship over the years. He had encouraged me to become part of the Colorado Council for Economic Education. I had lost Dr. Paul Ballantyne's home phone number, and the university was on Christmas break. I finally weaseled his home phone number out of some contacts I had through the Colorado Economics Council. When I reached him, he and his wife were just walking out the door on their way to spend Christmas with their son and his family. I had just barely caught him.

As fast as possible, I told him of my involvement with the Ukrainians and about Project C.U.R.E.'s humanitarian and economic mission. He listened quietly. I explained how I needed a real expert who could quickly and convincingly present the fundamentals of a free-market economy to a bunch of ex-Marxists who desired to reform their health care system.

When I took a breath, he nearly knocked the telephone right out of my hand with his reply. "Jim, how very interesting that you would call. I have thought of you many times and wondered if you were still working with the Brazilian government on their debt repayments. Let me bring you up to date on what I have been doing in addition to my work at the University of Colorado. I have been teaching free-market, democratic capitalism courses at the Sumy State University in Ukraine! In fact, my wife has been accompanying me and teaching English courses at the university, using the Bible as her English textbook. We have had a marvelous time in Ukraine, and one family has adopted us and has made us godparents of their children. I would be pleased to help you in your efforts to aid Ukraine, and I have the dates of January 11–13 open and available. That's between semesters at CU. Now, I had better run or I will miss my plane. Here is my son's telephone number. Let's talk more about the details when I arrive."

I hung up the telephone and sat in my chair, and I cried. I was overwhelmed that I was being allowed to be part of something so much bigger than everything I could have dreamed or imagined.

Dr. Johnson not only was able to get the right Ukrainians lined up to make the trip on such short notice, but also was able to raise almost seven thousand five hundred dollars in twenty-four hours to cover the airline tickets from Kiev to Atlanta. In addition to Dr. Ballantyne, I was able to secure Dr. Michael Tanner of the Cato Institute (a prestigious conservative think-tank organization in Washington, DC), and Mark Litow, a consulting actuary, for our group of presenters. The speaking participants made it clear they were willing to come without charging any fee at all! We were going to have a powerhouse symposium.

The president of Ukraine, his cabinet, and the leaders of the legislature worked with Dr. Mark Johnson to determine who should travel to the United States for the training conference. We ended up with the most influential leaders of the government, along with their aids and politicos. It was an absolute miracle to have arranged for all those important people to get together in one place in the world. It was an even greater miracle to have gotten them all together in the United States with valid visas on such short notice.

On January 11 we assembled together in one of the large meeting rooms not being used by the American Association of Physicians and Surgeons for their Board of Directors meetings. Dr. Paul Ballantyne had been assigned the responsibility of handling the initial presentation. His assignment was to explain the basic principles of economics in terms that could be convincingly re-conveyed on the legislative floor of the Ukrainian Parliament in Kiev. It would probably be the first time anyone had ever taken time to explain the basic concepts of free-market capitalism to such a delegation from the old Soviet Union. I was so confident of Dr. Ballantyne's ability to share the simple, basic rudiments of economics to open-minded individuals, that I found myself relaxing and thoroughly enjoying the presentation. Never once did my toes curl up inside my shoes with anxiety.

He began by focusing on a brief overview of Adam Smith's work written in 1776 entitled, *The Wealth of Nations*. He explained the definition of wealth.

"Money is not wealth," he said. "Just look at the example of Germany in 1913 when it cost one mark to buy a loaf of bread, but by 1923 they needed to carry seven hundred and fifty thousand marks to the store to buy a loaf of bread. Money can nearly destroy an economy."

Next, he helped them see that "Resources are not wealth." Look at India. The country has incredible resources, but it is not wealthy. Japan has very few resources, but is wealthy.

"Wealth is income, and income comes from production."

He walked them through how to figure a country's gross domestic product (GDP) by taking the measure of the total value of everything the country produces in a year and dividing it by the number of the population. The GDP per person, per year (1997) for certain countries would look like this:

| India = $1,000 | China = $1,300 | Japan = $21,500 |
| USA = $25,000 | Russia = $1,500 | Ukraine = $1,600 |

"Why is that?" he asked. Dr. Ballantyne then circled back and quickly explained the essential conditions for the successful operation of a society, which are: 1) the pursuit of self-interest; 2) competition; 3) private property; 4) the rule of law; 5) freedom; 6) respect for human rights, and 7) democracy.

"Above all, voluntary exchange is the key to the market system," Dr. Ballantyne said, with emphases. "The top line and most important word in a successful economy is *people*; people must benefit; people must become better off."

Dr. Ballantyne skillfully explained how the free-market system worked as it did because of voluntary exchange. People could choose among the goods and services that they wanted from a variety of providers, and these voluntary exchanges were key to getting both production levels and pricing right, following the principle of supply and demand.

Occasionally members of the Ukrainian delegation would lean over to me and say, "We've never heard anything like this before. No one ever told us that this was capitalism. This makes sense!"

When Dr. Ballantyne finished, Dr. Mike Tanner from the Cato Institute took over. He began to build slowly on the basis formed by Dr. Ballantyne. He explained logically why long lines of people wait in Ukraine to receive health care: because neither the doctors nor their patients are concerned about cost. He also showed them with simple graphs why their system pushed some of their best people into criminal activities of the black market.

Dr. Tanner reinforced what the delegation had just heard in the previous session about the three necessary elements of a successful health care delivery system. Included must be the recognition of the factor of self-interest, the need for the encouragement of competition, and the absolute necessity of including and honoring freedom of choice. He pled with them to allow into their new plan the right for the patient to legally contract with the doctor of his choice. That way there would be a relationship of accountability established between the doctor and the patient, rather than the doctor and the government. The relationship of accountability between the doctor and the patient would be absolutely essential. Dr Tanner recommended the inclusion of three main points into the new Ukrainian health care system:

1. Right of contract between the patient and the doctor.
2. Reform how the payment is made (i.e., have the patients pay the doctor, rather than having the government paying the doctor).
3. Develop some rational formula for the people to purchase adequate health care insurance.

By this time the Ukrainians were really beginning to understand the benefits of a free-market system approach to health care delivery.

Dr. Tanner carefully explained the cost formula: V_a (actual value) and V_i (value to the individual or perceived value) = C (cost). When both values (V_a and V_i) are equal to the cost, the patient will purchase the optimal health care possible. The V_a (actual value) could be zero if the V_i (value to the individual) is equal to the cost. For example, if the doctor is very pretty, you may pay for the visit even if there is no actual medical value to you at all. The big problem is where the V_a and V_i are greater than the cost. Then the people will use too much health care service—they will waste the system's time on sniffles that would go away on their own, or simply use a doctor's appointment as a way of getting out of work. The people who really need the health care will be excluded because of the long lines waiting to see the doctor. Dr. Tanner told them that when the formula for health care has to be reformed there were really only three ways to do it.

First, there's the traditional way, in which the government intervenes and rations out the health care i.e., "You can only see the doctor once a month."

Second, there is managed care, in which the insurance company steps in and says, "You can only come in and see the doctor once a month."

Third, there is the option to increase the cost. Take the control away from the government or the insurance company. Allow the individual patient to pay with his own money for the cost of basic services.

In recapping his first session, Dr. Tanner encouraged the inclusion of insurance for serious or catastrophic illness. The patient should pay the doctor directly for most routine services—or at least a good portion of these services. Serious and catastrophic illnesses, however, should be covered by insurance, spreading the risk of such eventualities among large populations.

By the time Drs. Ballantyne and Tanner were through with their first sessions, a world of difference had taken place in the minds of the delegation. The group began openly asking questions about the possibilities of creating medical savings accounts for individuals and families. Nowhere else could they have accessed the information, intelligence, and expertise available to them than in Atlanta that weekend. And perhaps one of the strongest factors being made available to them was the gift of love and concern for the people and the future of Ukraine. They were for the most part responding with appreciation. Each had lived an entire lifetime under the old centralized system, however, and occasionally I could see that it was difficult for them to break from the security of the old system.

Dr. Mark Litow, the actuarial consultant, used his presentation time to identify and explain some of the strengths and weaknesses of the US health care system. He spoke of the types of systems involved in the six distinct market groups receiving health care in the United States. He pointed out how, as the United States had moved toward a socialistic centralized health care system, the United States had increasingly been pushed further and further into debt to underwrite the program. "Today, half of the US deficit is the result of Medicare costs alone."

Following dinner that night we combined our group of the Ukrainian delegation and our presenters with the entire Board of Directors of the American Association of Physicians and Surgeons for the final evening session. I had been assigned to speak during the first half of the session. The final segment would include a round table discussion where the Ukrainian leaders would explain their health care system and present their urgent situation. Then the entire group could ask questions and offer any insights for help.

I had thought about what I was going to say for several days, and I had also used the flying time from Denver to Atlanta to crystallize my thoughts. I did not want to denigrate the Ukraine health care system. I did not wish to speak as an American looking down my nose at their plight in a condescending manner, emphasizing only their problems. So, I had decided to share with the whole group some of the observations that I had made in my needs assessment studies of hospitals and health care systems all around the world. The Ukraine leaders could readily identify with each of the problems, but I would not be pointing my finger directly at them. I announced the title of my presentation as simply, "International Health Care Observations."

I am continuously crisscrossing the avenues of a bankrupt portion of the world while viewing the aftermath of a great social and economic experiment of the past eighty years. It promised everything and ultimately delivered nothing. Why? The answer is, because you can only pursue the philosophy of redistribution for a limited period of time. Here are some of the observations I shared that night.

First, in theory you can argue for the advantage of efficiency provided by a centralized health care delivery system, but lost-opportunity costs are unacceptably high.

Then I explained the economic principles of scarcity, choice, and cost. Items are *scarce* because they have two or more alternative uses and there will always be more possible alternative uses than there are items. But eventually you must narrow your *choice* down to one alternative for the use. The next highest-valued other use that you gave up was the real *cost* of what was chosen, because it went wanting.

In North Korea the health care system was very centralized and extremely regimented. It appeared to be efficient, but the rigidity of the system disallowed for any creative or altered approach to a medical procedure. The lost-opportunity costs were very high, as they are in any regimented system.

Second, the centralized system does not allow for keeping pace with medical discoveries and new technologies.

Here's an example. The head doctor in one of Cuba's largest hospitals begged me to bring in new medical procedural and research books. "We are so restricted. We don't even know current medicine."

Third, healthcare that is freely available to all is the same as equally unavailable to each.

An example of this is that in Brazil and Peru I had seen people coming to a clinic in ox carts, old buses, or on foot. They would stand in line all day only to have to return the next day and get back into another line because they were unable to receive help because the lines were so long.

Fourth, the centralized system produces over-specialization and under-training in general family medicine.

In Uzbekistan I had a young doctor tell me, "I am trained to remove gall bladders. I don't have to be responsible for anything else." I had one man in Moscow tell me, "I'm sorry the hallway is completely dark, but the man who is trained to change light bulbs doesn't work here any longer. I don't change light bulbs." (An increasing shortage of general practitioners has already occurred and is predicted to worsen in light of the latest US health care reforms.)

Fifth, in a centralized system there is a built-in disincentive to take any risks or make any decisions to do anything new or creative.

For example, in Minsk, Belarus, I had watched a medical team in a burn unit just stand and watch patients die in agony rather than deviate from the standard care procedure, for which they were not at that moment equipped. In a centralized system there was no way to experience reward or approval for doing something new or different. But there was always a possibility for experiencing loss for trying something different.

Sixth, when the centralized system controls a single source for medical supplies and goods, usually the level of quality suffers, and the delivery system for those goods becomes inadequate.

Many of the hospitals I've visited experienced the same thing. "Dr. Jackson, we have not been able to get the medical supplies we have needed for several years now."

Seventh, a centralized medical system can seldom get the cost-vs.-value ratio correct.

In countries where the value of the health care provided was greater than the cost paid, people would use too much health care service. Long lines would form and the people who really needed the care would be excluded because of those long lines. On the other hand, if the cost charged is greater than the benefit received, then no one can afford the health care services.

Eighth, hospital stays are longer where there is a centralized health care system.

In Kazakhstan and Uzbekistan it was not unusual for a patient who had experienced a heart attack to stay in the hospital seven or eight weeks. The hospital received its budget allocation based on the number of patient days. There was no incentive for the patient to be dismissed and sent home any earlier.

While I was talking, one of the association board members raised his hand. I stopped and acknowledged him. He asked, "Dr. Jackson, just why are you doing what you are doing, and why are you so determined to help the Ukrainians in rewriting their laws?"

I began to tell them what a dramatic difference God had made in my life. How he had changed me from a person who was totally consumed by seeking wealth only for myself to a person devoted to sharing God's love by helping hurting people around the world. I glanced around the room as I spoke, and I saw Dr. Raisa Burchak, the wife of Dr. Fedir Burchak. Dr. Fedir Burchak was the legal advisor and personal confidant of the president of Ukraine. She had her lace handkerchief out and was crying. Perhaps it was the first time she had ever heard such a thing.

I finished my part of the speaking agenda by challenging everyone there to consider moving from a personal position of success to a position of significance in his life. "Do something significant that will last forever."

After the session, both Drs. Burchak came up and hugged me. Dr. Raisa Burhack said, "I have learned many things during these hours. But perhaps the greatest thing I have learned, I have learned from your heart."

I tried to keep close tabs on the activities of our Ukrainian delegation as they returned to their busy schedules back home in Kiev. I was later informed that they had returned back with a new confidence and determination to see the reform measures enacted. The distinguished members, upon returning from Atlanta, successfully represented the proposed laws for reform on the legislative floor of Parliament. The economic policies and national legal reforms were introduced and accepted. Historic change was accomplished in the old Republic of Ukraine.

The next time I was in Kiev, I had the opportunity to meet up with some of our Atlanta delegation. When I met with Dr. Nikolaev, one of our delegates, it was a very emotional occasion. He spotted me across the lobby of the Parliament building and came running to hug me. He just kept expressing how much everyone appreciated someone who would love the people of Ukraine enough to become actively involved in helping them at a time of crisis.

We had wanted to strike at the heart of the systems that had set into motion endemic sickness, poverty, unemployment, and corruption. We had wondered if Project C.U.R.E. could be the change agent needed to influence the economic direction of a country or a national system. We had actually had the privilege of experiencing the miracle of such an involvement. We had been able to set the stage for a very large number of people to become better off.

I have to admit that this memory is now a poignant one. There we were in the old Soviet Union, helping them reassemble their broken health care delivery system, while we in America were getting poised to learn the harsh lessons of universal care: Health care that is freely available to all is the same as equally unavailable to each.

JACKSON MEMORIES

Jimmy Jackson

Anna Marie Johnson

"Best Friends Forever"

1987: First donated medical goods to Jackson's garage

Making friends in Brazilian "favela" shantytown

Financial consulting with top Brazilian officials

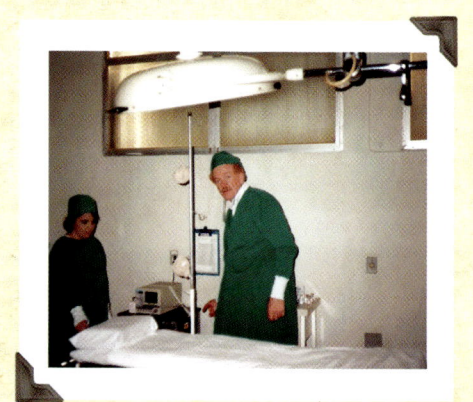

Preparing for surgery in Brazil hospital

Lorena and heads of Medical University in Brazil

First Project C.U.R.E. loads to leave Phoenix for Brazil

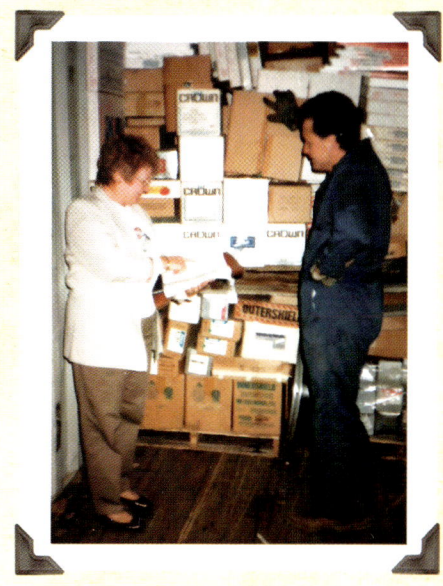

Loading cargo containers in Denver for Brazil

Jeff Martin installing Cath Lab in Brazil University Hospital

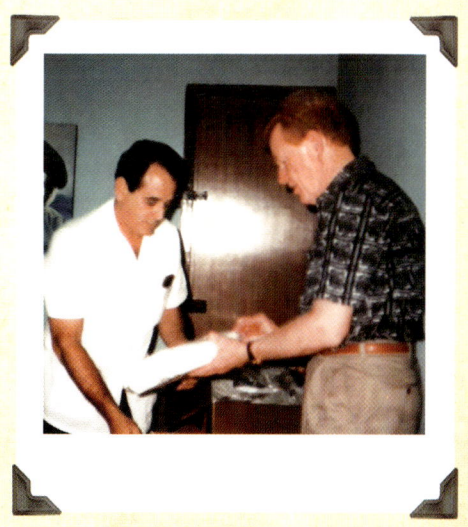

Jackson delivering medical goods to Havana, Cuba

Jackson presenting flowers at North Korea celebration

Jackson appearing on North Korea television

North Korea Ambassador in Denver hosted by Jacksons

First donated medical goods into Pyongyang, North Korea

Project C.U.R.E. repairing flooded clinics in North Korea

Loading out medical goods for North Korea

James and Jay Jackson: one of eight trips to North Korea

Hero's welcome for Dr. Jackson in Pyongyang

Trying to reach flooded Vietnam hospital

Millions of dollars of Project C.U.R.E. goods to flooded hospital

Dr. Jackson and new Vietnam friend

"No one else came to help but the tall American."

Project C.U.R.E. medical team in Senegal

Sharing happiness in Senegal

Presentation of donations to Senegal President and Minister of Health

"This is a miracle...no one has ever done this for Senegal!"

Making Dr. Jackson into an "Uzbek man" in Uzbekistan

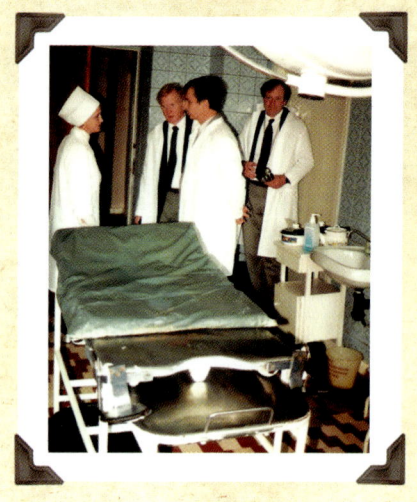

Preparing for surgery in Ukraine

Jackson: "lecturer and mentor" at University in Kiev, Ukraine

Student friends of Dr. Jackson at Kiev University

Dr. Kunar's clinic for the "Rock Breakers"

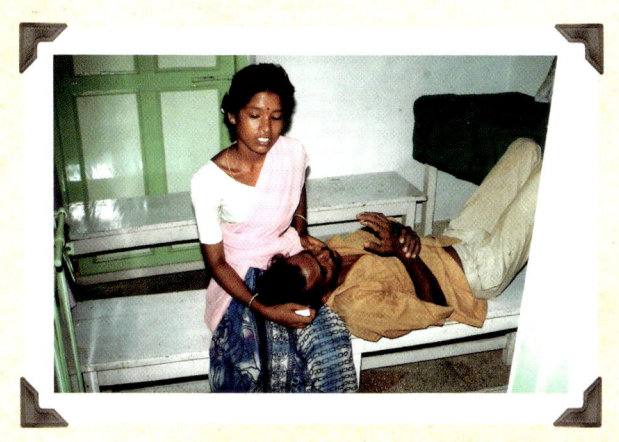

Injured from breaking the rocks by hand

"Untouchables" relegated to eke out living breaking rocks

Life expectancy: less than 30 years in rock breaker villages

"My angel Vera" and husband "Innocent" in Lagos, Nigeria

Little Alifa and baby Moses in Malawi

Brenda and brother orphaned in South Africa

Anna Marie searching for shanty "828"

Dr. Jackson crowned Royal Chief of Africa

New "Chief Uzoma of Nkume People" with King Onyeka and Cabinet

Project C.U.R.E. furnished Nigerian University Teaching Hospital

Denver West Metro Fire Dept. donates two fire trucks and one ambulance for Nigerians

Dr. Jackson and Dr. Larry Sthreshley deliver medical goods to villages

Dr. Jackson greeting new friends in Congo villages

Thousands of people are alive today because of Project C.U.R.E.

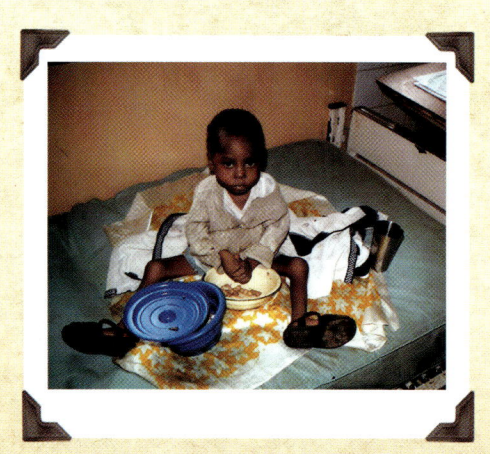

Abandoned orphans dying of HIV/AIDS in Congo

Jackson presenting millions of dollars of goods to Burma's leader

Traveling in dugout canoes to visit village clinics

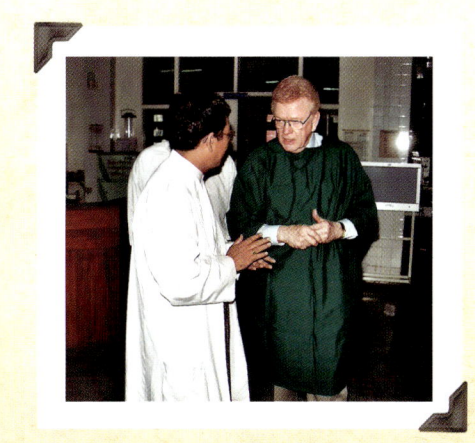

Performing "Needs Assessments" at hospitals in remote Burma

Burmese nurse receiving needed supplies from Project C.U.R.E.

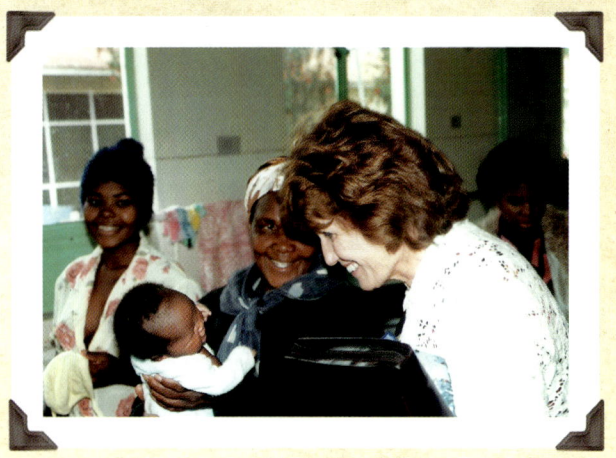

Dr. Anna Marie Jackson with patients in Swaziland

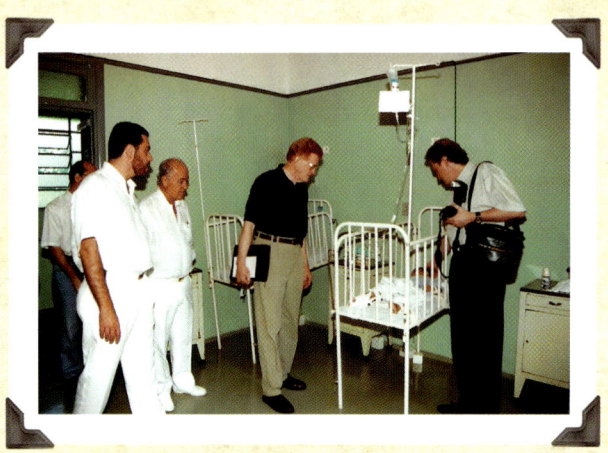

Dr. Douglas Jackson and Dr. James Jackson in Brazil

A new buddy in jungles of Tanzania

Jackson in burned out tank after Hutu/Tutsi genocide

Negotiating with War Lords in Afghanistan

Dr. Jackson offering "free clinics" in Afghanistan

Assessing needs and delivering hope in Iraq

Negotiating logistics for shipments into Iraq

Some of Project C.U.R.E.'s fleet

US Air Force C-140 delivering Project C.U.R.E. donations

International Headquarters Office and Denver Warehouse

Millions of dollars of donated medical supplies inside one of Project C.U.R.E.'s warehouses

18

Cultural Economics

Within nearly every person, there's a deep longing for justice to be done and for the world's ills to be cured. The Christian understands why this is so, and can recognize beliefs that—however devoutly held—work against justice and the betterment of social conditions. A current trend in our cultural thinking has come to be dominated by political correctness, characterized by a misunderstanding of "tolerance" that treats all truth claims as equally valid. The secular social entrepreneur is, on principle, committed to treating all worldviews as equal in positive contribution.

That's not so, however. It's a nice thought, but it's just not true.

For example, not many Westerners realize or understand the insidious nature of the Indian caste system—the stratification and social restriction of society embraced by the Indian people and culture. The constitution of India, adopted following the involvement of the British, makes the discrimination of the caste system unlawful. However, the constitution has not changed the Indian social mores to any great degree. It is claimed that none of the Hindu scriptures actually endorses the system, but many of the passages are interpreted as sanctioning the practice.

At the top of the hierarchy are the Brahmans—priests, teachers, and scholars. Next, are the Kshatriyas, the kings and warriors. Following them are the Vaisyas, represented by the merchants, agriculturalists, and traders. Finally, there are the Shudras, that include all the artisans and service providers. Below the sanctioned four levels are those known as the Dalits or Harijans. They are the downtrodden or untouchables. About 16 percent of India's population, more than one hundred and sixty million, are considered untouchables.

Syam Kunar is a Brahman. His family is privileged, well-educated, wealthy, and accepted. At an early age Syam felt compelled to access his educational opportunities and become a medical doctor. He determined that he would not set up practice in the socially elite areas of India, however. He vowed that he would finish his education and go directly to work with those of India who were shunned and had absolutely no access to medical care. He was warned repeatedly that he would pay a very high social price and would be accused of abject neglect of his family. He paid the price, and it was indeed a high one. But was it worth it?

In May, 2000, I traveled to India to perform the needs assessment studies along the foothills of the great Himalayan Mountains in the northwest, and also to go over the scary mountain passes into Tibet. Additionally, I was to visit some cities along the eastern seacoast. I was to meet up with Dr. Syam Kunar and his wife, Mary Jean, at the airport in Vishakhapatnam. We would then drive for seven and a half hours from Vishakhapatnam to Rajahmundry, where Dr. Kunar had established a medical clinic.

His Request for Assistance form indicated that he wanted to build a hospital in the same area. Dr. Kunar's paperwork had caught my attention immediately, and I was looking forward to meeting him and getting better acquainted with his work. An organization near Seattle had already agreed to cover the assessment costs, as well as the shipping costs of any of our donated medical goods into India, should Project C.U.R.E. agree to assist the doctor.

We stopped about halfway between Vishakhapatnam and Rajahmundry in a city called Tuni. Mary Jean's parents lived there. Mary Jean and the Kunars' little boy were going to stay with them because the temperature in Rajahmundry was deemed too hot. I should have taken that as a clue to the one hundred and twenty-five degree weather that we were in for. I was served dinner at the parents' home.

Usually in India the women never eat with the men, but instead wait until the men are finished, then take what is left over and go to the kitchen to eat. At Mary Jean's parents' home not even the household's men ate with me. They set a little wooden table in front of me and brought out a plate, spoon, and bowls filled with fried rice, spiced meat, and spiced vegetables. Always, the entire host family just stood around me and watched me eat. They jumped in to wait on me hand and foot, but none would ever sit down.

On our continued trip to Rajahmundry we saw terrible highway accidents. At one scene, two of the huge TATA truck drivers, who were Dalits, had played a game of "chicken" on the narrow road, and neither one had given in. I was told that the desperation of the hopeless untouchables affects how they value their lives to such an extent that it influences their everyday behavior—in this case, it seemed, leading to recklessness. There were five dead bodies on the road and several others injured. Six other times there were huge trucks off the road and smashed into something or turned over. A number of cars and scooters was also involved in accidents, and perhaps the worst was a head-on collision involving a passenger bus. We didn't stop to count the dead. Bodies were everywhere, but no emergency vehicles were anywhere.

One of my greatest fears in traveling the roadways of developing countries is to be involved in an automobile accident. In those countries there is no such a thing as emergency service, as we know it. In India, for example, it is not unusual for people to just drive by without anyone helping at all. At best, you might get thrown into the back of a truck if you were unconscious, and taken to an inadequate facility. There, the only trauma care you could expect would be to get injected with a contaminated needle. For that very reason, I have carried my own sterile needles and syringes and medications with me at all times while traveling around the world.

Once we had arrived in Rajahmundry we went straight to a hotel and I checked in. Dr. Kunar was packed and was ready to stay in the room with me to protect me from the bad and desperate locals.

I thanked him profoundly for his kind thoughtfulness, but told him that would not be necessary. I explained that I was accustomed to traveling around the world in pretty bad places, and that I would be just fine. "I would welcome you to walk with me to my room and check it out and protect me as I shut and lock the door. Then, I can happily stay there until the following morning until you come to my room to collect me. I will be all right."

"We would never forgive ourselves," he said, protesting, "if anything should ever happen to our very important guest from America while he stayed in our city. There are some very bad people here."

"I understand completely, Dr. Kunar," I said, "and I want to express how very much I appreciate your love and concern for me, but I will be just fine."

"Don't answer your phone or answer your door for anyone! In the morning, about seven thirty, you can answer my phone call from the lobby. You must not take any food from the hotel or from anyone who might offer. I have arranged for my wife's friend to cook all your meals, and you will eat in my home. You will always eat there," instructed Dr. Kunar emphatically.

The next morning I went with Dr. Kunar to his clinic. Scores of people were already crowding around the clinic waiting for a chance to be seen. Dr. Kunar was a gifted physician and possessed a very high level of energy. His daily schedule at the clinic started early and extended late:

6:00 am to 10:00 am—simple surgical procedures
10:00 am to 2:00 pm—general clinic patients
2:00 pm to 6:00 pm—more minor surgeries and emergencies
6:00 pm to 11:00 pm—general clinic patients

As we drove to the clinic, Dr. Kunar began telling me about his life. "You see, Dr. Jackson, it is a miracle that I am a doctor in India at all. I was the very first Christian to graduate from the medical school. I was second in my class even though they did everything they could to turn me out and keep me from passing my exams. They even changed answers on my exams to try to make me fail. But God wanted me to be a doctor to the poorest people in this area, and it is now happening. But, Dr. Jackson, I need your help because, as you will see, I have nothing in my clinic except sick people and God."

Dr. Kunar's clinic saw two hundred to two hundred and fifty patients a day. Nearly all the women we saw that Monday were severely anemic. The community people could only afford bulk-type food, like rice. They would boil the rice, eat the bulk, and drink the broth. They could not afford vegetables, fruits, or meats. I would estimate nearly 80 percent of the patients—men, women, and children—had serious respiratory problems and often glandular infections. Few men in the community lived past the age of twenty-seven years old.

One thirty-year-old mother with five children had joint and muscle deterioration so severe that she could hardly walk up the few steps into the clinic. Her back, neck, arms, and hands were terribly affected. She was not alone; there was an unusual prevalence of joint and bone problems, and the onset of arthritis at an early age.

The peoples' respiratory illnesses came from their living conditions—huts with dirt floors under dirty banana leaf thatch roofs. The mites and insects and dust filtered down from the thatch and into their lungs. The hot, humid atmosphere, coupled with the filth and dust of India, irritated and infected them with each breath. The same conditions allowed ringworm, scabies, parasites, and a variety of skin ailments to become endemic.

One woman had come in with a sinus infection and severe facial pain. Additionally, she had a blocked septum. Minor surgery would have taken a doctor about ten minutes, and with some antibiotics the woman would have found some relief. Dr. Kunar literally begged me to send him an electric blood cauterizer so that he could successfully perform such procedures, along with removing bothersome tonsils from both children and adults.

One man showed up with a swollen and bloated intestine. Quack doctors had taken all his money and had performed two surgeries on the man. One scar ran from the rib cage to the pelvis area. Another scar was about twelve inches in length and ran diagonally from his hip to above his navel. Twice they had sliced him open and sewed him shut again without finding the problem.

Dr. Kunar quickly diagnosed the problem, but he did not have the facility or any of the necessary equipment to successfully do the procedure.

We saw many cases of middle-ear infection with considerable discharge. Lots of women suffered with OB-GYN problems. Add hormonal imbalances and universal anemia to all the other problems, and you come up with a lot of suffering folks. Before Dr. Kunar had come to open his clinic those people had no place to turn for help.

I inquired and found there to be no government hospital or free clinics in the geographical area. I did find, however, that there were a lot of self-taught doctors, more commonly known as "quacks," who had simply hung out a sign and started taking the peoples' money for their services. For an extremely qualified doctor, like Dr. Kunar, to open a free clinic in an area of extreme poverty, inhabited by the untouchables, was radical and revolutionary.

To extend help to the untouchables was not looked upon favorably by the rest of the society. In my many trips to India, I had requested that the higher caste groups, including the Brahman caste, help me in getting aid to the neglected and hopeless people in the untouchable groups.

The answer was always the same. "Why, Dr. Jackson, would we want to do that? Why would we want to interfere in the lives of those people by making their lives easier? You see, they are in that position for a reason, and they must learn the lessons of life that they are now assigned to learn. They obviously have done something in a past life to deserve the plight in which they now find themselves. Of course, it is deplorable, but they now have the wonderful opportunity to learn the appropriate lessons in this life. If we interfere and deprive them of the opportunity, they will only have to return again in the next life and learn them then."

My response? "Do you mean you would rely on such an honorable and lofty defense," I would ask these people, "in order to get out of helping your hurting brother in his time of great need, and yet take advantage of his position for your business labors?"

"Oh, Dr. Jackson, we are sorry that you cannot understand the richness of the great teachings. Everyone is very happy."

The quack doctors were not appreciative of Dr. Kunar's competing clinic either. They had figured out a way to take advantage of his free services. They began sending their patients to Dr. Kunar to get him to give them a legitimate diagnosis, since the quacks could only guess. Then they would instruct the patients to return to them for treatment. The quacks also conspired to flood Dr. Kunar's clinic with their patients in order to get any free pharmaceuticals he might give away.

I asked Dr. Kunar just how he planned to handle the problem. "It is really not my problem," Dr. Kunar said. "It's God's problem. If I know the patient has come to my clinic having been sent by a quack, then I will simply turn him around and send him back. If I find the patient truly has a need, then I take care of him." He gave a quick laugh. "You see, I really rather enjoy the other doctors trying to flood me with thousands of patients. The patients soon know that I am a legitimate physician when they come to my clinic. When they come here we treat them with respect and dignity, and allow them to feel God's love working through us. After all, it was God who impressed upon me that I was to come here and help these untouchables with their needs. No one else is here to really help them. Everyone else wants to take from them."

I was quite overwhelmed when I realized that it was ten o'clock at night, and we were still at the clinic. Dr. Kunar actually worked the hours that were listed. His energy and commitment were exceptional.

The longer I was with him, the more I was impressed with his intelligence and medical expertise. I quizzed him about his diagnostic abilities. He told me that after he had graduated from medical school he had gone to work for a well-established Hindu doctor. He had quadrupled the doctor's patient flow, putting his fellow physician in awe of his quick and accurate diagnoses. His reputation grew, and he was asked to consult with other respected doctors and hospitals. Dr. Kunar ended up making a lot of money for the other doctors, and they begged him not to do such a stupid thing as to set up a clinic and hospital for the untouchables.

I kept thinking about Mother Teresa, quoting Jesus: "As ye have done it unto the least of these ... ye have done it unto Me." Mother Teresa would have understood Dr. Kunar perfectly, if few others in India did.

Tuesday, Dr. Kunar notified his staff that he would not be into the clinic until ten o'clock that morning. He had things he wanted to show Dr. Jackson. He wanted to let me see why he was giving his life to India's poorest of the poor. "I want to introduce you to my friends, the rock breakers."

One of the Rajahmundry groups of untouchables had to break rocks in order to eke out a living. Small rocks were needed in construction.

Paved roadways are not constructed in India like they are in the United States. There are no large pieces of paving equipment that glide down the interstate highways laying down a magical carpet of smooth blacktop miles at a time. In India the roads are constructed by first laying a bed of small rocks, each no bigger than three inches in size. Then the small rocks are tamped into place.

Alongside the area of roadway where they are working, laborers dig pits about three feet deep and fill them with burning charcoal. Troughs of tar are placed over the fire pits until the tar is hot and bubbling. Laborers then pick up the smoldering troughs by hand and dump the hot tar over the top of the bed of small rocks. This method is repeated one small area at a time until a stretch of roadway is paved.

Imagine the number of small three-inch rocks it requires to pave a mile of road. There are no huge rock-crushing machines in India to supply those small rocks. Each rock is chipped by hand with an individual hammer. The poor families of the untouchables are the ones who swing the hammers hour after hour, day after day, year after year. Mother, father, teens, and even little children, sit or stand on the rock heaps swinging their beat-up hammers. Boulders have to be split into smaller stones and those smaller stones into the rocks of desired size. As soon as a child is old enough to swing a hammer, he is placed in a rock pile and expected to break rocks.

One day each week a large TATA truck comes to the local rock-breaking work area and dumps huge boulders. The members of each untouchable family gather around their massive granite boulders and begin to chip away at it, and break it down into smaller and smaller pieces. They have one week to break the massive rocks into small, three inch rocks. The TATA trucks return with more boulders and the families must load all their small rocks into buckets and load the large empty truck with their rocks by hand.

For one week's work the family is paid the US equivalent of four dollars in Indian rupees. Out of that they pay all their living expenses. They have no other opportunities. When you are on the bottom of the caste system, or beneath the whole system, as were the untouchables, you simply accept your lot and hope that in the next life you can at least be a street vendor. In the meantime, the Brahman caste is counting on your slave labor. There is no alternative to the untouchables' dwellings of dirt floors and banana-leaf roofs and walls. They live on rice, no meat, no vegetables, no milk. For shoes, they might have a simple pair of thongs. They fetch their own water in their own pots from a rusty metal pipe on the edge of the village.

We drove to one of the rock-breaker villages, parked the car, and walked. The people recognized Dr. Kunar and laid down their hammers in respect as he walked by. He was the only person to come and help them. The people were not ugly, but fine-featured and attractive, albeit dirty from working in the rock dust day after day. They were eager for me to take their pictures, and a little troupe of young kids started gathering around and following us until the rock-pile foreman yelled at them to get back to work.

I will carry to my grave those vivid scenes. I will never be able to erase or bury the emotion of that first walk through a rock-breaker village. The people were eager to smile and talk and welcome us. They were totally given over to their fate, and did the best they could during the present life in hopes they would come back in their next life as something better. Perhaps one day they would be good enough to pass out of the caste structure into a better world of peace and rest.

I determined then and there that if there were any ways Project C.U.R.E. could join Dr. Kunar, and help him fulfill his dream and vision, we would do it! I had found a whole other set of "the least of these" that needed our help. We could help change eternity, as well as the here-and-now, by bringing help and hope and medical care to the rock breakers of Rajahmundry.

I could better understand now why so many young mothers and fathers came to the clinic with deteriorating joints and bones in their hands, elbows, and shoulders. I could now see why so many suffered nerve and muscle damage. I could see why the expected length of life was only twenty-seven years. How they could breathe in the rock dust of the breaking areas, go home to breathe in the dust, parasites and bacteria of the thatched huts, and be able to breathe at all by the time they were adults was a mystery to me.

An Apostolic Lutheran Church had given Dr. Kunar five hundred and fifty dollars per month to purchase antibiotics and other pharmaceuticals. Applied to his daily patient load, that amount did not go far. I did not find guinea worm there, as was so prevalent throughout Africa, but occurrences of elephantiasis and grotesque results of heart disease were very common. Many times Dr. Kunar would write out a prescription for the sick patient to go to a pharmacy and purchase an antibiotic or hypertension medication. He would find out later that they had not taken any of the prescribed medication because they could not round up enough money to purchase the medication. So, their problems would continue to persist.

One young man arrived at the clinic leaning heavily on a stick in order to hobble his way to the doctor's attention. He had fallen from a rock pile and dislocated his hip. He was in great pain, as the muscles had contracted around the dislocation. Dr. Kunar told him to go get an x-ray, which would cost him four dollars at a quack's office. The man was caught in an economic quandary. He didn't have four dollars, and the other members of his family were too sick to break rocks. He was the only provider, but could no longer even get to the rock pile, let alone swing a sledgehammer. If he did not receive help for his hip, he would be permanently unable to work for food for his sick family or himself; he was trapped.

"This is why, Dr. Jackson, I desperately need an x-ray machine of my own," said Dr. Kunar pleading.

I reached into my wallet and took out enough to set up an economic emergency fund for cases such as this man's. It would be for people who were totally caught in the trap, needing a bit of money to get their need met so they could get back to work.

Most of the untouchables were illiterate. They didn't have radios, televisions, or access to any simple or accurate information about life. One mother brought her two sick children to see Dr. Kunar. He translated their conversation for me. She wanted to know when she would have more children. He asked her if she was having intercourse. "Not since my husband died," she replied.

The doctor then told her that children came as a result of intercourse.

She was shocked. "I had heard that when I was younger, but I had intercourse with my husband many times and didn't have a child, so I never believed that story anymore."

Lots of patients came with hands swollen from terribly infected blisters or wounds from imbedded rock fragments. Almost all of the first-time patients received an injection that included antibiotics, vitamins, and tetanus.

Wednesday morning Dr. Kunar got up from his chair in the clinic and motioned with his head for me to follow him. "I only have you here for such a limited time, Dr. Jackson, and the patients can wait a bit while I show you more of my dream."

The doctor drove me across the river that flowed into the Bay of Bengal at Rajahmundry. The city included about two million in population. Another group of untouchables lived across the river. These did not break rocks in their villages. They worked seasonally in large plantations of wealthy individuals and corporations. Their plight was just the same, however. They were paid less than fifty cents per day, when there was work for them. Again, they had no access to legitimate health care. Dr. Kunar's plan included opening a clinic on that side of the river as soon as possible.

Then we drove to a site where Dr. Kunar believed God was going to give him the ground needed for his new hospital. "Somehow we will see it built if Project C.U.R.E. could agree with us to come and furnish the hospital with supplies and necessary pieces of equipment," he said. (Dr. Kunar was a great advocate for his cause!)

The site was nearly one acre in size, easily accessible, and had a couple of small buildings that could be used for storage during the construction phase. Dr. Kunar had already been dealing with the owners who had agreed to sell the property for a hospital at a greatly reduced price. Several of the family members who owned the property were already patients of Dr. Kunar.

"As you can see, Dr. Jackson," Dr. Kunar said, as we walked the perimeter of the proposed site, "this property is situated directly across the road from the main entrance to the city refuse dump. Several more villages of untouchables work at the dumping site. From this strategic location we will be able to serve the untouchables who dwell and work here, as well as the rock-breakers and the plantation workers. Oh, we have such a wonderful and exciting opportunity here."

We then rushed back across the river and back to the long lines of hurting individuals waiting patiently to see their beloved doctor.

Later in the day the doctor spoke to his staff and told them that he and I needed to travel back to the city of Tuni before it got dark. I checked out of the simple hotel where I had been staying the past few nights. We traveled for nearly four hours back to the home of Mary Jean's parents for another dinner, where I ate while others watched.

After dinner I was once again taken to a local shabby hotel. This one was located right on the main street of Tuni. People were crowding the street in front of the hotel trying to sell fruits, vegetables, even pots and pans. The room that was to become mine for the night was situated on the ground level. As was the case with most hotels in India, there was no shower or bathtub in the room. There was, however, an old toilet instead of the usual footpads where you were expected to just squat over an open sewer hole in the floor. I was pleased and thankful to see the old toilet.

Instead of a shower or bath, there was usually a water spigot located about a foot up from the floor. That was where the plastic buckets could be filled with the unsafe water. In the bucket, or near it on the skuzzy floor, would be a plastic dipper. In order to have a wash, I needed to fill the bucket and use the dipper to pour the water over my head. Since most Indians who were privileged to have access to water had washed themselves in such a manner since birth, they believed it to be the normal and natural way to wash oneself. I always had trouble washing out the shampoo, but that was *my* problem.

Dr. Kunar's in-laws had given me a clean towel, a bottle of purified water, and a glass to use in my room. They also had given to me a clean sheet to use on my bed so I wouldn't have to lay my face on the dirty mattress. Those amenities had not come with the price of the room.

My doctor friend gave me the same stern lecture about there being lots of mean and desperate people in the vicinity, and that I was to be extremely careful because I had what they needed—money! Dr. Kunar then offered again to stay with me to protect me.

I thanked him, and assured him that I would be fine. I secured the door as best I could. I finally was able to fall asleep by seeing myself walking alongside the sparkling, splashing mountain stream that flows in front of our Evergreen home in Colorado. I imagined that the slightly cool air from the ancient hotel air conditioner, placed in the street-level window of my room, was a breeze wafting down my creek from the fourteen thousand-foot peak of Mount Evans.

About three o'clock in the morning I was awakened by the smell of smoke. I thought, in my sleepy daze, that perhaps someone out in the lobby was burning incense to one of the three hundred and five Hindu gods. Still in the half-awake, half-asleep stage, I dreamed about a man riding on an ox cart, smoking an ugly, hand rolled cigar. I had seen such a man the day before on the road from Rajahmundry to Tuni. I thought perhaps that man was out in the hallway smoking his long, ugly cigar.

When I finally realized what was going on, I jumped out of the bed onto the dirty floor and turned on the single raw light bulb in my room. Survival instincts, sharpened by millions of miles traveled in dangerous venues around the world, had me fully alert. I began to search for the source of the smoke in my room. By that time the room was hazy.

Once awake, I could tell that the smoke wasn't coming from a fire; instead it carried the cloying scent of dope.

I checked the bottom of the door into the hallway and the rectangular transom vent above the door. The bathroom did not have a window, but had louvered slats high up on the wall. Someone was trying to put me into a sleep too deep for self-defense.

In previous years, I had been warned while traveling in the old Soviet Union to throw a blanket, rug or shirt along the crack under the door of the hotel room whenever I was sleeping. Also, I had been instructed, after some of my acquaintances had been victimized on the old Russians trains, to use a belt or wire to secure the train coach doors at night. Additionally, it was wise to cram dirty clothes under the train compartment door when traveling because thugs would force chloroform or other knock-out types of drugs under the door. Once the victim was unconscious, they would break through the door into the compartment and rob him.

My son, Jay, and I might actually have been victims of such a robbery once before. We were in London, and our hotel room had been emptied of valuables during the night without either of us waking. Scotland Yard detectives suggested that the thieves might have drugged us.

I located the source of the smoke coming into my Tuni hotel room: it was coming in through my air conditioner. Someone was outside my room letting the intake fan swoop the highly toxic smoke right into my room.

The natural response would have been to unbolt the door and hurry into the hallway. That would have been exactly what the robbers wanted. Once I left the protection of the room, the robbers would have had complete access. I would have been totally defenseless, and in my underwear.

I thought of what my son, Jay, the respected fire chief of our town, would have told me. I knew that a predator counts on his victim reacting without thinking. I needed to stop and figure out what I needed to accomplish, and then respond, not react. I listened to what Jay would have suggested, and I grabbed my handkerchief and the bottle of clean drinking water. I doused the handkerchief with the water and tied it around my face.

I then figured out how to disconnect the two hundred and forty volt air conditioner to stop the inflow of the toxic smoke. There was a ceiling fan in the room, and I quickly got it started. Now, I had the source of smoke stopped and the air pressure from the ceiling fan blowing the smoke out of the vent slats in the bathroom and the cracks around the door and window.

The smoke started to clear out, but I could still taste the nasty residue in my mouth and feel the sting in my eyes. I left the light on in my room for the rest of the night, and sat back down on the bed. To make a little better breathing filter, I kept the handkerchief soaked with fresh water from the bottle, and tied a T-shirt about my face and over the wet handkerchief. I never went back to sleep, but at least the smoke continued to clear out of the room.

When I got up to take my bucket bath, I reconnected the air conditioner to get a little relief from the stifling heat. The sweet, toxic smoke had absolutely saturated the air conditioner, however, so I quickly disconnected it again. Better to be hot, than dead. Apparently, when I turned the light on and stopped the air conditioner, the thugs, whoever they were, decided to move on to another foreign victim.

I was happy to receive Dr. Kunar's phone call to my room from the lobby at seven thirty that morning. I let him know that I had not left the room. When I related the night's episode to my friend, he began to tremble. "They were intent on robbing you, and they certainly would not have hesitated to kill you in the process."

Dr. Kunar's reputation for his work with the untouchables was beginning to spread. He had been invited to speak at a conference in London, England. He had never flown on an airplane, and had never been out of that area of southeastern India, but he had agreed to go to the conference to tell about his efforts. He had been praying that God would send someone to help him make his way through the mysteries of traveling for the very first time. He knew nothing about passports, visas, airports, tickets, fees, luggage check-in, boarding gates, and airplanes. When I sent him my travel itinerary, he discovered we were traveling together all the way from Rajahmundry to Vishakhapatnam to Hyderabad, and on to Bombay. God had directed my travel plans to coordinate exactly with his.

I could help and mentor him until we got to Bombay. He would then depart and go to London, and my flight would take me to Frankfurt. His friends would meet him at London's Heathrow airport.

I put Dr. Kunar through a graduate class in international travel. I explained everything to him, from how to find his seat on the plane and fasten his seatbelt, to locating a monitor to learn where his flight was boarding. His eyes were pretty big as we took off from Vishakhapatnam runway and he looked out the window of an airplane for the very first time.

As we parted in Bombay, and I watched Dr. Syam Kunar walk bravely from his gate onto his plane, I was proud and greatly humbled at the same time. Dr. Kunar was a prime example of a cultural entrepreneur—someone who paid the price to change the lot of the "least of these" for the better.

At the Bombay airport it was night, and still one hundred degrees Fahrenheit. I stood in line to check into my 2:40 a.m. flight to Frankfurt, and watched the sweat run through the fabric of my shirt and down behind my belt. I was ready to leave India and go to cool Colorado. We had been able to ingress into an unethical and unholy practice of discrimination and cultural abuse and apply our values of integrity and grace.

On my return flight I had time to write and reflect on my busy and event-filled trip. I received a profound insight from God concerning a passage of scripture from the Apostle Paul's writings in the book of Philippians. "I want to know Christ and the power of his resurrection and the fellowship of sharing in his sufferings, becoming like him in his death, and so, somehow, to attain the resurrection from the dead" (Philippians 3:10–11).

Everyone wanted to know Christ and the power of His resurrection. He walked right through walls to where his disciples were meeting. His resurrected body knew no limits of time and space. He would never again experience pain or death. But the truth I experienced on my flight from India to Colorado had to do with the second part: "the fellowship of sharing in his sufferings."

I came to believe that the Christ of the universe had allowed me intimate fellowship with Him through the experience of joining in His suffering. I used to think that meant getting beat up, or having thorns placed on my forehead. Over the years of traveling throughout the world, though, Christ had allowed me the high privilege of experiencing the brokenness of the world in a way that broke my heart. I often saw more pain and suffering in thirty days than most people would in an entire lifetime.

I would never get over the pain of meeting and experiencing life with the untouchables of India. I would never completely heal from the shock of seeing dead bodies in Nagorno-Karabakh, or the results of the bloody massacres in Rwanda, Uganda, Burundi, or West Africa. How many times had I looked upon human bones sticking up out of shallow graves, or seen the marks of torture on people in Bosnia and Kosovo and Cambodia? I had seen atrocities with my own eyes, and my heart had been broken like a crushed egg shell.

On the airplane flying home, God seemed to speak to my heart. *You have obediently followed Me and I have allowed you to enter into a unique fellowship of sharing in my suffering. You have now seen what makes My heart hurt. I want you to continue to reach out to those I created and those I love with a passion that will result from this fellowship—then when it's time, you shall also know the taste of death, but greater yet you shall truly know the power of the resurrection. Our life, forever, together, will be splendid.*

19

Despair

Cultural economics, as exemplified in India's caste system, can have such devastating effects that I was tempted to despair, as every social entrepreneur can be. At times maintaining our stated distinctive of keeping a singleness of purpose and a "can-do" disposition was almost impossible. India broke my heart, but in India I could see how a false conception of human destiny had become a ready excuse to the plight of the poor. The AIDS epidemic that began sweeping Africa in the 1980s and 1990s—an epidemic that goes on killing millions today, despite the introduction of retroviral drugs—presented scenes of such sadness and horror that I came to live with an aching in my marrow, the screams that I feared to voice lest I never stop.

In the 1990s and early 2000s it was common to hear people say, "Africa is gone," implying it was already too late to save the continent. Hundreds of millions would eventually die. The widespread dissemination of retroviral drugs has modified this view and given the story less play in the West, where AIDS has been largely confined to the gay community and IV drug users. There is still no cure for AIDS, but people like the former basketball star Magic Johnson have become symbols of how the disease can be managed.

Still, a conservative estimate puts the number of people afflicted with AIDS in Africa today at 22 million. The disease continues to spread throughout central Asia. More people have died of AIDS in our time than died of the bubonic plague in the Middle Ages. Most countries minimize the number of people afflicted with AIDS because they are under pressure to meet percentage targets from relief agencies, including the United Nations. It's easy to lie about the mortality rate from AIDS because no one dies directly from it. AIDS wipes out the immune system, allowing its victims to die of malaria, tuberculosis, and whatever infection happens to come along. Governments regularly ascribe many AIDS deaths to these immediate causes.

Even so, if the world woke up tomorrow to find that 22 million people in Africa alone, and millions more elsewhere, were afflicted with a potentially deadly virus, wouldn't we consider that a catastrophe of historic proportions? We have lived with this plague for so long that many have become insensitive to its real dimensions and challenges.

I was schooled in the horror of AIDS at a time when no help, and virtually no relief, could be found. It's the essence of the experience that I want to get at here, because social entrepreneurs will almost inevitably run up against similarly defeating conditions. It is part of being in the midst of the world's brokenness and finding out what that truly means—not as an abstract theological doctrine, but as a day-to-day, brutal, and unremitting reality. Every social entrepreneur will have his own AIDS epidemic to deal with—his own potentially overwhelming situation.

Africa, particularly sub-Saharan Africa, has been turning to Christ in massive numbers since the turn of the twentieth century. This process has accelerated greatly in the last three decades. Many times, in the midst of the AIDS epidemic, I was dealing with my Christian brothers and sisters, both as those caring for the ill and as the ill themselves.

As many people have remarked, though, for many, Christianity in Africa is a mile wide and an inch deep. African Christians often find themselves straddling the ways taught by their new Christian faith and those of their tribe. Because of cultural inheritances like polygamy and animistic religion, Africans tend to be promiscuous even after marriage, and could be hard to convince that AIDS was something more than a western invention.

I know that sounds like a typical white man going on about the promiscuity of black peoples. Haven't Westerners been having their own sexual liberation party? That's true, which is why we have our own epidemic of venereal disease. Consider this: in Africa, the general health of people is often compromised, and their sanitation and personal hygiene resources are fewer. The more fluid structure of the African family—with extramarital affairs being taken for granted—has combined with these factors to make AIDS a bigger threat in Africa than anywhere else.

If the people of Africa—and elsewhere in the world—began practicing the chastity and marital fidelity to which their faith calls them, the AIDS epidemic could be stopped within one generation. It's notable that the most successful AIDS programs in Africa have been those advocating abstinence and remaining faithful to the marital bond. Those that are less countercultural, emphasizing the use of condoms, have been less successful.

My first eye-opening introduction to HIV/AIDS took place during my early involvement in Kenya. I was assessing a rural district hospital when I was taken to the rear property line of the hospital site where a small, whitewashed building stood alone, housing the serious tuberculosis patients of the district. As I walked through the facility, I asked if all the patients were tuberculosis patients. "No," the director answered. "We also place all our HIV/AIDS patients here."

My jaw dropped a bit, and I asked, "Don't you know that putting an AIDS patient right next to a dying tuberculosis patient is a surefire death sentence for the AIDS patient?"

"We don't know what else to do with them," he confessed. "We have no other space or money, so we really don't have any other options."

Later on, I kept hearing references to tuberculosis as the "Angel of Mercy" in connection with AIDS patients.

In chapter one, I introduced Dr. Larry Sthreshley, who was on assignment to salvage what was left of the Presbyterian medical mission's heritage in northern sub-Saharan Africa. I had traveled all over Cameroon and Congo assessing hospitals and clinics with Dr. Larry. At times I would shake my head in wonder as to where Larry was coming up with the patience to put up with the incompetence and inadequate conditions he was trying to fix. He kept quietly pushing for excellence and accountability in his rebuilding efforts. I was discovering that Dr. Larry Sthreshley was perhaps one of the finest examples of a cultural entrepreneur that I had encountered.

In 2004, Dr. Larry and I were traveling together again. There were six institutions that we were to assess in the general area of the capital city of Kinshasa, Congo. Our third hospital was called Boo Nsuba. I was impressed with the facility's appearance and the way the hospital was being run.

Dr. Larry informed me that the doctor who was directing the facility was a tremendously talented man of about forty years of age. "I have invested a lot of money in his training by sending him to the US and Johannesburg and he has turned out to be a splendid director. But now …." His voice trailed off and he did not explain further.

As we proceeded down one hallway of the hospital, we stopped at what looked like the doors to a supply closet. Dr. Larry reached for the handle. It was just a shallow room with an old trolley bed pushed up against the back wall. There in front of us was a man who might have been one hundred years old. His arms and legs were the size of gnarly ropes. He was lying on an old, dirty mattress with no sheets on the bed or pillowcase on the tattered pillow. The man's face was shriveled, his eyes sunken, and his head bore so many lesions it looked as if he had grown scales. Oddly, he wore a pressed dress shirt, business slacks, and a pair of nicely polished dress shoes. The small, darkened room reeked with the nauseating smell of death.

Larry introduced me to him. Here was the once-talented director of the hospital.

The director signaled for Larry to come a little closer so he could speak to him. "Larry, I know you can help me," he whispered. "Even though the treatment is expensive, please bring the medicine that will cure me."

Larry gently took hold of the doctor's emaciated arm and said quietly, "You and I both know that there is no cure for what you have. The virus has taken over your body and allowed the disease to advance to where you are now. I am your friend, and I am really sorry."

We turned and slowly walked back into the hallway and Larry closed the doors.

Once outside, Larry explained how disappointing and frustrating it was to pour time, money, and training into his top staff people, and then have them contract the virus, when they should be the ones most aware of the absolute consequences. "We are quickly losing our good people," Dr. Larry said slowly and deliberately. "Just this year I have lost seven of my best administrators and doctors to HIV/AIDS."

"Did the director inadvertently get stuck with an infected needle?" I asked.

"No, no such thing. The director was a fine, married, Christian man. The hospital directors and staff members were having a retreat at the lake. There was a very cute, young nurse who was bopping around in her starched nurse's cap and uniform. The director arranged for her to have a room close to his at the retreat. He had sex with her. She failed to tell him that she had just ended a relationship with her boyfriend who was HIV/AIDS positive. The director then came home and unknowingly infected his wife and impregnated her at the same time. She died and the baby died. The wife's mother was so humiliated that she stopped eating and starved herself to death."

Commenting on such episodes, an African doctor told me, "The tradition of promiscuity is so prolific that it probably will result in the wiping out of the majority of the population in the future. Further, the people not only don't intend to change their practices, they don't want to even acknowledge, or discuss, the explosive situation. It is worse than denial."

On another such trip to the Congo I landed at the Kinshasa airport, where Dr. Sthreshley once again picked me up. The city of Kinshasa had a population of about six million. Together we visited the Kananga City facility located on the Lulua River. From there we traveled into the highly-restricted area of the war-torn Congo to an interior city called Mbuji-Mayi, then back to Kanaga. We continued traveling to the Hospital du Bon Berger located in Tshikaji.

When we arrived we were informed that the five main doctors in charge of the hospital could not agree on who could take holidays at that time. Since they couldn't agree, they all just left at the same time. There was no coordination of plans, and there was no one really left in charge. All was chaos.

I was introduced to a fine retired gentleman, Dr. Bill Sager, who had been appointed to travel from the United States to help instruct in some procedural classes at Bon Berger. Dr. Sager agreed to accompany me on my needs assessment tour, since the director was gone. He then invited me to join him on the medical rounds that afternoon. One of the first patients on our rounds was a young, sharp and very intense business-man. He was using his briefcase as a pillow and was busily working on his paperwork. As soon as Dr Sager and I approached his bed, he began angrily to rebuke the doctor. "I told you to x-ray my knees and give me either medicine or surgery to make my knees better. You have done nothing for me, and I have been here for a long time. I have not seen any of the regular doctors for a long time. They must have gone somewhere. But I am demanding that you immediately do something to fix my knees. I can't just stay here, I have business to do."

Dr. Sager smiled warmly at the patient while he gently pushed around on his knees. Then he turned his back to the patient and showed me his chart. "In the States you might think this man had arthritis in the knee joints, as well as his other joints. But you can see here on his chart that he has HIV/AIDS. Infection is settling in his joints, as well as elsewhere, like his lungs. He is a dead man. There is absolutely nothing we will be able to do for this businessman but watch him waste away and die in pain."

In the next bed was a man with a terribly swollen face and head. He was in so much pain that he could not lie down. He just sat there and moaned and tried to look out from the tiny slits of his disfigured eyelids. His lips were grotesquely huge, so that he could not close his mouth, but he continually drooled onto his bare chest.

"This man had a toothache," explained Dr. Sager. "He went to the local tooth man who took a reed and scraped the tooth and gum line thinking that there might be some leftover food lodged around the tooth, making it hurt. All he really accomplished was to infect the mouth and gums with his reed scraper, so the infection has uncontrollably ballooned to the proportions that you see now." Dr. Sager then pointed to the man's chart at the letters HIV/AIDS. "This man has no immune system left that is strong enough to fight the infection. He is not responding to treatment. The infection has taken over his body in just a short time. He won't leave this hospital alive."

On the next bed was a small boy sitting with his legs wrapped around a pan containing some groundnuts, or peanuts. His arms and legs were skinny and fragile, and he just looked at me with a blank stare. His mom had just died of HIV/AIDS, but not before passing on the virus to her son. No one knew for sure what to do with him until he died. So, he just sat there on the bed, trying to eat the peanuts.

The situation at the next bed turned my broken heart to anger. There were two female nurses and one male nurse who had been closely following us on the hospital rounds. They were graduates of the nursing school on the hospital campus. When we arrived at the foot of the next patient's bed, Dr. Sager studied the chart and examined the patient's foot. The patient, a young lad about fifteen years old, was very sick. He was burning up with a fever and was crying aloud because of the pain. He had stepped on a rusty nail where he was working and had become infected with tetanus.

Dr. Sager looked sternly at the nurses and exclaimed, "I told you very plainly, and even demonstrated to you, how I wanted this wound treated. I also left instructions that the wound was to be cleaned, medicated, and redressed three times per day. I come here now and the wound has not been treated at all, and there is no dressing even now on the foot. I suspect that you did not follow any of my instructions."

"Well," said one of the arrogant young nurses in a defiant tone, "you are not an African doctor, and you simply don't know how to treat wounds here. Here wounds heal by leaving them alone and letting the air take care of them."

"So, you defied my instructions for this patient?" asked Dr. Sager.

"But, of course," retorted the snippy little nurse.

"I think it would be well for you to remember who the doctor is and who the nurse is," reprimanded Dr. Sager.

He looked at me and rolled his eyes as we walked from the bed. "It is almost impossible to work under these conditions. She does not know that he has AIDS, so that did not influence her thinking. But the least that we could have done would have been to try to slow down the infection and give the boy some relief from the excruciating pain."

Every bed in every ward of that hospital was filled with an HIV/AIDS patient. They were all dying of infection, malaria, cholera, injuries, diarrhea, or some other ailment. They had no hope of recovery because somewhere along the line they had contracted the HIV/AIDS virus.

As we finished the rounds, I confessed to Dr. Sager that there was something I didn't understand and needed to have explained to me. "Why is it that those with HIV/AIDS in Africa are never informed that they have AIDS? No one ever mentions it to the patient. They are left to believe that they have malaria, or African sleeping sickness, or swelling of the joints, or something else. Wouldn't it be better for them to know so that they wouldn't go around spreading the disease to lots of other people before they died?"

"That really is a strange medical phenomenon, isn't it?" Dr. Sager answered. "It is a big, big problem, and quite culturally complicated. A sickness like HIV/AIDS is very taboo here. Even a tuberculosis patient's family, when they discover the family member's disease, will actually mourn for them as if they had already died, and completely abandon them. Hardly ever will a family return to the hospital to take care of, or feed, the patient. It's their way of taking care of the healthy members at home."

Dr. Sager went on explaining the cultural ramifications of an AIDS diagnosis. "AIDS in Africa is taboo. If the patients you saw today were to be told that they have AIDS, their families would conclude that their condition is the hospital's fault. Their families never saw them with symptoms of AIDS before, so they draw the conclusion that people get AIDS when they go to the hospital.

"If that conviction took hold, no one would enter the hospital doors for legitimate needs and problems. Further, in this area, AIDS is believed to be a 'white man's disease,' and it is being spread to do away with the Africans and their culture. Mothers will forbid their daughters to allow a man to use a condom during sex, saying that the whites want to ruin their natural enjoyment and change their culture. The women are warned that if condoms are used, at least one of two things will happen. First, they will get pregnant anyway, but the baby will be born with severe deformities and will die shortly after birth. Second, if the condom should happen to come off inside the woman during sex, it will stay inside her and rot her out and make her die, or at least make her go crazy."

Dr. Sager wasn't finished. "Another problem exists. There are a lot of superstitions here regarding HIV/AIDS and other STDs [sexually transmitted diseases]. Over the years men have come to believe that, if they contract a sexually transmitted disease, they can be cured if they have sex with a virgin. To cure a more severe disease a younger virgin must be found. So, if a man discovers he has contracted HIV/AIDS, a likely reaction would be for him to go out and find an eleven- or twelve-year-old girl and rape her in order to cure himself. Of course, he doesn't get cured, but he has just infected another innocent girl.

"There are just a lot of reasons in this culture why AIDS will not be recognized or talked about. And in the meantime they are losing the entire working segment of their population," said the doctor.

Dr. Larry Sthreshley had gotten in on part of our conversation and was aware that I had just recently been to Malawi, just south and east of Congo. Larry had been in Malawi just prior to flying to meet me in Congo. "Jim, you have been to both Blantyre and Malamulo in Malawi and are aware of the HIV/AIDS crisis there. Just since you were there the problems have become much worse. It is quietly recognized that over 65 percent of the entire population now prove HIV positive."

I told Larry that his figures reinforced what I had found when I was recently talking to the surgeons and lab people in the local hospitals.

Larry went on, "Men and women and children are already dying at a shocking rate. In the area where I was, there are five Presbyterian churches that are trying to take care of the young children whose parents have died of AIDS. One church was trying to feed and clothe three thousand such children. Another church was trying to take care of about two thousand children. It is an impossible task. Of course, many of those children are infected at birth and are now dying.

"It has become such a huge problem that now, when a mother dies of AIDS and leaves a baby, there is no longer anyone available to take care of the infant. So, the live baby is placed alongside the dead mother in the coffin and buried with her. No one even wants to think, much less talk, about what will surely happen in the future as the HIV-positive victims enter into the 'dying stage' and the death-rate skyrockets," Dr. Larry said sadly.

In the early part of 2003, I traveled to Nairobi, Kenya, to meet up with my good friend, Frank Dimmock. He was the overseer of the Presbyterian USA work in South Central Africa and health coordinator for all the Presbyterian hospitals and clinics in the region. Together, we visited and performed needs assessment studies on hospitals and clinics in the countries of Kenya, Malawi, and Zambia.

We met up with Frank's wife, Nancy Dimmock, in Lilongwe, the capital of Malawi. The population of Malawi was somewhere around 12 million, with just over 2 million living in Lilongwe. Ninety percent of all Malawi's people lived as poor subsistence farmers, dwelling in mud huts or houses with thatched roofs. Even the population in the cities lived mostly in small mud-brick houses. The country managed to export quite a bit of tobacco, some tea, coffee, sugar, and wood products. Life expectancy in Malawi had only been thirty-seven for males and thirty-eight for females. But those figures were changing daily now because of the prevalence of the HIV/AIDS problem. The average worker brought home about five hundred US dollars per year.

Nancy Dimmock was a second generation missionary kid who had been born in Congo and had only left Africa long enough to attend college in North Carolina, where she also received a master's degree in community health. She and Frank had met at school in the United States. After marrying, Frank and Nancy became official Presbyterian missionaries, returning to Africa. Frank was very much a counterpart to Larry Sthreshley. The drive, intensity, and creativity of Frank and Nancy definitely made them candidates for the cultural entrepreneur designation.

In addition to their missionary assignments, the Dimmocks had started personally adopting abandoned children. These kids were left at their doorstep or dropped off along the road.

One of these children, little Moses, was found in a maize field. The HIV-AIDS-infected father had died and the mother, who was also infected and weakened, was on her way to the hospital, but could go no further. She wandered off the side of the trail. She gave birth to the baby among the corn stalks, and then died. The baby had not been cleaned up after being born, and the afterbirth had dried and hardened around him. He was extremely dehydrated, but someone heard his faint cry, like baby Moses in the bulrushes of Egypt. The Dimmocks saved his life and adopted him. There were over one million abandoned babies at that time in Malawi, and in the big picture, saving babies one at a time didn't seem so significant. To Moses and the Dimmocks' other adopted children, the couple's actions made all the difference in the world. When their family had grown to six children, they organized the Crisis Nursery in their home.

I also had the privilege to meet little Alifa. An AIDS infected father and mother had both died, and had left a baby girl. Many of the old grandmother's children had already died, and she was now trying to take care of more than thirty of her abandoned grandchildren. It had been determined that the best option was to bury the baby with the dead mother since there was no one else left to take care of her. As the small funeral procession slowly moved on its way to the burial site, the sister of the dead mother stepped in and took the baby away from the procession and determined to raise little Alifa herself. Hers were good intentions. But reality settled in when the woman who had stepped up to take Alifa also died shortly thereafter because she too had been infected.

The Dimmocks heard about the situation and determined that they would try to help Alifa. They gathered up her fragile body; she was nothing more than skin and bones and weighed nearly nothing, even though she was over two years old.

"There was nothing to her, and I thought she would only be with us a short time," said Nancy.

They took immediate measures to save her life. At the hospital they quickly connected her to IV feeding tubes and medications. Little Alifa began to respond to the medical attention and love, and, amazingly, she survived. It was nothing less than a miracle from God.

Alifa sat on my lap with her bright eyes sparkling and told me that she was five years old. Now she goes to school and is a cheerful, happy little girl.

Nancy told me, "I put Alifa on a diet of bananas and peanut butter and watched her fill out from a skeleton to a cute little girl. Her height is stunted right now, but she may overcome that, too."

It was not uncommon for a child to be orphaned two or three times, as the child would be taken into a home of perhaps an aunt or uncle, only to have that relative die from AIDS. Young children were becoming heads of households, trying to raise their brothers and sisters and cousins after the death of their parents.

One major problem began to be recognized: with no adults around, who would be available and responsible to teach the children how to cook, to plant the crops, tend the goats, or even fetch the water? Traditions, skills, and even identities were being lost forever from the core of the culture. With 65 percent to 70 percent of the population infected, and deaths occurring mostly among people between the ages of fifteen and forty, the whole future labor force of a country could be lost, paralyzing an entire economy.

I had now traveled in more than one hundred fifty countries of the world. Project C.U.R.E. had been involved in shipping donated medical goods into over one hundred and twenty of those countries. I had been given the opportunity to observe with my own senses what was taking place in the cultural economics of a large portion of this planet. I will forever be grateful for such a privilege. But to whom much is given, much is required. It takes a steady hand to move a full cup.

One stark aspect of the HIV/AIDS tragedy posed an acute ethical dilemma. African hospitals, where AIDS patients resided with patients suffering other afflictions, became death houses for nearly everyone. Should Project C.U.R.E. restrict its medical help only to hospitals that segregated these populations? If the populations were not segmented, little long-term benefit was being derived from our donated medical supplies. But how could these populations be segregated in Africa?

One day a Request for Assistance form landed on my desk from South Africa. It concerned sending medical donations to a hospice facility. I asked Anna Marie if she would put the South African request toward the top of my travel agenda. Would she also go with me to do the assessment? We had an assessment trip request from Swaziland as well, she said. Perhaps we could combine the assignments. What a wife!

In August, 2004, Anna Marie and I headed from Denver to London and on to Johannesburg. Our host there would be Phillip DeLange, a former black politician who had previously been elected to parliament from the Alberton metro area. Based on Project C.U.R.E.'s previously successful work in the South African communities, the US Embassy in Johannesburg had encouraged Phillip to contact us and fill out all our paperwork.

Surrounding the Alberton area three major shantytowns had grown up. No one really knew the population of the shantytowns, but Phillip said there were well over one hundred and ninety-five thousand households, with at least five hundred thousand to one million illegal squatters. There was absolutely nothing the South African or municipal governments in the area could do about the expansive growth. The squatters would come, find building materials—corrugated tin, wood, cardboard—and build a shack for themselves. Should a property owner or a farmer on whose field the shanties were being built object, the insurgents would simply kill the landowner and keep on building shacks. Many of the shanties were only one-room dwellings with dirt floors and provisions for a fire pit on the floor or just outside the structure. Beds and interior furniture would be made of whatever the occupants could find and carry to their dwellings.

Fearing outbreaks of diseases like cholera, typhoid, or other communicable illnesses, the various government entities would try to cut roads into the encampments and erect toilet facilities and pipe in fresh water to various stations in the shanty areas. Many of the people had flocked to the cities to find work, or were displaced from other parts of South Africa. Many came even from surrounding countries because of civil unrest or droughts.

The unemployment situation only added to the explosive cultural problem. At least 65 percent of those who were able bodied could not find work, or refused to look. They just hung out with nothing to do. Most who had left their old communities or tribes to move to the cities were young people who were sexually active. Now, when you have sexually active young people in new surroundings, seeking acceptance and intimacy with nothing to do but socialize, you have a very big potential problem culturally. But to have those factors coming together in an area like Africa, where the HIV/AIDS virus was already running rampant, you suddenly have the possibility for unspeakable disaster.

Phillip DeLange and his wife, Vivian, with their "Eagle Excellence Hospice," were trying to deal with aspects of the problem. They were concerned with those in the shanty communities who were terminally ill and dying with the AIDS virus. HIV/AIDS carriers were pretty much left alone to die with whatever disease finally attacked them. The ravages of the disease, or diseases, would usually kill the patient in Africa in two to five years. That was different than the situation in the United States, where the virus, because of its victim's otherwise good health, might remain latent for seven to ten years.

Phillip and Vivian had watched scores of dying victims be shunned, neglected, and abandoned. They wanted to comfort, and give dignity to, the pitiful victims in the last weeks of their lives. "We had watched those people lie in their own puss and excrement, and nobody would even stoop to help them," Phillip said, passionately. "We believed that God still loved them, and would be pleased to have us show His love to them, especially in the last stages of their lives."

They also wanted to promote the idea of reconciliation between members of families who had shunned the AIDS victim when the facts of the infection had come to light. Many families would have already gone through the death and mourning process and considered the victim dead to them. The DeLanges wanted to bring those families back together in their hospice and serve as mediators of reconciliation.

Phillip was trying to purchase a facility on a piece of land. He had managed to raise enough money to lease the property, and had begun to set up his hospice. Because of the shortage of money, the "Eagle Excellence Hospice" had been put together with mostly ragtag pieces of equipment, ratty beds and mattresses, and terribly worn linens and blankets. It was almost impossible for him to acquire bandages, disinfectants, salves, or creams, to treat the AIDS patients. The local government health system had refused to give even wound dressings or aspirin to Phillip for treatment of his hospice patients.

Our first night staying at the hospice, Anna Marie and I watched, stunned, as Phillip and Vivian picked up dying AIDS patients and put them gently in the bathtub. They would wash their hair, their sores, and their fevered bodies, trying to protect themselves as best they could.

Phillip said, "Vivian and I believe that Jesus would have loved like this. He would have touched these who are dying like he did those with leprosy and other illnesses."

It didn't take long for us to determine that the DeLanges, and their needy "Eagle Excellence Hospice," qualified for help from Project C.U.R.E. I thought the hospice approach to the care of terminal AIDS patients was promising because this allowed for an appropriate separation of the sick from those who simply had no hope. If hospices became common among countries where the AIDS epidemic was spreading, then Project C.U.R.E. could better direct the type of supplies needed for patients to heal to hospitals, and palliative care to hospices.

Anna Marie and I stayed at the hospice for five nights. We were able to obtain a firsthand education about dying from HIV/AIDS in urban Africa.

In fact, the first night we were there, one of the women patients died a very traumatic and messy death. In her dying moments she called us close to her bedside and made us promise that we would return to her shantytown and try to find her small daughter, Brenda, and baby boy. She did not know for sure where they might be.

After the woman died, Philip and Vivian filled us in about the woman's situation. She had been living with a boyfriend who also had HIV/AIDS. Phillip repeated what Dr. Sager had told us in Congo: "Somewhere between 85 to 87 percent of all African men ardently believe from their cultural upbringing that, should they ever be infected with a sexually transmitted disease (STD), or sexually transmitted infection (STI), they could be cured from their disease of gonorrhea, syphilis, etc., by having sexual intercourse with a virgin. The more severe the disease, the younger the virgin needs to be."

The boyfriend of Brenda's mother had zeroed in on Brenda. Little Brenda was only five years old when the boyfriend had started raping her. She had been too traumatized to tell her mother what was happening, but eventually had told an older woman about the boyfriend. The boyfriend had infected little Brenda with AIDS, and then had run away into the big city of Johannesburg to die.

Early the next morning the four of us started out over the dusty dirt streets and winding paths of the shantytown to keep our promise to the dying mother. There were more than one hundred thousand refugees living in the collection of shanties where we were walking. The hovels where the people lived were about ten feet by twelve feet in size and constructed with a random collection of pieces of sheet metal, cardboard, plywood, and wood scraps. Occasionally, a resident might be lucky enough to scavenge a window from somewhere and build it into the derelict structure.

Our first stop was at a hovel about fifteen minutes away from the hospice. The shanty had a chain and lock threaded through the planks of the front door and looked abandoned. Phillip inquired at the shack next door. "Where is the woman and where are the little kids who live here?"

"They took her away to some place because she was so sick. I'm sure she's dead by now. She's never been back," said the neighbor. "The kids went off somewhere to live, but nobody seems to know where. The man hasn't been around for a long time. He was very sick."

The next stop was at another shack, where we went to the front door. On the greasy piece of plywood that had been propped up as a front wall, the numbers 828 had been scribbled in chalk. An older woman, dressed in a soiled T-shirt and a piece of dirty print cloth wrapped around her waist as a skirt, invited us in. The inside of the building was really bad: dirt floor, a partial tin roof, cardboard to sleep on, and a lot of collected pieces of junk and plastic stored in the corners. "We are here to check up on a little girl named Brenda and her three-year-old brother," said Phillip. He then asked the old woman if she knew where Brenda and her little brother might be.

The older woman brought them out from behind a blanket that was being used as a divider wall. The little three-year-old boy came out dressed in an old sweater four times his size, but he seemed relatively normal. When Brenda came out into the light, I noticed that she was very weak and had difficulty walking. Her lower chest and abdominal areas were enlarged, and the swelling continued downward. She obviously had received massive internal damage from being raped. Brenda's eyes were clouded over with a hazy film, and she had white skin blotches on her dark brown face, especially under her nose and around her mouth.

Right away the old woman said to Phillip that she wanted to keep the little boy with her, but she wanted Brenda to go away. She could do nothing to help her, and Brenda was getting worse every day. The boy had not been tested for HIV/AIDS, but Brenda was a very sick little girl and was dying from AIDS-related problems.

Phillip and Vivian explained that we were trying to fulfill her mother's last request that someone check on her children.

Once again, the old woman insisted that we take the dying Brenda with us because she did not want her there anymore. Phillip tried to tell her that he would need to notify the authorities and seek their permission to take little Brenda.

We waved good-bye as we walked away. The little brother waved back, but Brenda just stood and stared at us without a flicker of emotion.

"I want the government to release Brenda to our hospice," said Phillip. "I can't think of a reason why they would want to let her die out here without any help."

India could break your heart, but Africa could make the effort to help seem a hideous charade.

I have marveled at the unparalleled beauty of the continent of Africa—

with its Rift Valley, Serengeti, Massa Mara, exotic animals, snow-capped mountains, savannah grasslands, and tepid jungle watering holes. I have walked the halls of hundreds and hundreds of hospitals and clinics, and met thousands of doctors, nurses, and helpless patients. I have sat around the evening village fires and eaten from the common cast-iron cauldrons. I have laughed, prayed, and sung with people whose hearts are pure gold and whose joy and enthusiasm often know no bounds. But when I lay my head down to sleep at night, my memories come back and waves of unacknowledged despair roll in. I have seen stacks of dead bodies in morgues with no provision to refrigerate or embalm them; prayers rising to heaven for the TB angel of mercy to come and silently kill the suffering HIV/AIDS patient; the senseless dying of African leaders because of promiscuity; the raping of innocent young girls out of damnable superstition. I have seen the Alifas in coffins with their dead mothers, and the Brendas with irreparable physical and mental damage, and have staggered with despair.

The world is too broken for me to fix it—nor can it be fixed by all the cultural entrepreneurs and their well-meaning kin put together.

I know what the Dimmocks and DeLanges are doing is right, though. They are not building a utopia of their own construction, but God's Kingdom. God will finally be sovereign over history and everything done at His behest gathered up into that final victory. I don't see how anybody who lacks this faith keeps at it—and most don't. It's hardly easy comfort, though, and it doesn't keep me from remembering Brenda watching us leave.

20

Cost of Petrol Just Went Up For You

Involvement in cultural entrepreneurship brings risks beyond emotional burdens; there's often physical danger. Some of the dangers I witnessed in my traveling were obvious: plane crashes—particularly small planes on hops into mountainous or jungle regions; car accidents on highways where the locals are apt to ignore victims, instead of helping them; getting caught in the midst of a war, as I did in Ramallah on the Palestinian West Bank, or Serbia; being asphyxiated in my hotel room in India for the sake of my valuables; and the constant threat of becoming seriously ill via parasites, flesh-devouring bacteria, and a host of other causes.

There are other dangers, too, that apply to anyone trying to change the world, even in seemingly sedate settings. Those dangers are learned in a hurry once one is out on the front. The war between Good and Evil is real. Anyone who begins to act on his or her faith will quickly see how many cards the devil has to play, including physical injury, serious illness, and untimely death. And the inability of peoples to get along, rapidly comes into play.

Military strategists say that the first thing to go out the window in a war is the battle plan, and that war's first casualty is truth. In the midst of the spiritual war, the cultural entrepreneur encounters that it's difficult to hold onto the truth that set him or her into motion in the first place. God's sovereign control of history, and the circumstances in which we find ourselves, may seem at times a delusion, particularly when we are physically threatened and afraid.

I had to learn the working meaning of "the just shall live by faith" (Habakkuk 2:4, KJV). I learned by experience that heavenly instruction comes in installments, not as a package deal. I had to keep moving through hazardous situations, expecting to receive the next bit of divine instruction on a just-in-time basis. It takes courage to wait for God's guidance.

I learned this lesson in many places, but especially in Nigeria.

Project C.U.R.E. had become involved in shipping donated medical goods to Mission Hospital Onitsha in Anambah, Nigeria. From the beginning, our in-country partner, E. C. Okoye, had run into trouble negotiating entry of the container loads into the country. Everyone wanted a bribe.

I made an executive decision that Nigeria was a "no-no" destination, and we were finished with the Nigerians!

But E. C. Okoye would not let us so easily quit helping his country. He came all the way to Denver, Colorado, and met with me and invited me to return to Nigeria to verify that the customs problem and others had been corrected.

My opinion of Nigeria remained, however: it was the most lawless chunk of real estate I had ever encountered. It appeared to be regulated, not by the rule of law, but by the rule of the lawless. Still, I told Mr. Okoye I would visit Nigeria and him between upcoming trips to Ghana, Benin, and Senegal.

When my Air Kenya flight landed in Lagos, Nigeria, my fear blossomed into a walking nightmare. The only uniformed security-looking person on the airport premises was the immigration/customs woman in the arrival area.

I left the customs security point and started looking for Mr. Okoye. A small army of predators surrounded me as soon as I had placed a foot outside the customs security area. One woman and one man were especially aggressive. They were pushing and grabbing me and literally trying to wrench my bags away. They pushed their homemade plastic photo ID cards in my face, told me that they were in charge, and I would be going with one of them to Lagos Island.

I pushed free of them and told them I didn't need their help because a friend was there to pick me up, even though I could not spot Mr. Okoye.

The man trying to intimidate me said, "There isn't gonna be nobody to come here to pick you up. There is no petrol available today for private cars, so you got no other choice but to go in one of my taxis."

He grabbed at my luggage again. "What hotel you goin' to?"

I brushed him off and kept walking inside and outside the arrival area hoping to locate Mr. Okoye. The incoming passengers were beginning to thin out and I was one of the few still remaining. All the locals now zeroed in on me as their last available pigeon.

I stopped behind a concrete pillar and opened my briefcase to pull out my Nigeria file. I needed to find a phone number to call Mr. Okoye. Why was he not there to greet me? Had something happened to him? If so, what would I do?

Boom. Out of nowhere the pushy man with the homemade badge was right over the top of me laughing, "See, I told you nobody come to get you today. Now your taxi will cost you much, much more. The cost of petrol jus' went up for you."

I told him gruffly to back off. He seemed to enjoy getting a reaction out of me. There were absolutely no police or uniformed military people on the site. The bullies had free reign at the airport.

I stayed close to the pillar as I carefully shuffled through my file trying desperately to locate Mr. E. C. Okoye's phone number. I had lots of correspondence and notes, but even on the Application for Assistance forms the phone numbers given were for Mr. Okoye's contacts in the United States. The addresses I had were post office box numbers for the town of Onitsha in Anambra state.

I carefully replaced all my papers into my briefcase and decided to take another walking tour of the nearly empty terminal. From a short distance away the big man and the woman followed me, hollering, "I told you nobody come to get you today. Now all the cars is gone and you is in trouble." No kidding.

As I walked I searched for a ticket sales counter. I would purchase a ticket on the next flight out. It didn't much matter where, although I hoped I would be going in the direction of my next stop, Dakar, Senegal.

There were no tickets available for purchase at the Lagos airport, I discovered. I would have to go to Lagos Island to purchase a ticket from a travel agent there.

As I walked back toward the customs security area, the customs officer approached me. She was the only person I had seen wearing an official uniform. "You seem to be having a problem," she said. "You should not be just walking around. That is dangerous. Go over there and stand against that wall, and put your luggage in front of you for protection."

And wait for what? I wondered. "I do need someone to help me," I said. "I saw only one telephone book in this terminal, but it did not have the names and phone numbers of individuals. It was just advertising. The phones require the use of a phone card to use the system, right? I can't find the number I need, though, and I don't have a phone card even if I could. What do I do here?"

The customs woman looked at me blankly and asked, "Didn't you arrange for someone to meet you?"

I took out one of the letters from my Nigeria file and showed it to her. "My problem is that my man did not come after me, and I don't have his phone number to call him. How would I find out his number?"

"You wouldn't," she said. "He lives in Onitsha, so you can't find out his number."

The big obnoxious man and the aggressive woman were leaning against a counter about thirty feet away, grinning at me. They knew I was in their trap.

The uniformed woman proceeded to instruct me in very firm tones,

"Do not talk to anyone at this airport. Do not go with any of them, and do not do business with any of them. Don't give them any information, and do not have them change any money for you. I tell you to not trust anyone here, not even me. The people here are very dangerous, and they will kill you for what you have. No one will find you or know what happened to you."

While we were talking, a short, plump Nigerian woman came and stood at the left elbow of the customs officer. She stood there while I was getting my warning. Then softly she asked me, "You are a Christian, aren't you?"

"Yes, I am." I answered her.

"My name is Vera. I was upstairs in an office, and God told me to come down here because there was someone in trouble and needed help. I am here to help you." Vera took the information I was showing the customs officer and told me to follow her. I pulled my luggage across the terminal to a secluded spot where there were some old rickety chairs.

"You sit here and don't go anyplace," Vera said. "I will take this information and see if I can find a phone number."

Vera and the customs woman walked away, and it was all I could do not to go after them like a frightened child.

Then my suspicions kicked into overdrive. I had never had the "God told me" approach used on me before in Africa. America, yes; Africa, no. If this was a ploy to gain my confidence, it was a clever one. I was going to have to confide in someone, though, or I was not going to get out of there.

Thirty-five minutes went by, but they seemed like thirty-five hours.

The intimidating couple cruised by a couple of times. On one run, the man pointed at my face and said, "That is chewing gum in your mouth. Give me some. I want some now!"

He wanted more than chewing gum, that was for sure. I took the gum out of my mouth and offered it to him, then put it back into my mouth.

Finally, Vera returned. "I am going upstairs to try again," she said. "So far I have not helped you at all. You are not speaking to anyone, are you?"

"Look, Vera," I said, thinking how to speed things up. "I don't want you to be helping me without my being able to pay you for what you are doing. I will give you five US dollars if you can locate this man on the phone, and I can talk to him."

"I knew I would help you even before I saw you," Vera said. "I am gonna help you for nothing, even though I really do need money. But you must not have anything to do with the people around here. You must not even trust the customs officer. I am going to try something else. I'll be back, so don't move from here."

Another half an hour passed before Vera returned. "I've tried everything. I can't get any numbers for that name. The customs woman even let me use her phone card. Is there something else I can do?"

"Yes, Vera," I said. "How would I go about calling my office in the US? If I could call them, they could either give me a phone number, or call Okoye from there and find out why he was not here to pick me up when my plane arrived. How much would it cost to call America from here?"

"Let's start with a twenty dollar phone card. Do you have Nigerian shillings? They won't take any US money here," Vera said.

"Can I go to an exchange desk or a bank here at the airport?" I asked.

"No," she replied, "I will have to find someone who is willing to exchange with me for the right rate away from the airport. Do you have twenty US dollars?"

Everything with Vera had gone well up until that time, but I was faced with acting contrary to everything I had ever learned about being in such a dangerous situation. Hadn't Vera warned me not to trust even her?

I reached into my wallet as inconspicuously as possible, pulled out a twenty dollar bill, and gave it to Vera. She went scurrying out the door of the terminal. I didn't know if I would see her again.

In about fifteen minutes, though, Vera came hurrying back to where I was standing. She motioned to follow her to the kiosk where they sold the phone cards. Before we went to the telephone, I took Vera by the hand, and said, "Look, Vera, I don't know who you are, but it does not surprise me that you have come to help me. I believe that God sent you at just the right time. I consider you to be an angel. This is not the first time such a thing has happened to me. And I thank you for responding the way you have, and I thank God for once again taking care of me. Now let's see if I can contact my office in America."

Eventually, I was able to talk with my son Douglas, in Denver. He said, "Yes, someone will be coming for you, but … *click*."

I had run out of units on my prepaid phone card, and Douglas and I had been disconnected. The smallest US currency bill I had left was a one-hundred-dollar bill. Did I really believe what I had previously said about plump little Vera being an angel, or not? How about trusting her with one hundred dollars? To a local Nigerian, one hundred dollars was like all the money in the bank.

I began to breathe a little easier when I saw Vera reenter the airport doors. She had not run away with my one hundred-dollar bill. We walked over to the kiosk, and I purchased a new phone card with twice as many units on it. On the next call Douglas was able to finish his sentence. "Somebody will be after you, but the town of Onitsha is five hours away."

I informed Douglas that I was getting out of the airport terminal just as fast as possible. I would find a hotel, and then call him back. He could communicate with Okoye and tell him where to pick me up.

I discovered that Lagos Island was over an hour away from the airport. I already knew a taxi would be very expensive, if not lethal.

Vera had a better plan. She called her husband to come and retrieve us from the airport mess. She also knew of a small neighborhood hotel closer to the airport in the district where she lived. They would take me there to see if they had a room.

I broke into a grin when I saw Vera's husband walk into the terminal. He could have suited up and played guard or tackle for any NFL football team in the United States.

"Doctor Jackson, I want you to meet my husband. His name is Innocent."

"I love it!" I blurted out. "First, I get an honest-to-goodness angel named Vera to help me, and now I get a bodyguard with the name of Innocent. What more could I ask?"

We picked up my luggage and headed for Innocent's car out in the parking lot. It was an old 1974 Mercedes sedan, beat up on every square inch of surface. They had tried to pound out the dings, and then had given it a fresh coat of metallic-blue paint with what looked from the brush strokes like a whiskbroom. It must have traveled hundreds of thousands of miles before Innocent ended up with it.

On the way out of the airport the group of men and the one woman that had been tormenting me actually tried to pick a fight with us. They had waited a long time to pick my bones clean and now these scavengers were being denied their meal! Innocent forcefully pushed a couple of them away until we were able to crawl into the safety of his old car.

The Heritage Guest House/Hotel was not far from the airport in a neighborhood of torn-up dirt roads and dilapidated houses. The small concrete building was completely surrounded by a high, cement wall with rolls of razor wire strung across the top. Armed guards patrolled the perimeter carrying AK-47s. There were two guards, similarly equipped, just outside the front metal gate. Innocent talked them into opening the gates and we drove into the small compound. All three of us went inside where the Arab proprietor asked me, "How many nights you want?"

"Only one," I answered.

"I will charge you for three nights in advance. That's the way we do it just in case you stay longer. I also take one hundred US dollars cash in advance just in case you eat anything while you are here. If you don't use up the additional nights, or eat a hundred dollars of food, then I will give the balance back to you when you leave. That's the way we do it here!"

I did it his way, being that I was "here."

I called Douglas as soon as I could, partly to let him know where I was staying so that Okoye could contact me, and partly just to get grounded again in reality.

Later, Vera and Innocent returned, and we had a lovely time over dinner. I told them that I did not have a good feeling that Okoye would contact me. If he had not called me by morning I suggested that we make plans for me to purchase a plane ticket to Dakar, Senegal. (I kept thinking what might happen if Vera and Innocent lost interest.) I told them that I had found out that I could not purchase a ticket at the airport.

Angel Vera had another surprise: "My aunt owns a travel agency in downtown Lagos. Those tickets could be very difficult to obtain, but she knows the people who will help us." Vera had some advice about waiting for Mr. Okoye. "Since your contact needed five or six hours to drive here, he may stop over at a friend's house to sleep overnight and arrive here in the morning. So, we won't check out and leave for my aunt's business until about nine o'clock. Innocent and I will take off work and both go with you into the city."

I was so relieved that they were making my cause their own!

I didn't even leave my room the next morning to go down to breakfast because I didn't want to miss Okoye's telephone call. He never called or came by, however.

Innocent and Vera did come back that morning, and we left to go do business at the travel agency.

In the morning light Innocent's car looked even worse, as if it had been one of the wrecks left by a chase scene. Miraculously, it could still be driven.

Traffic was heavy on the road to Lagos. A large portion of the trip was made traveling on a bridge that spanned the coastal waters. "This is the longest bridge in all of Africa," Innocent told me as we drove to the city. "Once you get on this bridge there is no way to turn around. The traffic can get very bad here."

We made it safely to the travel agency called, Tess Travels, Ltd. Vera's aunt went right to work in securing my needed tickets to Dakar. It took us most of the day trying to finalize the reservation.

At a little after three o'clock that afternoon, with tickets firmly in hand, we headed the old Mercedes back toward the airport. The longest bridge in Africa proved to be a scenic drive, even though the drivers in the six lanes were aggressive, and not particular about staying on the right side of the road. Still, we proceeded in the left-hand lane, trying to make good time, as my flight left at seven o'clock that night and I should be there two hours early.

Without warning, the engine in Innocent's tired old auto just quit. It didn't belch, bang, or bubble. It stopped. The drivers of the other cars were agitated as Innocent tried desperately to cut his way over into the right lane before the wheels stopped rolling. There was no such thing as a pull-off lane on the tight bridge. The best that Innocent could do was to get as close as possible to the bridge railing.

Innocent was totally perplexed, as well as irritated and embarrassed, because this happened in front of his new friend, the American. He just sat there grinding the starter, hoping something good would happen.

I was in the front seat and started to pull the handle to open my door. "No, no," Innocent insisted. "You stay in the car. I don't want them to see you out there."

I knew he was serious, so I sat back as he gingerly opened his door into the traffic and squeezed out. He popped the hood open and began to take a bewildered look at the engine. He opened the radiator cap, wiggled several wires, and made a slap with his hand at the air breather.

I thought to myself, *Oh, my goodness, he doesn't know the first thing about automobile engines.* The irritated motorists were honking and yelling and swerving around him. Innocent slid his massive body along the side of the car and carefully opened the door. He made his way back into the driver's seat again, turned the key and began cranking, to no avail.

I looked at my watch. It was already four fifteen and the plane left at seven o'clock. As Innocent stopped trying to turn the engine over, I offered some advice. "You know, I used to have a car like this, and I am somewhat familiar with them. The way it sounded when it stopped, and the fact that it did not sputter as if it were out of petrol, I would guess that the problem is electrical. The Mercedes I used to have had a problem with the little contact ignition points inside the distributor cap. They would burn and stick together, and then there would be no more spark to ignite the fuel." This was all Greek to Innocent, I'm sure.

Out went Innocent again into the traffic to have another look-see at the engine.

Out of nowhere came a scruffy looking young man walking very closely to the bridge railing and carrying a white plastic shopping sack in one hand. He came by the car, and Innocent and he talked briefly.

Then the scruffy man came to the door and got into the driver's seat, turned the key, and tried starting the car. He only tried it once and then went back out to the engine compartment. I was watching what was going on in the engine compartment by looking out from the windshield and between the hood and the firewall. Who was this scruffy passerby and just what was he going to do?

To my absolute amazement he reached into his plastic shopping bag and pulled out a rusty screwdriver. He went straight for the distributor cap, popped the ears from the little latches with the screwdriver, and removed the rotor. With the rotor out, he used his screwdriver and loosened the two screws holding the breaker points and removed them.

"Yes!" I said right out loud. "This guy knows what he is doing!"

Vera leaned up from the back seat and said, "I'm sorry, what did you just say?"

The passerby reached once more into his white plastic shopping bag and pulled out an old worn piece of sandpaper and began filing down the burned spots on the ignition points. Then he did something very unusual. He yanked the gas line from the carburetor, put the end of the gas line in his mouth, and started sucking until he had a mouthful of gasoline. He leaned over the distributor and spat the gasoline into the open distributor. Once again, into the bag he went, and pulled out a greasy rag. Carefully he cleaned the gasoline-soaked distributor parts with the dirty rag.

I remembered that the contact points had to be set precisely at fourteen thousandths of an inch. When the scruffy fellow had the points reinstalled he used only the sight of his eye to set the precise gap, instead of using a feeler gauge. Could anyone do this successfully?

The mystery man climbed into the car. He turned on the key and—varooom! It started! I was impressed and thankful to God beyond measure. I never knew that some of God's angels wore greasy clothes and traveled by walking on busy bridges in Africa. I shook his greasy hand and smiled.

He jumped out. Innocent gave him some money and slid once more behind the wheel. Into the moving traffic we went. About fifty feet. The engine died again almost immediately.

Innocent jumped out of the car and ran back to where the man was still standing by the bridge railing. I think he simply picked the little man up by placing his huge hands around his neck and lifting him back to the parked car. "I paid you to fix the car, now fix it!

Up went the hood again. I was watching intently from the front passenger seat and second-guessing the problem. It still had to be electrical and it wasn't the points anymore. That meant the ignition coil was probably the problem.

If so, we were hopelessly in trouble because an ignition coil to fit this old Mercedes would be as rare as hen's teeth. Where on a long bridge in rush hour traffic with no tow trucks—in Nigeria—would one go to get spare parts? I was going to miss my flight, and I really did not want to stay another night in Nigeria, ever.

Out from the scruffy mechanic's mysterious white plastic bag came a short wire, maybe eight inches long. He used the wire to jump the connection from the battery side of the coil to the engine and got a spark. Then he jumped the connection from the distributor side of the coil to the engine and got nothing. "You got yourself a bum coil," said the scruffy man to Innocent, and shrugged his shoulders. I rolled my eyes and sighed. I had such great hopes of leaving Nigeria in just a short while!

Right then another inexplicable thing took place. Walking toward us on the bridge was another man hugging tightly to the railing. Yes, he was carrying a white plastic shopping bag.

When he got close to our car the scruffy man stopped the new visitor, and they talked a bit. The new fellow came over, looked under the hood. He listened carefully as the first visitor tried starting the car. He then took the wire and performed the same crude test on the coil. Down went his hand into his white plastic sack and out came a small wrench. Once more he reached into his plastic bag and withdrew a black electrical ignition coil. He removed the old coil from the fender well and held the two together. They were identical, and even had the same Mercedes markings on the casing.

I felt a lump form in my throat and warm tears began to make their way down my cheeks. I didn't even shake this man's hand as he got in and started the car. I just sat there stunned. I kept asking myself, *What were the odds?* What I had just seen with my own eyes would have been absolutely impossible without divine intervention. The whole episode was a miracle.

I wondered if it had been divinely staged to give to me an indisputable lesson in accepting the awesome occurrence of miracles.

Innocent let the first scruffy man go with his pay. He opened up the back door, scooted Vera over, and threw the second man into the back seat of the car. "We are going to get Dr. Jackson to the airport on time and you are going with us to guarantee your work. When we get there I will pay you for your labor and your parts. But you will stay with us."

A half hour later, we pulled up in front of the infamous airport. I had prepared a thank you note in an envelope with a cash gift to help out my new friends, but our friendship had gone far beyond money. We had become battle-tested fellow soldiers.

The Nigerians wanted forty dollars US as exit tax upon leaving the country. I gave the airport people my money and smiled as I said to them, "Please take this. This is one of the greatest bargains I have ever made. To get to leave Nigeria for only forty dollars is a real deal. I would gladly pay twice that much."

When I got back into the safety of the airplane seat my thoughts were racing. I bowed my head and said to God: *Let's make a deal. I know I said that I would go anywhere and say anything to anybody as long as I knew that was what I was supposed to do. But if it is all the same to you, I would like to never go back to Nigeria again, OK?*

I figured that would be the last time I would ever see Nigeria as long as I lived!

Within a short period of time, Project C.U.R.E. was getting inundated with new requests for us to help out in Nigeria. Our reputation had spread like wildfire throughout all of West Africa because of the donated medical goods that had been sent into the needy areas.

Dr. I. C. Ekwem, and his wife, Linda, who was also a medical doctor, were doing a great work in building a new hospital in the Port Harcourt region at Nigeria's southern tip. They traveled all the way to Colorado to present their case to us personally and stayed in our guesthouse in Evergreen.

Finally, the persuasion outweighed the logical objections, and I agreed to travel and assess the Ebony Hospital in the city of Port Harcourt. My heart was softened, in part, when I learned that the mistake that led to my Nigerian nightmare had been made in our office; we had never informed Mr. E. C. Okoye of my arrival! This detail had been lost among the many others in planning the trip.

Still, I really did not want to go back to Nigeria, but deep down I felt that I needed to return. It was the right thing to do.

Then, within hours of the time I had consented in writing to Dr. I. C. Ekwem and his wife that I would make the trip, I received a travel warning regarding Nigeria from the US State Department:

> Thousands have been killed in ethnic and religious violence in recent clashes between the Hausa tribe from the predominantly northern Muslims and the Yoruba tribe of mostly Christians in southern Nigeria. US citizens should be warned that ordinary criminals, as well as persons in police and military uniforms, perpetrate violent crimes.

Kidnapping for ransom remains common, especially in the Niger Delta area. The use of public transportation throughout Nigeria is dangerous and should be avoided. Taxis pose risks because of fraudulent or criminal operators and poorly maintained vehicles. Most Nigerian airlines have aging fleets and there are valid concerns that maintenance and operational procedures may be inadequate to ensure passenger safety.

I still had a strong sense that I should make the trip, and flew to Port Harcourt located on the southernmost tip of Nigeria.

Upon finishing my needs assessment study in Port Harcourt with Dr. Ekwem, our driver took us north to the city of Owerri, the capital of Imo State, where we were to perform a needs assessment study on the Cecilia Memorial Hospital and Clinic. In route to Owerri we encountered three separate sets of military roadblocks.

Our driver was a very skinny, middle-aged, tall Nigerian, who was possessive of his car and took great pride in his driving. Our driver spotted the first roadblock a full kilometer away. With the armed military trying to wave him over, he simply gunned his worn Peugeot sedan. By the time we ran through the roadblock, we were traveling at the speed of one hundred and thirty kilometers per hour with the roadblock people just yelling and shaking their fists at us.

As soon as our driver spotted the second roadblock, I could feel the surge of the Peugeot engine as his accelerator foot went straight to the floor. Once again, we virtually flew right through the armed roadblock. Could the driver's French sedan outrun automatic weapons fire?

I never figured out what was so different about the third roadblock set-up on a desolate stretch of blacktop. For reasons known only to our driver, he slowed down and pulled over in a compliant, if agitated, manner.

As the soldiers in black uniforms surrounded our car, one officer aimed his automatic weapon right at my head and started shouting orders in his tribal language. Our driver began muttering and pounding the steering wheel as the officer began shouting louder and louder.

The more intense and irritated the officer became, the more his large nostrils flared. Soon they were so huge that I would have sworn I could see straight into his sinus cavities.

To keep the situation from escalating, Barrister Joe Emenaha, our in-car attorney, stepped out and began speaking to the officer. Pretty soon the officer stopped aiming the barrel of his automatic weapon at my head and pointed it at the ground. His nostrils constricted.

By then the driver had reams of paperwork pulled out from his car's glove compartment and was shaking them in front of the blockade soldiers. There was a big wad of money in the car's glove box when the driver retrieved his papers. When he put the papers back the money was gone.

When Joe got back into the backseat with me, I asked him what he had said to calm down the officer. "I explained," said Barrister Joe, "about the American having come here from all the way across the ocean to help us have a good hospital. If he didn't settle down and be nice in front of the American, he would probably not ever come back, and it would be the officer's fault for not getting a hospital in Imo State."

"You gave him the gift that keeps on giving, Joe—guilt!"

The driver put his gas pedal foot back down to the floorboard and away we flew on toward Njaba.

The road was lined with plantation groves of cashew nut trees as we neared Njaba. Our driver pulled off the roadway in front of some large steel gates. From inside the gates a man stepped out and approached my door. As I opened the door and stood up the gentleman introduced himself as the secretariat of his majesty's cabinet of Nkume. Then he bowed politely and said, "The king sends his greetings, and you are welcome to this place."

Behind the secretariat was a man that I later learned was over seventy years old. He was decked out in his Royal Chief's regalia, including his bright red skull hat with a clipped tassel. He carried a large, hollowed-out elephant tusk with elaborate carvings, and had a long string of reddish beads around his neck. Around his wrist was a leather thong that was attached to his scepter. The scepter had been made of the long flowing hair of a horse's tail. The old Royal Chief also welcomed me, and as I moved to walk away, he raised his ivory elephant tusk and blew a trumpeting blast.

When would we be moving on to assess the Cecilia Memorial Hospital and Clinic? I didn't understand what was happening.

I was then escorted by the king's secretariat into a reception room of a large house and told that I had entered the honorable home of the lawyer Joe Emenaha and his family. After being seated, I was allowed to view many old pictures of the tribe and especially pictures of the late Royal Chief S. N. Emenaha, Okpe Udo I (Peacemaker I) of Nkume, and his wife and eight children.

They certainly highly respected their Royal Chiefs, I thought to myself.

After extended family members arrived and welcomed me, Joe asked me to come with him. We were going to take a little car ride to the next venue. Joe kept the exact destination vague. I kept looking for a hospital somewhere on the landscape.

A couple of miles from the Emenaha home we parked the car, and I was asked to follow Joe through some trees to a clearing. A rectangular building about fifty feet by forty feet stood in the clearing. I walked into the building constructed with very large grilled windows on all four sides and open to the outside. As I entered through the doors, two deafening explosions went off. I quickly looked for a safe place to jump and hide, remembering the State Department warning about war in the area.

I was assured that everything was just fine, and that the explosions were simply mortar shells fired from cannon to celebrate and announce my arrival at the tribal headquarters where the king, his chiefs, and cabinet conducted official business. The cannon fire had not gone *bang, bang* but rather *ker-phoom, ker-phoom*, setting off percussive shocks that I felt in my chest.

Already seated within the open-windowed room were distinguished-looking tribesmen in chairs lined up around the perimeter of the building. From the ceiling down about three feet to the tops of the window openings hung antique photos, sketches, and portraits of past kings, chiefs, and tribal dignitaries, as well as documentations of historical events. After being personally introduced, and after shaking hands with all the men, I spent some time walking around, acquainting myself with old photos and artifacts.

A car drove up quite close to the building, and all the men stood to their feet and began a call-and-response type of a chant in low tones. Out of the car stepped a portly gentleman dressed in a bright red and gold robe with a felt skull hat and other paraphernalia. His Majesty, King Eze A. N. Onyeka had arrived. I noticed as he entered the building that he shook hands with some of the men and with others he took his round fan made of animal skins and struck the back of their hands three times before he shook their hands. He embellished shaking the hands of his cabinet members with the same fan gesture.

Then the king approached where I was standing, shook hands with me, and invited me to sit in the big chair to the right of his large throne. As I was introduced to the king, I inquired as to where he was raised. In Africa the children of the Royal Family are rarely raised in their own countries. Instead, they are sent to London, Paris, or another nation to be educated. This is done partly as a precaution against the entire royal family being assassinated at one time by an enemy. They tried to plan ahead so that there would always be royal blood left alive to lead the people.

The king was pleased that I had some knowledge of African culture and smiled as he told me that he had spent a lot of time in India to prepare for his role. There he was educated in English private schools.

His Highness called on Barrister Joe Emenaha to formally introduce me to the honorable group. Then the king responded and finished his remarks of welcome by requesting a two-tier wooden bowl be brought to him. In the bottom of the upper level of the bowl were placed some strange-looking objects. The king patiently pointed out each and explained its significance. There were dried pepper pods and several samples of nutmeats in the bowl. His Majesty summoned a sharp knife, and then picked up a chococa nutmeat that was about the size and shape of a Brazil nut. He began cutting the nutmeat into slices. When finished, he took one of the slices and began chewing on it. Then he handed a chunk to me and motioned for me to start chewing. The slice of nut was moist, but very bitter, and it made the inside of my mouth feel raw and puckered. While we were both chewing, he explained that only those accepted by the Nkume people, and welcomed, were offered the nut. "You, Dr. Jackson, are accepted and welcomed into this people." Then he picked seven of the different objects from the bottom of the upper bowl and placed them into my right hand and closed my fingers around them. "You must put these someplace in your home so that if there is ever any question about your approval or acceptance by our people you shall show these objects of official welcome. Any Nigerian will see these and know their significance. Keep these proofs."

The king then requested me to stand. "Our council has talked of all the noble things that you do. We have never honored a white man since the English colonization of our sacred land. But, today, it is the unanimous decision of my royal chiefs, the cabinet members, and the elders to honor you and make you a full, Royal Chief of Nigeria."

The king took a magnificent robe of black velvet, with embroidered heads of male lions stitched of metallic gold threads and highlighted with purple-colored tongues. He had me stand up, and the three royal chiefs helped place the robe over my head and down over the length of my body. Then the king fastened the three gold buttons that were connected by a gold chain through the button holes allowing the chain to hang naturally with the end clipped by a brad to the pocket on the front of the robe.

As I was seated, His Majesty leaned forward and placed around my neck the official necklace of red and white stones. "These are the beads of loyalty," he stated, and told of their importance. Next, he placed the bright red, wool felt hat with the clipped tassel onto my head. "No one is allowed to wear one of these red wool hats except a royal chief. Wear it with pride and dignity."

With the hat on my head that represented my royal crown, with the robe and with the necklace, I was then asked to stand and face the rest of the officers and elders. Then they brought the scepter that was about twenty-four inches in length and made of white hair from a horse's tail. Two more mortar shots were fired from the canon.

Next the king demonstrated the ceremonial handshake that could only be exchanged among African royalty. I was expected to perfect the ritual. We faced each other and hit the backs of our hands, or our royal animal-skinned fans, together. Next, we shook hands and allowed our hands to slide out of the handshake until our fingers came close to the knuckle of the last joint of the middle finger. Then, each used the other's fingertip to snap, as you would snap your own fingers together, only using the other person's finger for the snap. Having learned the royal handshake, I tried it with the other chiefs.

The next part of the ceremony required that we move outside the building. The king led me past a clump of bushes to a clear spot on the pathway. Everyone else cleared the building and circled around. His Majesty took out a bottle that was sealed. He broke the seal, opened the cap, and knelt down in front of me. He proceeded to pour libations out on the ground in front of me, and around my feet, and finally over the tops of my shoes.

As the king stood to his feet again, another of the royal chiefs handed a framed certificate to him. Someone had produced all the artwork and design on the certificate by hand. On the document was written my new name, Chief Uzoma of Nkume People.

"All of the legal work has been accomplished in our national government to make you a royal chief as of this 29th day of November," the king explained to me. "The Nkume people proudly have given this name to you. 'Chief Uzoma of Nkume People' has been entered into the historical books and chronicles of our people, and no other person shall ever be given, or have, that name."

The king went on. "The name 'Uzoma' means 'good road' or 'good pathway' or 'good direction.' You have chosen a good pathway for your life, and now the Nkume People will join you, and look to you to lead us on the good road in the future." On queue, the mortar canons shot off two more explosions.

As our nervous driver finally drove us out through the gates of the compound to get us back to our hotel room in Port Harcourt, my new friends cheered and waved. In the early darkness of the African evening I could see the bright flash of the canons, as the tribesmen shot the last three mortar blasts into the sky.

I had some quiet time as we drove very fast through the African night. Our driver actually stopped at all the roadblocks. When the guards approached the car with their guns drawn, Barrister Joe Emenaha would officially announce that their passenger was Chief Uzoma. The guns would be lowered, and the guards would take a step back and salute as our driver sped away. I grinned like a little schoolboy, even though no one could see me.

As we rode along I could hear, *You did the right thing in returning to Nigeria to help these people, even though you had decided that you would never be here again. Let the experience of today serve as a positive reinforcement that in your pursuit of goodness you will never be without guidance and direction, and it will come at just the right time. If I have given you a part in the battle, a share of my suffering, I will also supply my resurrection power.*

The president of Nigeria was keeping a close watch on all that was being accomplished in his country through Project C.U.R.E. He summoned several of the governors and appointed a delegation to travel to Washington, DC. They met there with the Nigerian ambassador, and then traveled together to Colorado to visit the International Headquarters of Project C.U.R.E.

When we gave them the tour of our sorting centers, our huge warehouse, and headquarter facilities, they could hardly believe what they had found. In our conference room they explained to us about their ambitious plans to expand the Owerri Regional Hospital into the new University Training Center Hospital. The ambassador told us, "We will be able to handle all the building requirements, but we have no way on earth to come up with the funds necessary to equip, supply, and facilitate the new University Teaching Hospital. Would Project C.U.R.E. please help us with the teaching hospital and allow our dreams to come true? We simply cannot do it without you!"

Since I had already performed the required assessments while I was there, we were able to enter into an agreement and give them the confidence that we would be proud to be part of the exciting venture. We ended up sending seventeen forty-foot ocean-going cargo containers with an approximate wholesale value of over 7 million dollars to the newly constructed training hospital site in Imo State.

During the late summer of 2004, the honorable ambassador delivered a message from the president informing me that I needed to set aside some days during the end of November and the first part of December for the commissioning ceremonies at the University Teaching Hospital. It would be a great celebration. Since the hospital would not have become a reality without Project C.U.R.E., they were all insisting that Dr. Jackson be there dressed in his Chief Uzoma royal robe and paraphernalia.

The day of the ceremony, I was placed in an official car with lights flashing and sirens sounding, and whisked to the site of the new hospital about thirty minutes from the hotel. My hosts had arranged for me to be delivered to the new hospital site about forty-five minutes before the rest of the entourage would arrive. They were going to give me an unhindered opportunity to tour the facilities and view all the items in the hospital that had been donated by Project C.U.R.E.

As I walked into the new facility, I was overwhelmed with emotion. Even the desks and chairs in the reception area had come from one of our warehouses. As I walked down the first hallway, I immediately began to spot pieces of medical equipment and shelves loaded with supplies that once had been in our Project C.U.R.E. warehouses throughout the United States.

I saw examination tables, otoscopes, blood pressure equipment, needles and syringes, and wound dressing kits that had been carefully sorted and packed into large ocean-going containers by Project C.U.R.E. volunteers. Now those items filled the offices, examination rooms, and procedure rooms in every department of the hospital. The only mammography machine in that part of Africa had made it safely from our Nashville Project C.U.R.E. facilities to Nigeria, and had been successfully installed by bio-med technicians. The large x-ray machine had already been installed in the radiology department, and the portable x-ray machine was proudly displayed in the hallway just outside the operating theaters. I recognized the beds, the gurneys, the EKG machines, the defibrillators, the baby cribs and incubators, and all the overhead lights, anesthesia machines, pumps, surgical instruments, and operation tables in the operating theaters.

The doctors were so proud and excited when I visited their departments. The nurses were in their best-starched outfits and busily scampering around making sure that everything would be perfect for the tour of the president, the governor, and all the media. All of the hard work of the past nearly twenty years at Project C.U.R.E. suddenly seemed validated. I was humbled as I viewed the new facility, and caught the smiles on the faces of the hospital people, and sensed their newfound hope for a better day in Nigeria.

I kept thinking about the impact the Imo State University Training Hospital would have on the future of the African health care delivery system. Hundreds of doctors, lab technicians, and nurses would be trained at the teaching center and affect the lives of thousands more patients who would be cared for over the next decades by people being trained at the hospital. Long after I was dead and gone, the impact of the teaching hospital would live on!

I couldn't help but smile as I compared the present situation with the situation of my original travels into the uncomfortable nation of Nigeria. Then, I was scrambling for my life and safety, surrounded by people who would have killed me to get what I had that day at the airport. God had to send an angel named Vera, and a bodyguard named Innocent, to get me out of the mess. Now, I was being met and escorted through the passport and customs lines at the airport by designated dignitaries. Now, the president of Nigeria and the governors were scheduling meetings with me. Now, I was being sped from one meeting to another in escorted vehicles to hotels where a twenty-four-hour security guard was placed on a chair just outside my hotel door, and up to eight security guards with automatic weapons were roaming the seventh floor hallways to keep me safe. Now, instead of having folks threaten to take from me all my belongings and perhaps my life, folks were lining up to help make me comfortable.

God, the original and eternal rearranger of resources, had divinely intervened to move components out of a position of lower value into a position of increased yields and fruitfulness. God had allowed me to be part of helping many people to be better off in my role as a cultural entrepreneur. He had intervened in human affairs to give me wisdom and favor and acceptance so that He could fulfill His will in helping Nigeria. He could not have told me ahead of time how all of this was to come into being. I had to trust, take courage, and accept risks.

Those risks had proven worthwhile, and God true to His character as sovereign over all things.

21

Empowering Others

As Project C.U.R.E. matured I was discovering that the economic and cultural principles we were implementing were affecting world relief globally. Part of our success—perhaps the greater part—lay in our commitment to working with others. This was an inherent part of our model, as we always worked with sponsoring partners who contributed the money for medical shipments and the partner institutions in the various nations that received these shipments. We found ways to extend our working relationships even further through embracing the work of other cultural entrepreneurs. These strategic alliances multiplied our effectiveness exponentially. People like Dr. Larry Sthresley, the Dimmocks, and the DeLanges in Africa were among those with whom we allied, as well as Dr. Vinh Ngoc Le, and many others. These cultural entrepreneurs either were part of established ministries or established their own.

I want to stress that cultural entrepreneurship usually does *not* entail founding a new work to address an unmet need. It should be our working assumption that, if we sense a need in a given area, probably someone has already been called to address that need. In fact, usually there are multiple organizations available through which to address most of the world's needs.

Ask first, second, and third whether that's the case before starting up a new non-governmental organization or ministry. Many of the world's problems can only be addressed by organizations with sufficient scale.

Frankly, the proliferation of "mom-and-pop" organizations in world relief and other crucial enterprises is one of the world's problems and betrays an unsightly egotism. We are not willing to do much unless the organization through which we do it is seen as our baby. Those who participate in large cultural entrepreneurial enterprises deserve the distinction of "change agent" just as much as the founders of these enterprises. Every volunteer at Project C.U.R.E. is a "change agent."

Daniel Kalnin was such a "change agent," and a prime example of a cultural entrepreneur with whom Project C.U.R.E. formed a strategic alliance with exponentially positive results.

In 1995 Daniel arrived at my office in Denver. The man and his story immediately intrigued me. He was a quiet, dignified Asian in his fifties. His placid demeanor prompted me to look for signs of deeper traits flowing beneath. Daniel had come to ask me to help him with his Barefoot Doctors program. Barefoot Doctors operated out of the city of Chiang Mai in northern Thailand. This organization trained village people from the closed country of Burma in basic health care and medical procedures. Then, Barefoot Doctors sent them back into the hill-tribe villages where they were the only form of health care available.

"I don't have equipment and supplies to send back with the people," Daniel said. He also needed to upgrade the quality of instruction his Barefoot Doctors were receiving. "Dr. Jackson, could you and Project C.U.R.E. help me in Thailand and Burma?"

His request was straightforward, and the urgency of his cause compelling. I traveled to Bangkok and Chiang Mai, Thailand, to evaluate Daniel's work and to see where we could best help. I needed to see what medical goods would be most appropriate to send. Almost immediately, Project C.U.R.E. began furnishing Daniel and his Barefoot Doctors with tens of thousands of dollars of donated medical supplies and small equipment pieces from our warehouses in Denver and Phoenix. One of my trips even saw us riding on motorbikes all through the hill-tribe villages of northern Thailand.

The more I was with Daniel, the more he began to confide in me about the deepest dream of his heart. He wanted to someday go back personally to his home country of Burma and help and train the Barefoot Doctors in even more efficient and effective ways.

I kept pushing Daniel and questioning him as to why that was such an impossible dream?

He began to tell me his story a bit at a time. For context, I read international security reports and histories of old Burma (today's Myanmar). Burma had a storied past as a British colony, played a key role in World War II, and a recent history of isolation and dictatorship. The government carried on an ongoing struggle with an active insurgency.

The rush to colonization had driven European governments to occupy every valuable piece of real estate around the world. Burma was one of the last targets. England sent its royal troops, and soon valuable tribute was being transferred from Rangoon to the queen. Many advantages were also transferred from Great Britain to Burma all the way from Rangoon to Mandalay. Roads were built, railways extended, schools sprang up. Bridges were built over dangerous rivers that had previously separated the people and commerce of Burma. Doors were opened to missionaries to tend to the needs of the local people. Hospitals and clinics were established throughout the land.

Along the borders, the English built military forts to prevent countries like China—which had pillaged the country throughout history—from disrupting the peace and security of the Burmese people. Then one day in 1948, the Brits decided to call it quits and go home; they gave Burma its independence. Unlike many of England's colonies, Burma was not so keen on being left abandoned. The Burmese had grown accustomed to the rule of law and economic development, enjoying reliable health care, civil rights, and well-run courts.

Of course, there were those who could hardly wait for the Brits to leave so that they could inherit their political positions, sturdy homes, and well-built office and commercial buildings. They looked eagerly toward the last ships sailing.

When the English decided to pull out of Burma after World War II, they did it in a hurry. The years that followed Burma's independence were chaotic. Power struggles ensued; tribal positioning and bloodshed became the agenda. Burma turned inward, living off the residual benefits of British rule. But the Burmese had not acquired the necessary knowledge to utilize the resources and systems the British had left, nor to put them to work for the advancement of their country.

Daniel Kalnin was born into the political, economic, and social turmoil that followed Burmese independence. By the time he turned eighteen, he had decided to escape to a better life somewhere else. But that would prove a test. No one simply ran past the oppressive military. Still, Daniel dared to dream. He read books about people who had gone through suffering in order to succeed politically. He determined that he would escape, go to law school, and return to help his country.

Daniel's mother was a devout Christian and a prayer warrior. He was confident that she would always pray for his success and safety as long as she lived. But he couldn't bring himself to tell her what he was planning; leaving was going to break her heart.

Then, one day, while Daniel was working on a labor team in the border town of Maessi, he was allowed to cross the bridge for materials. Once on the other side of the bridge, he realized that he was in Thailand. The other workers returned across the bridge back into Burma that evening, but Daniel kept on walking. Surely he could find someone who would help him keep going and escape repressive Burma. Well, it wasn't that simple. By quietly keeping to himself, Daniel was able to join up with a Thai work team in a mountainous village named Lahu for the next three months. He had left on the first day of November, 1965. Now it was January. He lived every day knowing that he would be shot as a spy if he were found to be a Burmese in Thailand without any identification or papers.

After January, he moved on and worked for another three months in a hill-tribe village. His goal was to eventually make it to Chiang Mai. The fact that part of the country was embroiled in the Vietnam War made things all the more precarious. As a worker, Daniel was arbitrarily sent to a rebel military camp, and was forced to help them work. They would not allow his escape for another three months. Eventually, a sergeant of another rebel group offered to take Daniel to Chiang Mai. Daniel was loaded into the back of a large truck hauling sacks of rice. He was wedged between the top of the truck's metal covering and the load of rice. The sergeant stopped at a town called Faang, and Daniel quickly made his way to the local bus station.

On the way to Chiang Mai, Daniel sensed that if he could link up with some Christians, they would be able to help him. So, upon his arrival at the bus station, he took the only money he had left and paid a rickshaw driver to take him to a Baptist center. Eventually, he arrived at the Baptist place only to discover that everyone was suspicious of anyone from Burma traveling without proper papers or identification.

To put some distance between themselves and the strange young traveler, the Baptists sent Daniel out into another area in the mountains to work in the fields north of Chiang Mai. The young escapee had to keep moving from village to village. At the third location he was staying at the home of a family in exchange for work. But the man's neighbor had a running grudge with the farmer, and to spite him, he went to the authorities and told them that the farmer was harboring a military spy from Burma. The Thai police moved quickly and surrounded the farmer's house. Daniel had just finished bathing in the evening after a long day's work.

"I was standing next to the outside cooking fire trying to stay warm after my bath," Daniel told me. "The police grabbed me without even letting me get dressed, or retrieve anything, and promptly threw me into jail as a foreign spy. I had no papers and no defense, and they had a signed complaint that I was a foreign spy from Burma."

In early April the Baptists heard of Daniel's being thrown into jail and sent a fellow with an old Volkswagen sedan to bail him out of jail. It wasn't until August that Daniel appeared in court on the spy charges. At the trial the judge made a very strange and unusual ruling. He charged Daniel five hundred baht, but signed a paper that gave Daniel permission to stay in Thailand.

Daniel still didn't have any official identification papers. With just the signed paper from the judge, some of Daniel's new friends helped him get a Thai passport. By that time it had been observed that Daniel was bright. Soon someone agreed to sponsor him to America to be educated at a small college in Cincinnati.

Even though Daniel's mother had warned him never to marry an American girl, he met a girl named Beverly, at college, and on New Year's Day, 1974, they were married. Daniel told me, "Beverly was from Toronto, Canada, so I kept faith with my mother and did not marry an American girl." They both graduated in June, 1974 and returned to Chiang Mai as quickly as possible.

Their common dream was to help the suppressed people in Burma. Daniel and Beverly tried helping the people in the northern hill-tribe area of Thailand known as the Golden Triangle. That was where the people of Burma, Thailand, and Laos produced some of the highest yields of heroin for the international market. The Kalnins designed a plan whereby the natives could break away from growing opium poppies for a living by switching to coffee as a cash crop. They were beginning to see some encouraging success. Additionally, Daniel and Beverly started an endeavor called The Home of Blessing, a safe house for young ten- to twelve-year-old throwaway girls who had either run away or been kidnapped. At their early ages they had become child prostitutes or indentured child laborers. When I first visited Daniel and Beverly they were taking care of forty-seven such girls.

Then, in 1983, reports of an unexplained explosion began to filter down out of the hill-tribe villages. The mountaintops near the border area of India, China, and Burma had one day blown up and many native villagers had observed the terrible devastation. The villagers reported that the snow on the tops of the mountains simply exploded and the mountains blew into the air. The explosion covered about one hundred miles square. Entire populations of villages died instantly. Fish in the lower streams were found to have bodies that were half-rotten. People who ate the fish, or any other food from the area, would either die or become terribly sick.

Years later it was discovered that the mysterious explosion had been a test of China's nuclear bomb. None of the authorities or governments would give any answers at the time. Because of all the sickness and dying, and because there were no doctors to help in the mountainous areas, certain hill-tribe folk from Burma illegally came down and crossed the border into Thailand. They were looking for a Burmese native named Daniel who had traveled to America for education and had reportedly returned to the northern areas of Thailand.

When they found Daniel, they begged him to find medical people who could go and help the sick. Daniel knew very well that the common mountain people were never allowed access to professional doctors or nurses, and there was no training available in Burma for them. Under the new repressive military government in Burma, many of the universities and institutions had been shut down to guarantee that there would be no protests or opposition movements that would spring up against the insecure leaders.

It was then that Daniel determined to set up a medical training program for the common people of Burma. The leaders of the villages would select the right people to travel out of the mountains of Burma into Chiang Mai, Thailand, to be instructed in first aid and rudimentary health care skills. The training process would stretch over a three-year period. The trainees would come each year to Chiang Mai and reside there for one month. During that time they would receive instruction from volunteer medical personnel and medical teams. Then they would return to their homes and travel from village to village to give medical care to their people. Daniel Kalnin's "Barefoot Doctors" was born.

The term Barefoot Doctors described well the picture of the simple Burmese villagers who would walk barefoot among the hill tribes taking medical care to the sick and injured natives. But the system of training was not to be simple, because Burma did not approve of any persons coming into, or leaving, Burma. The first candidates would need to walk for approximately four weeks down out of the mountains and illegally cross over into Thailand and travel on to Chiang Mai. Then after receiving their month of instruction they would be required to slip quietly back across the border.

Sometime later Daniel was able to negotiate an exit visa policy for the trainees. But the price for each visa was in excess of four hundred US dollars. That was an absolutely impossible amount for any of the villagers to muster. So, it was necessary for Daniel to go out and raise the necessary funds to pay for the visas to encourage the candidates to travel to Chiang Mai. The providing of the visa money for the trainees worked as a symbol of honor because the trainees then felt even more privileged to have been chosen to receive such expensive training.

The first time I visited one of the "Barefoot Doctors" training sessions in Chiang Mai there were twenty-one candidates enrolled. Daniel's staff had already trained one hundred and thirty villagers who had returned to their home areas and were tending to the medical needs. Barefoot Doctors had rented a large, walled home inside Chiang Mai where the candidates slept in dormitory rooms, were trained in the parlor, and would eat wherever they could find sitting room. Miraculous stories were beginning to be told of the simple effectiveness of the newly-trained medical people.

By early 1998, Project C.U.R.E. was furnishing supplies and pieces of medical equipment, and some medical training props, for the Barefoot Doctors training institute. We were also sending in more and more medical supplies for the candidates to strap on their backs and carry on their heads back across the border into their mountainous Burmese villages. A huge difference was being made in the health care delivery system of the hermit country in spite of all the obstacles. Daniel and I talked many times, and I agreed to help him build and equip a new training center for the Barefoot Doctors on the outskirts of Chiang Mai. But it was strange that each time we talked the subject would eventually turn in focus onto Burma.

Daniel's heart was really in Burma, and his thoughts were concentrated on returning. It had been more than thirty years since Daniel walked over that bridge in Maessi. As much as he desired to go home, though, he knew that he would be considered a fugitive and thrown into prison. He suspected he might never have the opportunity to return.

At one point he received word that his mother had died after a botched appendectomy at a village hospital in the far northern state of Kachin. His mother had instructed the rest of the family that she wanted to be buried at the end of the old British military airport runway in Putao. When her son Daniel would one day return, her stone gravesite would be the first thing he would see from the air as she welcomed him back home.

During the ensuing years, Daniel's family had become successful in state politics. His older brother, Phe Ram, had become governor of the Putao region in the far north district. In 1995, feeling his family contacts might afford him leniency, Daniel decided to see if he could catch the Burmese government napping. Perhaps if he used his Thailand passport they would not connect the fact that he was the same man who was listed as a fugitive, and would allow him entry. He was flatly refused entry in 1995. But in 1996 they providentially issued him entrance when he tried again. For the first time he was able to return home for an emotional reunion. However, when he applied for entry the next year he was once again flatly denied. The one visit still whetted his appetite all the more for entry again.

Daniel came to me with a plan. "Jim, I believe that if the Myanmar government realized that they might be the recipient of much needed donated medical goods into their needy government facilities, they just might allow us to come in. Would you be willing for Project C.U.R.E. to request entry, and would you go with the idea of performing the needs assessment studies in the northern insurgency areas?"

I agreed to the idea. If we could get all our medical supplies into Burma with the government's blessing, that would make a whole lot more sense than requiring all the Barefoot Doctors to carry the heavy supplies on their heads and on their backs from Chiang Mai into Burma.

"Let's go for it," I said. I was willing to offer the Myanmar government millions of dollars of additional medical goods for their institutions if they would allow us to legally ship into their country. We would be the very first outsiders to be allowed into the country to help.

In the months that followed we began talking with the military leadership of Myanmar. Their commitment to a closed society reminded me of North Korea or Cuba. The areas north from Rangoon, all the way to the China border, were especially sensitive and tightly closed. That was where we were asking to go to perform the needs assessment studies. That was where all of Daniel's family still lived and where the work of the one hundred Barefoot Doctors had been so successful over the years.

Finally, we were granted visa permission to travel into Rangoon (Yangon), and were given verbal agreement that we would be able to travel into the restricted area of the north. Daniel and I both knew that the long-awaited trip into Burma was highly significant, even historic, and we were grateful to God.

Our flight from Bangkok arrived in Rangoon about ten thirty the night of Thursday, November 8. Two government officials from the ministry of tourism met us. One was a young lady named Khin Khin Swe. "But you can call me 'Ma Lay' if you would like. That is my nickname," she said.

As they were stamping our passports, Daniel told me how significant it was that Ma Lay had been assigned to us. She was very influential in the government, and with her streetwise experience she could be extremely helpful in opening political and cultural doors. Khin Khin Swe's home was in Myitkyina, the capital of the Kachin province in the north where we intended to travel. She knew Daniel's sister and brother-in-law who lived in Myitkyina, a city of about two million. Ma Lay had graduated from university and had become a science and mathematics teacher and had moved to the northern town of Putao.

As God's providence would have it, Ma Lay taught at the high school in Putao before being invited to join the ministry of tourism. For two years, while in Putao, she had stayed in the home of Daniel's brother, Phe Ram and his wife, Chin Lay Do. Phe Ram was the brother who had been the territorial governor.

The following day a man arrived at my hotel room door. When I answered his knock he stepped in and announced that the officials had reviewed my passport and visas, and had determined that I was welcome to stay as long as I liked in Rangoon, but then I would have to leave. I was not granted permission to travel to the restricted area of the north.

As in the business world, there is a split second of time during any transaction where you must decide your strategy and move with full force in that direction. I could have either responded to the man in milquetoast submissiveness, closed the door, packed and left Rangoon mumbling to myself, or I could spring into attack mode. I chose to attack.

"Who are you, and just who told you to come to this room?" I asked sternly, moving in close to his face. "I consider what you have just done an insult to me personally. I do not accept your message, and I demand that you return immediately to whoever sent you here and tell them that they also have insulted me, and that I do not accept the message. I have traveled half way around the world to be here, and I have brought gifts that I intend to give to the three generals who govern Myanmar! When you return to your superiors, tell them that I demand a meeting with them immediately to rectify this matter. I will be waiting for your reply. Thank you."

The diplomat's mouth dropped open, and he kept staring at me as he backed away before turning and leaving my hotel room.

By the time I got to Daniel, Ma Lay had just broken the news to him about our permission to travel north being denied. It wasn't long before the fellow came back to my room, however, and announced that there would be a meeting at the cabinet minister's office at ten o'clock the next morning.

At our meeting the next morning, I was cordial, but I asked the minister of tourism, Htay Aung, for an explanation. He said that since the 9-11 incident in New York, and the bombings in Afghanistan and other places, they were concerned that certain people there might want to take their anger out and kill me as an American traveling in Myanmar.

"We just don't want to accept the responsibility of an American in our restricted areas." Htay Aung said. "As you know, the US pulled their ambassador out of Myanmar awhile back, and they still have sanctions imposed against us. We just don't want to deal with another incident."

Then he made clear the government's true concern. "Recently there was a zoological group from Switzerland and Netherlands who talked us into letting them go into our lower Himalayan areas to study our rare butterflies and lizards. They had an American in their group who was an expert on snakes. We told him he could not travel. But the group persisted, and, against our better judgment, we finally gave him approval.

"We made a big mistake," the minister continued, "because the American got bit by one of our very poisonous snakes. We told him of the traditional remedies he should take if he wanted to survive the snakebite. But he refused and insisted on being flown out of Myanmar in an American helicopter. We explained that we did not have diplomatic ties with America, and that it would be difficult or impossible for him to be flown out in an American helicopter. Before we could provide help, the snake expert died. We don't want anything like that to happen again."

Now that I had the real story I could argue more effectively. "I want to thank you personally for allowing this meeting to take place today," I said. I reached into my jacket pocket and pulled out my very fat passport and laid it in front of him on his desk. "As you can see by my passport, I am not a novice traveler. I quit counting how many countries I had traveled in when I reached one hundred and fifty. I respect the fact that you are concerned that some person may want to kill me while I am here. But please let me respond and tell you what all is entailed in killing me. First, you must really be sure that you want to kill me and that I am the right person you want to kill. That takes time. Next, you have to study my actions, where I am staying, what door of the hotel I exit, where I sit in the car that is to pick me up. Studying my movements takes time. Then you must devise a workable plan to kill me. That takes considerable time. And how would you dispose of my body? You would need a good plan so that you would not be recognized and identified while killing me. That study would also take time. By that time, Mr. Minister, I would be gone from Burma! Oh, and by the way, Mr. Minister … I don't like snakes!"

The minister started to laugh. "OK, OK," he said. "I will take your passport and go talk to my colleagues. You and Mr. Kalnin and Ma Lay stay here and drink your tea until I return."

A full thirty minutes later Htay Aung returned. "I have successfully intervened on your behalf. The ministry of tourism has now signed your papers, but you will not be able to travel today because the defense minister must also sign off on all your paperwork. The defense minister is in charge of security in the restricted areas. He cannot possibly hear your case today because we have had some serious upsets in the government today."

Our new friend, Ma Lay, proved her incredible worth by working her way in front of the defense minister the next day, and she finally got my paperwork signed. All of that bureaucracy had delayed our flying to Myitkyina until Monday morning. And I didn't even like snakes!

Burma exists in a one-hundred-year time warp. Outside the cities, the country is very much like it was when the Brits moved out. When I returned I told my Project C.U.R.E. board members that, if there were one place I would like for them to travel with me, it would be into the restricted country of northern Burma. There is nothing like it left on the face of the earth.

On Monday morning we checked out of our Rangoon hotel and boarded a Myanmar Airlines flight north to the regional capital city of

Myitkyina (pronounced "mit cheena"). Daniel was as excited as a young schoolboy as he returned to the villages of his childhood.

We stopped in Myitkyina and met with the head military government official in the region, Colonel Myint Thein, to share with him our plans. That way he might help us if we ran into any difficulties. While in the city, we stayed for two nights with one of Daniel's sisters, a longtime resident of Myitkyina. You can imagine how thrilled Daniel's sister was to have us take all our meals in her home. She gathered five of her lady friends into her open-air kitchen and cooked for us over the wood-burning cooking fires. They were all relieved when they saw that I could efficiently handle chopsticks. The Burmese almost never see an American north of Rangoon or Mandalay.

At every meal we were served a different variety of noodle bowl with meats and vegetables and hot spices. Then we were served delicious deep fried rice breadsticks that we would dip into cliff honey and eat with our tea. For dessert we would have either *pomelo* or grapefruit sections drizzled with more cliff honey. Two servings of tea accompanied our meals: first, English black tea with milk and honey; then to finish, very hot green tea served in bamboo teacups.

Tuesday afternoon with our meetings finished, we were driven out of Myitkyina toward the China border. We followed the river where families were out panning for large nuggets of gold. From high up in the Himalayan Mountains, the river washed the gold down, especially in the springtime, and many people made their living panning.

Likewise, the highest quality jade could be found in northern Burma. Rubies and sapphires were also mined in large quantities in Kachin state. I had been aware of the fine Burmese rubies—the finest rubies in the world—from my days in Jackson Brothers Investments.

When we returned to Daniel's sister's home, I noticed that the yard was full of parked bicycles, and at the front door were lines of flip-flops. To my astonishment, the house was crowded with Barefoot Doctors who had come to greet us. Some had ridden their bicycles or walked for days through jungles and across rivers to be there and celebrate. Word had been sent out to the remote areas that they could come and meet Daniel, whom many had not seen since they had graduated from the training sessions in Thailand, and also the man from Project C.U.R.E., the organization that had supplied them with their desperately-needed medical goods. Every square foot of floor space was covered with excited people that night as we talked and sang and cried together. They simply could not believe that we had been able to travel into the restricted area.

Daniel asked about twenty of the Barefoot Doctors to share the recent miracles that had happened in their areas. They told stories of being guided providentially in their medical practices, often out of necessity, undertaking procedures about which they knew little more than the concept. God granted them success far beyond what they could have expected.

Eventually, the power generator ran out of petrol and stopped running, causing the single florescent light to go out. So they ended the session by holding candles and singing songs before leaving to return to their villages the next morning. I was the happiest man in the world.

As I dropped off to sleep in yet another unfamiliar bed, I thought about the beautiful people that had gathered in that humble Burmese home. I had tried to watch carefully the actions and reactions and attitudes of the people, and had endeavored to read past their physical features and into their souls. There in the dark bedroom, I suddenly realized something: "I really love these people."

I also had that feeling of active compassion the week before while I was in Bolivia, and in Dakar, Senegal, before that. I realized this sense of identification and compassion had begun to dominate my outlook, helping me to see people by the light of eternity. Now, when I had been in Lagos, Nigeria, under the threat of personal harm, that perspective had certainly vanished for a time because some of the people there I didn't like. But something had happened inside of me, and I felt a love for the people wherever I went.

I also felt, in a way I couldn't explain, that the people I met loved me also. On a daily basis, in Burma and around the world, I saw more suffering and pain than anyone I knew. I observed, as well, peoples' simple joys and satisfactions—the things that would make them smile. I saw the love they had for their children and for each other. I saw how rewarding they found their accomplishments. It pleased them when they reached out to me, and I would smile and try to say something friendly in their language.

I realized how very much God had changed who I was. He had changed my mainspring—my central motivations. Many Christians complain that they don't feel the love of God or know the power of God in their lives. The love I felt now for the peoples of the world was God's love, as God granted me the privilege of being that love's conduit. The love of God depends more than I ever knew on the second part of Jesus' Great Commandment: to love one's neighbor as one's self, with friend and enemy alike counting as neighbor, and no one excluded. If I had become the "happiest man in the world," as I had become fond of saying, it was because I felt the joy of the Lord more often than not in my life as I reached out to all the peoples of the world.

If you take nothing else from this book, take this: If you want to know the love of God, which is the ultimate destiny that God wills for us, do good to your neighbor. Put your Christianity into action—that's genuine faith.

Otherwise, you can assent to all the doctrines you want, but you'll never experience the full love of God.

I fell asleep praying for the individual Barefoot Doctors that night, that God would bless them, their families. and their troubled country.

The next morning we set out for the city of Putao, the old British military outpost not far from the borders of China and India. It held a population of about two hundred thousand. The streets were dirt and gravel, and, even though the British had pulled out more than sixty years earlier, it still bore the characteristics of a colonial outpost, with a central square of wooden Victorian buildings with metal roofs.

Our flight had taken us from the tropics of Myitkyina to the higher elevations of the Himalayan foothills. The airport had been engineered and planned by the British for the World War II fighter and supply planes. The Burmese locals had built it, and they took great pride in having Myanmar Airlines drop into their community three times a week. Government protocol stated that any visitors to Putao were required to stay in the old military barracks. Daniel's brother, Phe Ram, former governor, had stepped in on my behalf and arranged for me to stay with them in the compound of their home.

Most heavy transportation was managed by ox cart. Many of the people rode bicycles or walked. There were very few individual cars, and the bus system consisted of a few large, old, beat-up trucks where the passengers rode stuffed in the open cargo bed.

Filth and poverty did not riddle northern Burma, however. It might be behind one hundred years in terms of economic development, but the houses and properties were meticulously tidy, and the people remarkably neat and clean. Like most Asian cultures, they grew and ate a lot of rice and homegrown vegetables and fruit. Emphasis was placed on the importance of the family.

The room Phe Ram gave me for my stay had plank boards for the floor, fresh mosquito netting over my bed, and a porcelain pot with a lid at the foot of my bed. On a handcrafted table next to my bed were extra blankets and a generous supply of candles. Everything was so neat and clean.

The city had no central water or sewer system, and the only consistent electrical source came from an individual's own generator. As I walked the streets and met the people, I was impressed with their sense of hope and quiet joy. I concluded that they were a happy lot and enjoyed living at the foot of the mighty Himalayan Mountains. I had been given the rare opportunity of going back one hundred years, or more, and seeing a highly functional culture.

Of course, Daniel and his brother, Phe Ram, reminisced endlessly as they sat together and talked. In the evenings, everyone gathered outside and sat around on chairs in front of an open bonfire and drank tea and talked with each other, and discussed the events of the day. There was no irresistible pull from the TV sets that drew folks into an incoherent group of zombies silently staring at the wall.

The next morning, before the clouds of cool mist drifted down to the lower valleys, we packed into the old 1945 military jeep and were on our way to perform the needs assessment studies on the existing village hospitals.

Our first stop was at the gravesite of Daniel and Phe Ram's mother. Sure enough, it was a large memorial made out of collected stone and concrete, large enough for Daniel to see when he flew in on his return flight to Putao. His saintly mother knew that one day her lost Daniel would come back home to her. Now, he was there. As we stood holding hands around the gravesite, they pointed out to me a very rare variety of rice that had sprung up around the stones shortly after their mother was buried. It was a very delicate and delicious type of rice, and each year there was just enough to harvest and divide up among the children. In the past few years the brothers and sisters had found a way to get Daniel's portion to him where he was living in Chiang Mai. The family believed that God had allowed the special rice to grow as a symbolic answer to the mother's prayers that God would always take care of the family and fulfill their every need.

Loading back into the old Jeep, we drove over the rough mountainous roads to a village located on the banks of the Malikha River. Pulled up to the sandy shores were two long canoes. They were about fifteen feet in length and had been hand dug with the help of ax and fire. There were no roads to take us to the village where Daniel had been born, Nam Kham. It was only accessible by river travel. Because we would be traveling with the rapid flow of the river, it would only take us about forty-five minutes to an hour. The guides slid their canoes off the bank and into the water. We climbed in and sat on pieces of split bamboo. No one even thought about life jackets. On each end of the canoe stood a young man with a large bamboo tree that had been split in half. From those positions they would guide and paddle our canoe down the Malikha River.

The river was so pristine and clear-flowing out of the Himalayan snow-pack that I could see directly to the bottom, even though it was quite deep. I could watch the fish swimming as we traveled. The lush, high-mountain jungle constructed delicate canopies over our heads. Behind me in the canoe Ma Lay began to sing a Burmese folk tune. I thought to myself, *I'll bet heaven is a lot like this*.

Just a little less than an hour later, the young men standing at the ends of the two canoes began steering us toward a sandy beach. We had arrived at Nam Kham village. Up on the shore I could see the village reception party eagerly waiting for us to beach the boats and come ashore. A half dozen of the village men had built a stone and sand walkway for me so I would not get my shoes wet walking to shore. The chief, and a couple of other village leaders, had walked down to the water to meet us and escort us up to where the rest of the official welcoming party waited.

Nam Kham village consisted of two hundred and eighty families and well over three thousand inhabitants. It was worth the whole trip just to observe Daniel's pleasure at returning to the place where he had learned to swim in the river and go fishing with his homemade bamboo spear. Back then he was the one who had driven the ox carts with the two big wheels pulled by the water buffalo. He was the one who had gathered the delicious fruit and had worked in harvesting the rice crop.

Many of the villagers had stopped their midday work to come to the riverbank to welcome us. Even the little children had come to sing to us, shake our hands, and present to us freshly picked jungle flowers.

The welcoming party and our group paraded over grass-covered trails back to the home of another of Daniel and Phe Ram's sisters. We would stay in her home for the following two nights.

The village elders and their people were so appreciative of how the

Barefoot Doctors had changed their medical world. They had heard all about Project C.U.R.E., and how we had furnished shiploads of donated medical goods to their people in Burma.

We excused ourselves from our meeting with the elders and climbed the stairs up into the stilted house, and were served a dinner fit for royalty.

As we walked with our lit candles back down the stairs to the grass courtyard below, I was taken back a bit. There were two large bonfires burning, and the whole yard was crowded with people. There was even a small choir from Putao. The choir had ridden their bicycles through the mountains, and then loaded their bicycles for the necessary canoe trip on the Malikha River. They were prepared to give us a mini concert that night. Another group of Barefoot Doctors had received word that we would be there, and they had walked and ridden their bicycles through the high, jungle mountains to meet us and thank us for our help.

The next morning, I was introduced to a middle-aged village woman named Pruperam Nang. The village leaders had chosen her several years before to represent their village. She had made the long and dangerous trek out of Burma and across into Thailand for three years in a row to be trained as a Barefoot Doctor. She had then returned to Nam Kham village, loaded down with our medical supplies, and had established a clinic near the village. She was so eager for us to join her and walk to her clinic and view her work. Pruperam lived in the space above her clinic and over the door she had hung a dignified sign reading, PUNG ZI PUNG CLINIC.

Her eyes twinkled as I performed a complete needs assessment study on her little clinic just as if it had been a three-hundred-bed hospital in the capital city. She was so proud, and all the village people who gathered round, and followed us down the grassy trails, were bursting with pride. We returned to the stilted house, gathered our belongings, and walked the mile from the village back to the riverbank, where we crawled back into our canoes for another four-hour trip on the Malikha River.

Every moment of our stay testified to the hero Daniel had become in the village of his birth. He had gone away so many years before, but he had not forgotten his people; he had gone away in order to return with medical help they desperately needed.

⁂

On the second leg of our journey on the Malikha River, we were close to the Tibet and China border. The two nations lay just over those eighteen-thousand-foot mountains. As we rounded a bend, we spotted the town of Machang Baw. It was the township headquarters, and boasted a population of more than twenty thousand. The governor was at the river's edge to greet us when we pulled our handmade canoes up on the sand.

Together we walked up the steep hillside and directly to the Machang Baw Hospital that sat high above the bend in the river with a spectacular view for miles. It, too, had been built and supplied by the British. That had been fifty or sixty years ago. Remarkably enough, the buildings were still in serviceable condition, but not because the Burmese government had invested much in their upkeep. The English had done such a commendable job in the beginning that their work endured.

The hospital had been without a government doctor in residence until just the day before we arrived. The medical situation at the hospital was disgusting, bleak. The equipment was very old and rusty. The beds were just board slats with no mattresses at all. All the medications and supplies were locked up in a separate little building, but no one knew where the key was kept. "Oh, well," said one male nurse, "there isn't anything of any value in there anyway, so it doesn't matter if we can't find the key."

The new doctor in charge of the hospital, Dr. Nanda Nyi Swe, was very embarrassed. "Our twenty-bed hospital is the only institution serving about eighty thousand people in our catchment area. I have just come here, but as you can see, I will not be effective unless I can get someone to help me here. I need everything for this hospital if I am going to help these people."

I promised Dr. Nanda that Project C.U.R.E. would do its best.

Eventually, we linked back up with our 1945 Jeep and scooted back to Putao. Much of Putao's old military community buildings still stood. Again, the Brits had left quality infrastructure, and the Burmese were still using many of the buildings. Putao's City Hospital had once been the British Military Hospital. Nothing on the inside, however, resembled anything of medical modernity.

Not only were we able to complete the needs assessment studies on the old hospitals, but Phe Ram was able to arrange meetings for us with all the military and civilian leaders of the north. No one had ever come there to help them since their independence. And the factious leadership in Rangoon over the decades simply had too many pressing political problems demanding their attention. The leaders certainly didn't have time to work on such things as health care issues.

When we began talking to the local leaders about Project C.U.R.E. bringing medical supplies and pieces of medical equipment, and perhaps teams of doctors and nurses on a visiting basis to help augment Daniel's Barefoot Doctors brigade, the high mountain sun really began to shine in their eyes.

When we returned to Phe Ram and Chin Le Do's house, we beheld a scene that was now becoming familiar. It was their yard and entry that was now packed full with bicycles. It was their doorway that was now stacked with flip-flops. Every possible Barefoot Doctor from around the regions of Putao had made his way to Phe Ram's home to greet Daniel and meet the man from Project C.U.R.E. We experienced another very emotional time together. All the rest of that day and into the night the whole group worked on plans for additional inventory that would be donated from Project C.U.R.E., as well as creative methods for distribution.

Malaria continued to be one of the most severe problems. The Barefoot Doctors begged, not only for medicine, but also for mosquito netting and spray. Tuberculosis was running rampant in the jungle areas, and there was no TB medication. They were almost completely out of emergency supplies, including sutures, casting material, blades, antiseptic agents and anti-bacterial ointments, bandages, tape, and latex gloves. Ear, nose, and throat supplies and medications were greatly needed. They were begging for eye surgeons to come from the United States to perform cataract procedures and lens transplants. There were high occurrences of fungus, ringworm, and other parasitic problems due to farming barefoot in the rice paddies.

Daniel's Barefoot Doctors were the only ones equipped to remove teeth with something other than a bamboo spike and a mallet. Still, they needed anesthetic, Anbesol, and simple dental equipment. There weren't any hospitals that could perform basic blood and urine tests. The Barefoot Doctors delivered a lot of babies, and they needed all the supplies entailed. Antibiotic medicines were desperately needed. The Barefoot Doctors, as well as all the hospitals and clinics in Burma, needed everything!

At the end of the long session, the past governor and the leaders came to where we were meeting and put on a little ceremony. The officials graciously bestowed on me the title of Honorary Governor of the Putao Province and all the Northern Areas of Myanmar. They shrouded me with the official robe of governor, and placed on me the unique headdress fashioned of tightly woven rice stalks, and adorned with four sets of ivory wild boar tusks. I now proudly display those precious tokens in my home in Colorado. What a great honor! Following a day of celebrating and saying farewells, Daniel, Ma Lay, and I returned to Rangoon and made our personal reports to the appropriate leaders there.

During the following years I tried to return to Burma as often as possible. At one point I returned three times in the course of twelve months. When the first containers arrived in Rangoon, the ruling generals contacted Daniel Kalnin and insisted that Dr. James Jackson should return with him and make a personal presentation of the donations. No one in the history of Myanmar had ever made such a large contribution to the aid of the country. The doors into the hermit country that had been so tightly closed for so long were now swinging wide open to Daniel and Project C.U.R.E.

At the presentation ceremony, all the Myanmar leadership had gathered together. They had made an impressive display of samples of the medical supplies and pieces of medical equipment that had been donated. The displays lined the walls of the banquet room. The leaders were amazed at the magnitude of the donation and at the quality of the medical goods. At that time the leaders begged us to return and perform the required needs assessment studies on all their hospitals so that they could qualify for our help. They even encouraged us to go immediately to the old historic downtown Rangoon General Hospital that had been constructed by the British and get started with our assessments.

One of the generals was making a presentation of appreciation to Daniel Kalnin at the capital. There was Daniel, mingling with the leaders of his beloved country. Once a fugitive, an enemy of the state, he had become an effective agent of change in old Burma—a national hero. I tried to think of alternate circumstances in which this reversal of fortune might have come about. If he had returned as an astronaut, a gold-medal athlete, the president of a neighboring country, or the U.N. secretary general, could the turnaround have been more complete? None of these stations in life would have afforded him the opportunity to help his beloved country as he had always longed to do. Now his dreams were being fulfilled. He was transforming his nation's health care delivery system.

Project C.U.R.E., in turn, had been able to ratchet the concept of cultural entrepreneurs one round higher by transferring opportunities to others. Hundreds of thousands would be affected. Such strategic alliances multiplied our effectiveness exponentially.

Daniel Kalnin and I knew that the glory belonged to God, for, "all that we have accomplished you have done for us" (Isaiah 26:12).

22

Darkness Comes to Call

Despite traveling into more than one hundred and fifty countries during the first twenty years of Project C.U.R.E., I had never become seriously ill. Anyone who travels into the Nigerias and Uzbekistans of the world will tell you, that's a miracle. I had somehow walked the halls of infection-ridden hospitals and escaped malaria, dengue fever, cholera, hepatitis, meningitis, yellow fever, and tuberculosis. I took this as an affirmation that God was protecting me, and was well pleased with what was being accomplished. On the road, I frequently quoted with gratitude Psalm 91: "He who dwells in the shelter of the Most High will rest in the shadow of the Almighty. You will not fear … the pestilence that stalks in the darkness, nor the plague that destroys at midday" (v. 1, 5-6).

I was coming to the end of 2006. I had already completed five separate trips to Africa that year in addition to making extended trips to China, Mongolia, Vietnam, and Bulgaria. I had two more trips scheduled into Africa before Christmas.

In early November, I left Denver for the West African, coastal nation of Togo. In Paris, I met up with a Jewish man named Amnon Leshem, who lived in Brussels and had agreed to sponsor the assessment trip to Togo. We flew to Lomé, the capital city, and were met by cabinet members of the government, and even the personal body guard of the president.

Along with the body guard, armed with a variety of weapons, and several other officials, we began performing our needs assessments on several of the major hospitals in and around Lomé. We then pointed our convoy north and drove all the way to the Burkina Faso border. For the next ten days we crisscrossed our way back and forth from the Ghana border on the west, to the border of Benin on the east. In our southerly trek back to Lomé and the coast, we performed assessments on nearly twenty of Togo's district hospitals. Much of our travel was over treacherous roads, and of necessity we stayed in the jungle villages and small towns of Togo. The specialty of the day on the village menus was always whatever was cooking in the black, cast-iron cauldron.

While in the city of Kara, I was reached by satellite phone and notified that Anna Marie's one-hundred-and-two-year-old father, Keller Johnson, had died. They agreed to postpone the funeral until I could get back to the United States. I finished up my work as quickly as I could and headed home.

It's a very long trip from Africa to Denver, during which I realized that I was running a fever. I dug into my emergency medical bag, that I always travel with, and started taking some Cipro. That should have killed anything bacterial in my body. I got home, slept two hours, and got back on an airplane headed for the funeral in Idaho. By that time I knew something was wrong, but the occasion was not one where there was the liberty of complaining about how I was feeling.

On the way home from Boise to Denver, I really got sick. Home in Evergreen, I found myself too weak to walk. The cold chills, sweating, headache, and dizziness were symptoms of serious problems in the urinary tract, the bladder, and the kidneys.

Anna Marie made an appointment with our family doctor, who scolded me for self-medicating, but said it had been very fortunate that I had gotten started on the Cipro. I went home and only got worse. As my fever spiked, I began to shake violently. I could not even hold a glass of water in my hand without spilling it. Was it possible that I had been infected with malaria? I had witnessed thousands of African, Asian, and Indian patients in despicable hospitals on their deathbeds suffering violently and shaking in the last stages of malaria. I had been careful to take my Mefloquine anti-malaria medicine regularly throughout the year. But as any African traveler would tell you, there is really no absolute and sure preventative measure from the many different strains of malaria when you are in the jungles. Anna Marie would heat up in the microwave oven the bean-filled bags we call our bed buddies and pack them around me to try to lower the chill and break the fever. Then she would wash my face, chest, and arms with a cool, wet cloth.

I still had one more trip to make back to Africa. I was scheduled to leave on Tuesday, November 28, flying from Denver via Frankfurt and Paris and finally on to Douala, Cameroon, in West Africa. All I could think about was staying quiet and healing over the weekend so that I would be ready to travel. I was confident that the medication would kick in soon, and I would be ready to travel again.

Monday, about noon, I got out of bed and snuck outside and tried putting up some Christmas lights and decorations before I left. By the time I was to return from Africa, the Christmas season would be in full swing, and we would have friends and Project C.U.R.E. members to our house for parties. I needed to get done as much as possible before I left.

No sooner had I begun to work than I felt sharp pains in my abdomen and lower torso area, and barely made it back into the house. My fever had gone to one hundred and four degrees. I knew I had pushed my luck. I leaned on the kitchen counter and told Anna Marie to get me in to see the doctor. I needed to get something from him to cure me so that I could travel early the next morning. My plane was to leave at four o'clock. My nonrefundable tickets had already been paid for, as had all my hotel rooms along the way. I could sleep on the plane and heal up en route.

At the doctor's office they ran some quick blood and urine tests. Things got very serious very quickly. "I have scheduled you to see Dr. Cohn, a urology specialist in Lakewood. He says he wants to see you immediately. We are dealing with something very serious. Here is his address, and he will see you just as soon as you arrive at his office."

I was able to reach Anna Marie on her cell phone and instruct her to meet me at the specialist's office. After some more tests, Dr. Cohn called in another doctor for consultation. "We don't know what is going on inside of you. You have been on Cipro for twelve days now, and it is not touching the infection. Whatever you have contracted is very aggressive and is attacking your kidneys, bladder, prostate, and urinary tract. We are going to schedule a CAT scan for you, to see if it might be a kidney stone that has lodged somewhere and has become infected."

"OK," I said, "just as soon as I return from Africa I will go in for the CAT scan."

They looked at each other and at Anna Marie and said, "Jim, we can't even change your medication if you leave for Africa, because then we couldn't observe you. You are not getting this. The infection inside you could explode at any time. If you get on that airplane tomorrow and go to Africa, you will not come back alive. You cannot go *anywhere*, except to bed."

The doctors further explained that my body chemistry was making my treatment more difficult, because I was allergic to penicillin, amoxicillin, ampicillin, and all the other penicillin-related drugs. Cipro had not touched the infection. The tetracycline family would not work, and sulfa drugs would be about as effective as they were in 1910. That narrowed down the options to two medications. They were going to start me on Nitrofurantoin. They hoped to find out from the CAT scan why my systems were shutting down.

When I finally understood I could die, my thoughts of Africa flew away faster than any supersonic jet. I had made my last African trip for the year 2006! Anna Marie would just have to take care of all the cancellations, and hope we could negotiate with the airlines a refund or rollover of my nonrefundable tickets.

About two-thirty the next morning, I had a very unusual experience. As I lay in bed, I turned toward my bathroom door. Between the door and my bed there was a tall man standing. He had on a pair of grayish white pants with a matching tunic. The tunic came below his knees but not below the calf of his legs. It was not a robe like the men wear in Africa, but more like what the men wear for formal dress in Pakistan or the Middle East. Because of the shadows in the darkened room, I could not see the features of his face, but I could tell that he was quite a bit taller than my doorway.

I was not frightened. I sat up and swung my feet to the floor and said out loud, "Who are you? What do you want?"

Actually, I already knew why he was there even before I sat up. He had been sent to carry me home.

My sitting up and speaking aloud awoke Anna Marie. She gently pulled me back into bed and cradled me in her arms. I looked back and the man was gone. I had been given an opportunity to go with him, or to remain.

I got up and took my second pill. I began to react violently to the medicine. I broke out in a red rash over my body. My head began to ache. My sinuses began to close and my breathing became more and more difficult. My kidneys hurt and I had a difficult time standing.

We called our paramedic son, Jay, and he told me to immediately take fifty milligrams of Benadryl, and contact the doctor. If we could not get hold of the doctor, he would meet us at the hospital. "Do not fool with this thing. It can quickly shut down your systems, and you will be dead before you can get to the help you need."

We were able to get in touch with the doctor, and he told us the exact same thing. The Benadryl stopped the reaction very quickly, and I could start getting my breath much easier.

Later my regular doctor called me and said that they had just received some further test results. "What we have determined is that you have hosted a very rare and aggressive strain of African E. coli. Most E. coli attacks the gastrointestinal tract, and is countered by Cipro. But this is strange. We've never seen it before, but it is moving rapidly to shut you down. I'm afraid we are running out of answers. As to medications, we only have one more arrow in the quiver. I am going to prescribe a Cephalothin medication for you to start on as soon as possible. We can only hope that you'll be able to tolerate it."

Many patients who are allergic to penicillin also prove to be allergic to Cephalothin. Needless to say, we were a bit apprehensive when I started to take the first pill of the last available medication. This had to work. In the meantime, I was still getting weaker and was now sleeping most of the time.

The good news: I was able to get down seven days worth of the new medicine without a reaction.

The bad news: after seven days my body reacted even more visibly than it had to the previously prescribed medication, and the full course of Cephalothin requires ten days of treatment.

I was back on the Benadryl immediately and called the doctor. "Come in now and we will see if the seven days on the Cephalothin was sufficient to kill the infection."

By noon on Saturday, December 9, we were in the doctor's office where they took more samples and did more lab tests. The results: I was clear! The antibiotic had killed the infection with just the seven-day regimen.

Then, I found out I wasn't in the clear after all. Dr. Cohn called me back in for some additional tests. "This is the worst news of all," he said. "The new tests show that you are as full of the infection as you were when we started, maybe worse! We must do something very decisive, and do it quickly. Go to this address; it is where the Western Infectious Disease Center is located. Dr. Jeffery Desjardin, a world-class specialist in infectious diseases, will see you immediately."

Dr. Jeffery DesJardin greeted me warmly. "Dr. Jackson, you are the founder of Project C.U.R.E., aren't you? We have been working with your organization for about eight or ten years now." Immediately, I knew that I was in good hands and felt grateful that God had prepared the way before me.

Dr. DesJardin prescribed special IV infusions through a PICC line. The line would run up to the top of my arm and follow the vein across to my neck, then carefully downward toward my heart, and end at the valve opening directly into my heart.

Checking into a hospital was one option. The other option was to start the process there in his disease center and then get someone to learn how to administer the infusions while I was in my own home, or hire a homecare nurse to perform the procedures.

"I would certainly rather not be confined in a hospital," I said to the doctor. "I have spent the last twenty years of my life in hospitals. People die there!"

Anna Marie volunteered to administer the necessary infusions, and followed us back to the procedures room to be trained by the staff in the infusion process. "OK," Dr. DesJardin said, "Follow me."

The nurses inserted a PICC line into my arm, just below the elbow, that would stay in place for the next four to five weeks. I was tethered to my chair, and that gave me time to slow down and analyze all that had been taking place.

I recalled the episode in 2004 in Kinshasa, Congo, when God had awakened me in that ramshackle, old, missionary hostel and had instructed me that I was to prepare to relinquish Project C.U.R.E. and start rolling off the responsibilities onto young leaders. God was saying that He didn't want the twenty-four hours in my day to limit what He could accomplish through Project C.U.R.E. He promised that if I would relinquish Project C.U.R.E., He would give me the true desires of my heart.

In that bug-infested setting I had agreed to relinquish control of Project C.U.R.E., and we had brought in my son Douglas as president, and added additional staff members. As to the global work of needs assessments, though, I was still operating business as usual.

God now had my full attention: *We are dealing with your willingness to totally relinquish Project C.U.R.E. and the touchy issue of leadership succession. Too many leaders hold on too long to what I allow them to build, and they think it should become their identity. Your identity must always be in Me and not what I create. Project C.U.R.E. must go beyond you, and you must go beyond Project C.U.R.E.*

That explicit message was coming to me as directly as the antibiotics dripping straight into my heart through the PICC line. I figured it was time to listen!

Finally, on January 5, after weeks of treatment at home through the loving hands of Anna Marie, the lab reports came back confirming that the infection was clear and the bug was dead. I was very pleased as I watched the nurses pull the long, lifesaving PICC line out of my forearm. I was free to go home.

But what was this message that I had received? Had I received new marching papers from headquarters? I knew that my life depended on a correct response!

23

The Final Surprise

I guess I had always seen myself as invincible when it came to health and strength. But the rare strain of African E. coli, coupled with the sheer exhaustion that came from twenty-plus years of hammering myself around in the toughest parts of the world, had left me surprisingly fragile and vulnerable.

Now the referee had blown the whistle and called for a time out. I didn't quite know how to handle that. The requests for needs assessments kept coming in cascading numbers from all over the world into the offices of Project C.U.R.E.

I wondered who would take care of all those requests and walk those hospital halls, put on all those scrubs, observe all those medical procedures, meet all the health ministers and country leaders, and see to it that the medical donations ended up where they were sent. I had foolishly slipped into believing that Project C.U.R.E. would have a hard time functioning without me performing those roles! God in His faithfulness was about to fix that. He was revealing to me that the success of Project C.U.R.E. was not dependent on my compassion, charisma, or acquired expertise. God had built the operation, and He was entirely capable of underwriting its success.

As I regained my strength, the devil tried to take advantage of my weakness. I would find myself asking: *Well, do you suppose the adventure is over? Did I push the total commitment to the Lordship of Christ experiment as far as it could be pushed? Is it over? In the final chapter of the saga, was Jim defeated by his own mortality? Do I now pull out the rusted fishing pole and reel, dip the line in the creek in front of the house, and wait for eternity?* The devil argued forcefully, *Yes, the grand experiment is over. You are done!*

One of my favorite places in the whole world is the small balcony on the front of the entry tower of our home. It stands no more than forty feet from the edge of the rippling Upper Bear Creek waters. Over the years, when I would be in some intolerable situation in Burkina Faso, or a dangerous truck stop in Mauritania, or in the crossfire of a gun battle in the Palestinian city of Ramallah, I would go to that balcony in my imagination for psychological and spiritual grounding. I would stand against the railing, turn my face fully to the west, and allow the gentle, cool breeze to waft over my face and across my body.

When the hot air of the plains on the east side of the Rocky Mountains begins to rise into the cooling atmosphere of the prairie sky, the refrigerated air from glaciers atop the fourteen-thousand-foot Mount Evans to our west rushes down the twenty-mile canyon, right past our house to the prairie below to fill in the vacated air space on the floor of the eastern plains. That breeze is perpetual. That breeze is moistened by the water from the creek and sweetened by the scent of a million pine trees. That breeze is a part of heaven, and it stabilizes my soul and instills peace and strength to my core. Wherever I am in this old world, I have found that my spirit can return to that favorite spot, and gain strength.

During my healing, I would go to that balcony and experience the presence of God. It was there that He reassured me that He always works with consistency and order, and that wisdom and understanding are always dispensed on the installment basis.

He gently reminded me, *I allowed you to be born into a righteous family and experience eternal truth as a lad. I allowed you to be exposed to stories of great people who believed and accomplished great things. I allowed you to understand basic principles of economics and business, and engineered opportunities for you to experience considerable wealth. I asked you to relinquish your wealth and give it away so that you would depend only on Me ... and you did. I gave you a block of time where you could think and articulate and write about God's economy and ideas of stewardship and relinquishment. Then, I instructed you to put away the formal teaching of the principles and embark on an empirical experiment that would serve as a show-and-tell expression of a new kind of business that would serve people around the world. This new business would be involved in repositioning assets that already belong to Me in order for millions of hurting and needy people to end up better off, and would give to them the opportunity to honor and praise the true God of the universe. You have only been allowed to experience these incremental steps based on your continued obedience to your newly recognized insights. The answer to your quandary is, no, it is not over. You do not get to go fishing yet! We are only now ready for the next installment.*

A strange thing happened at that point in my recuperation. God pushed the replay button of my memory, and I was taken back to the country of Ethiopia and the years of 1996 through 2000. By recalling vivid scenes from these years, God helped me reach conclusions that awaited rediscovery like da Vinci's drawings of flying machines by the first aviators.

In March 1996, I had been invited to Ethiopia to observe and evaluate the existing health care delivery system of the country, which had recently been freed from the oppressive rule of communism and the Soviet Union. Specifically, I had been asked to focus on the situation around Addis Ababa, as well as the cities of Axum and Mek'ele in the Tigray region. My invitation letters were signed by the prime minister, the minister of health, and the governors. The March trip would be one of many I would take to Ethiopia, and, in 1996, I was able to meet most of the new government leaders.

The new leadership came from the freedom fighters who resisted the Russian-backed communists. The story of their overcoming impossible odds and ultimately driving out the communists was an almost unknown story in America.

No one would come to the aid of the Ethiopian freedom fighters. The only guns, tanks, or other fighting implements they had were those taken away from the communists themselves. In order to commandeer a tank, they would run bravely alongside the tank being driven by the enemy, and jam a log or piece of steel pipe between the track and the boggy wheels. When the tank would come to a stop, or the track come off its wheels, they seized the tank for their own and put it back into operable condition.

The living heroes from that freedom war were now the creative and dedicated leaders of the new Ethiopia. They told me of their dreams for their future—the bulwarks they meant to establish against future oppressors. The communists had used famine as a weapon against the Ethiopian people. "Just drain the pond and the fish will die by themselves," as their former oppressors said. So the leaders determined to plant, raise, and harvest crops adequate to feed their citizens.

To do so they needed a healthy work force. They desired to build a health care delivery system that would begin, for the first time ever, to meet the needs of the ill and needy people of Ethiopia

Under the direction of Seeye Abraha, the previous commander and chief of the Ethiopian armed forces, and new president of such enterprises as the Commercial Bank of Ethiopia, and Ethiopian Airlines, several water conservation projects were being constructed. New hospitals were being built. Vocational training institutions taught young men and women to do carpentry work, heavy construction, welding, stone masonry, and other critical infrastructure jobs.

Seeye Abraha, Dr. Mesfin Minass, and Governor Gebru Asrat were eager to put me into a Land Cruiser and personally show me the project sites. Our first destination was the city of Mek'ele, five hours and two mountain ranges away. Accompanying us were ex-freedom fighters toting plenty of AK-47 automatic machine guns. In the city of Abiadi, near Mek'ele, we stopped and visited the new Teacher Training Institute, a splendid campus where about 75 percent of the new construction was completed. It was already in full swing, training five hundred new teachers at a time, preparing them to be assigned throughout Ethiopia to educate the children.

We then proceeded to the Youth Vocational Training Center. It was presently training three thousand young men and women in the skills of masonry and carpentry. They had already graduated one class out of the training center, and those students were now working throughout the country. The school took applications for those wanting to be trained, and the graduates repaid their tuition when finished with the course by working on government directed jobs for nine months. At that time they would hire out to development companies and international construction companies at regular wages.

There was now so much construction going on in Ethiopia that all of the graduates were immediately snapped up and put to work because of their skills. Even the vocational training center was being constructed by the students. They were divided into construction site teams and competed with each other, and were graded according to their finished product. They were taught in all phases of the construction business: framing and pouring concrete foundations, cutting stone blocks and laying them, framing the rafters, doing the roofing, and finishing the interior, including plumbing and electric.

I was extremely impressed with the training center. But the school lacked proper hand and power tools for the training of the students. Seeye Abraha literally begged me to help him by bringing desperately needed tools and pieces of construction equipment necessary for his new schools, "Dr. Jackson, what you have done with medical supplies and pieces of medical equipment you can do with hand tools and construction equipment to help me train my people."

We drove across the fertile plains of the Tigray region. As we rounded a small hill, Seeye suddenly stopped our Land Cruiser. To the side of the road was an old gnarly and weathered Ethiopian. He was walking behind an equally old and gnarly ox with a frayed hemp rope tied around its neck. The usable end of the rope was attached to a common stick about five feet in length and held in a direct vertical position. The lower end of the stick was pushed into the soil and was being guided by the farmer as it was pulled through the dirt by the ox. He was actually plowing his field with the end of one stick in order to go back and drop maize seeds into the furrow and plant his crop!

"Dr. Jackson," Seeye said, his voice growing passionate, "that is the perfect picture of the economic plight of Ethiopia! Until something is done to change the culture of subsistence farming in Africa, there will never be enough progress in the economic system or the development of markets. That man spends two or three hours walking to the river with a bucket on his head to fetch his water. Then he spends three more hours collecting banana leaves in order to patch the thatch on his roof. Then he gathers sticks to repair the corral for his ox. Then it is dark and time to go to bed. He knows nothing about Adam Smith's division of labor, so he does everything for himself by his own hands. He knows nothing of cooperation or supply and demand. He knows nothing about the market. He just burns up his life walking to the river and dragging a stick in the dirt behind his old worn out ox.

"That is why I am trying to train our new generation of freed citizens to learn specific skills, and the idea of competition and reward, and how to produce enough so that there is excess to take to the market and sell for money, so that they can purchase the needed things to make them even more successful. But I desperately need help!"

Then Seeye added the knockout punch, "James, you have changed health care systems all over the world with donated medical goods that bridged the gap between desperate nothingness over to hope and success. You know how to do it. You could turn Africa's economy around if you would take what you have done with medical supplies and do it with farm equipment. Please help me do it."

On my way home, I thought a lot about the possibilities of donated construction tools and also pieces of farm equipment that could be strategically placed into the African economy to bring about cultural change.

Growing up in the farmland of Idaho, I had always witnessed an abundance of good farm equipment that had been traded in for the newest and fanciest models. Every dealer wanted to sell the customer the new models on the showroom floor. There was plenty of available financing, and the government was even giving generous subsidies that helped the modern farmer to purchase the newest models and inventions.

Why not salvage the millions and millions of dollars worth of used farm equipment and save it from rusting into oblivion? Why not utilize the equipment to help feed the hungry millions in Africa?

When I returned to the United States, I contacted one of my old university chums who had become a CPA and had set up his business in the farmland area of Ontario, Oregon, located on the famous Snake River. Many of the clients he represented were successful and prosperous farmers of the area. During our visit on the phone, I described to him what I had seen as an opportunity in Ethiopia. "How do you think your tax clients would like to receive a contribution receipt in exchange for their farm equipment that they are just getting ready to trade in for the new big tractors with the fancy, high-tech, quad-stereo sound systems in them?" I asked. "Certainly, no one resents the opportunity for a farmer to get the nicest and fanciest and most efficient pieces of new equipment. But what are they going to do with the wonderful piece of equipment that had just given way to the new model? Do you think that they would get excited about helping to revolutionize agriculture in Africa?"

My friend's reply was very encouraging. He wanted to help in any way possible. "I'll make you a deal," said my past schoolmate. "I will have a nice lunch catered in to the community Grange Hall, and I will send out a little invitation and a sketch of our conversation to my clients. If they are interested in such a project, then I am sure they will show up. If they are not interested, then they won't."

I purchased an airline ticket to Boise, Idaho, rented a car, and drove the few miles to Ontario, Oregon. I could hardly believe my eyes. About a hundred farmers showed up. They loved the idea, and many stayed to help give advice on how to load the equipment for safe shipping, and some even asked if they could travel to Africa and help train the farmers how to use the equipment, along with imparting the techniques of modern farming.

I shared the phenomenon of Project C.U.R.E. with the farmers at the lunch about how we were utilizing entrepreneurial concepts of reallocating resources. I told them that we were just taking something that appeared to be in a position of lesser value and lifting it to a position of higher value for the benefit of everyone. They were bright guys and loved the concept.

Later that year I was on a flight and met a fellow who traveled around the world about as much as I did. He was an important official of a company that manufactured and distributed hand power tools. I had heard of his company and even owned a few of its tools..

We began talking about Project C.U.R.E. and our work in so many countries. I explained how we received supplies and pieces of equipment from both manufacturers and end users, and delivered them into the hands of the most needy people on earth. I even explained how I could go to manufacturers and, in essence, barter their overstock for donation receipts that could be used as "write offs" against their profits. If handled correctly, they could realize the credit and apply it to the bottom line of their accounting statements. And, in turn, people on the other side of the world could receive their equipment, never having dreamt of such a gift. Everyone would end up better off.

As our conversation progressed, I asked him what he did with all the hand tools they created when they were superseded by a new model with some new bells or whistles included.

"Suppose you gave those hand tools to me," I said, "and I went to someplace like Africa or India and set up co-ops where those individuals, who were presently struggling trying to make all their products with ancient methods, could suddenly be given the advantage of modern hand and power tools. What if they didn't have to purchase the tools, but I set up stores that would look a lot like tool rental businesses in the United States. Only those workers who signed up as members of the co-op would have the privilege of checking out one tool at a time from the co-op. The new members would have to pledge to pay back into the co-op a certain percentage of their business profits. That fee would be used to run the shop and keep the tools repaired and in good order. Suddenly, we would have enhanced and enabled those individual workers to increase their output many times over. As their incomes increased, the economy of their entire neighborhood would reap the benefit. Everyone would be better off."

The businessman grinned and said, "What a brilliant idea! Come and see me, and we will talk to our accountants."

The growth and success of Project C.U.R.E. consumed my time, however, and I was unable to give direction to these projects or find someone who could. With great regret I have to confess that the needed hand tools and pieces of farm equipment have yet to be delivered to Africa and India. The co-op organizations have yet to be implemented; the many willing volunteers from America have yet to be mobilized to go as mentors and partners to help the thousands of foreign entrepreneurs pleading for help.

I realized now, though, that these delayed plans could be taken in hand once more. In fact, besides farm equipment and modern hand tools, there were other areas in which the lessons Project C.U.R.E. had learned could be implemented. The story wasn't ending ... Not at all!

As I sat at home in the mountains of Colorado, my near-death experience still vivid, a new understanding of Project C.U.R.E.'s significance came into focus. Project C.U.R.E. was not only a successful humanitarian enterprise but a model that could be replicated again and again in many other areas. This business model drew its inspiration from deep wellsprings of Christian spirituality, a call to obedience and relinquishment. Project C.U.R.E. was a working example—a parable in action—that validated biblical principles as to the growth of the Kingdom of God.

It was all about good stewards who invest the talents they have been given and present the increase to the Master. Those principles, concepts, and distinctive characteristics are transferable. They can be duplicated a thousand times!

Many times during the past twenty-five years of visiting needy hospitals and clinics, the ministers of health would say, "I desperately need three more clinics in this region. Is there any way that you could help us build the clinics then furnish them with the needed medical goods?"

Or the director of a hospital would ask, "You see how badly we need a new surgical theater here. Is there any way Project C.U.R.E. could help us by building the facility for us?"

My answer was always the same. "I'm sorry, but we stay focused on collecting and distributing medical goods, and we are the best in the world at doing what we do. We don't ship used clothes, canned goods or toys, we just stick with medical."

Now, I was beginning to see a broader picture. Yes, Project C.U.R.E. needed to stick with medical items, but the same model could provide other desperately needed products and services.

In fact, it's already happening. I met recently with a group of my building contractor friends who just recently had gone through a disconcerting situation with their own version of Rev. Dr. Dimsdale. They were frustrated, disillusioned, and discouraged. After talking at length and examining the model, I helped them put their legal paperwork together to establish International Hope Builders. This organization is dedicated to going into developing countries for the specific purpose of building those needed clinics, hospital wings, orphanages, churches, and schools.

They are gearing up to build one hundred small houses in Cambodia and ten churches in Brazil—and are the happiest group I've seen in a long time!

Project C.U.R.E. will now have a partner to meet those requests from the ministers of health to build the clinics. In turn, Project C.U.R.E. will fill them up with medical supplies and pieces of equipment.

We have embarked on the most *exciting* part of the adventure, to expand the model, and launch a thousand such initiatives. You are invited and encouraged to participate in the next miraculous enterprise. You, too, can become a cultural entrepreneur and change your world!

As painful and scary as my E. coli near-death experience was, I am extremely grateful for the way in which God used it to redirect me once more from a narrowly focused, successful activity to a broader vision that can be of even greater eternal significance. The concept is transferable!

24

A New Wave of Global Transformation

> *Isn't it strange that princes and kings,*
> *And clowns that caper in sawdust rings,*
> *And common folk, like you and me,*
> *Are builders for eternity?*
> *To each is given a bag of tools,*
> *A shapeless mass and a book of rules;*
> *And each must make, ere life is flown,*
> *A stumbling-block or a stepping-stone.*
>
> —R.L Sharpe, A Bag of Tools, circa 1809

An individual is happy—fully alive—when his goals are clearly defined, consistent with the gifts God has entrusted to him, and he is positively engaged in pursuing those God-directed goals with all the energy he can muster. No one wakes up one morning as the happiest person in the world, because happiness is based on choices, and those choices always set into motion a series of consequences. How we manage and reconcile those consequences resulting from our choices determines our happiness. Those choices will position the person in the midst of the battle between good and evil, and this battle can only be fought through obedience and relinquishment. The stakes could not be higher. We are always in the process of becoming either fiends or saints.

Happiness is conditioned by one's relationship with others and the phenomenon of "goodness," love in action. Christ said, "Your concern for others is the true measure of your greatness" (Luke 9:48b, TLB).

Albert Schweitzer acknowledged, "I don't know what your destiny will be, but one thing I do know; the only ones among you who will be really happy are those who have sought and found how to serve."[4]

One of the greatest gifts ever offered to me was the opportunity to pursue this unique phenomenon of goodness at a relatively early point in my career. I grappled with the concept of "how much is enough?" It also gave me opportunity to experience the process of relinquishment.

The theory and art of accumulating assets, and the acquisition of influence and power, have become the curriculum and catechism of my culture. It affects the behaviors on all the different venues and playing fields of our clans. Rank materialism drives and shapes the behaviors of our business communities and entertainment enterprises. That same spirit of accumulation and power drives and shapes the entitlements of the welfare state. Greed, advantage, and one-up-man-ship are what we eat for breakfast.

The institutionalized church is no longer ignited by the compassion for lifting and helping the desperate and disadvantaged throughout the world, rather, it would seem it has given way to the infomercial approach to how much you will gain in temporal things, emotional thrills, and personal advantage if you will come and join the mega group. Historically, we have been accustomed to having the church lead the call with trumpets blaring for individual and cultural transformation. As I've noted, it wasn't that long ago when the great mission-sending groups in Britain and the United States were challenging the young to go to places like Angola and Congo, requiring them to pack all their belongings in wooden coffins so that their bodies could be shipped back home if they fell victim to malaria, TB, and dengue fever. Why is it that the charge has been abdicated by the institutionalized church and the responsibility for individual and cultural transformation been transferred to the secular entrepreneurs?

On Wednesday, August 4, 2010, famed investor Warren Buffet, chairman and CEO of Berkshire Hathaway, announced the names of forty of America's wealthiest families and individuals who have signed the Giving Pledge, a charitable project that asks billionaires to pledge to donate the bulk of their wealth. "We've really just started, but already we've had a terrific response," said Buffet. Each individual or family publicly announced that they had pledged to give the majority of their wealth to the philanthropic causes and charitable organizations of their choice, and agreed to follow up that announcement with a letter explaining their decision.

I applaud the incredible benevolence displayed by these families and individuals. Philanthropy and goodness just absolutely make sense. But will throwing money at the moral ills of this world be effective and sustainable without the authentic gospel of goodness? I think not. Who is going to carry the water that douses the inflamed problems of greed, crime, hate, tribal strife, political manipulation, and poverty? From where will the answers come that will not only salve the observable symptoms of want, hunger, and strife, but will also solve the underlying moral and spiritual causes?

The prophet Jeremiah was confronted with similar questions as he was directed to give his observations and conclusions to the king. "This is what the LORD says: 'Let not the wise man boast of his wisdom or the strong man boast of his strength or the rich man boast of his riches, but let him who boasts boast of this: that he understands and knows me, that I am the LORD, who exercises kindness, justice and righteousness on earth, for in these I delight,' declares the LORD" (Jeremiah 9:23–24).

"Kindness, justice, and righteousness" delight the heart of God; they make God smile. If you desire to delight the heart of God, then exercise kindness, justice, and righteousness with every ounce of energy afforded you and every minute of every day you have left to live. All of your energies should be focused on this one thing: carry out the mandate of kindness, justice, and righteousness on earth. Wisdom won't cut it; strength and manipulation will eventually turn into weakness and anarchy; riches will be fought over by others or wasted by inflation. Only kindness, justice, and righteousness will endure forever.

❦

This is a clarion call to the church holy and universal: stop competing on the turf of the secular world. You will lose the day and be pulled into their realm. The institutionalized church can't out-entertain the entertainment world. The church can't out-program the programs of the social government. The church can't outsell the "fuzzies" and "warm feelings" of the pop philosophies and hot trends. Leave the low plains of "me, too" and once again inhabit the high ground. Start doing what the church was ordained and set apart to do. Start living out the entrusted gospel the church teaches and preaches. The world as we know it today would experience a transformation—a renaissance—of epic proportions.

The jury is still out as to whether the institutionalized church is capable of making such a dramatic turn. It may not be possible to emerge into the light of a "renaissance" without first experiencing another round of historic "dark ages." I am hopeful, though. I believe there is still both the time and the willpower to turn things around.

As the reader has learned, I didn't just sit down and design and implement Project C.U.R.E. As is usually the case, most enterprises are step-by-step children of other enterprises. And those enterprises are based on true need. The manifestation of Project C.U.R.E. into real life and flesh came about on the installment plan. That progression amazingly followed the "insight, opportunity, and obedience" sequence.

God would allow me a bit of an insight into the realm of "what if." That insight would incubate for a while and within a short period of time I would be presented with a real, live opportunity to do something about which I had been thinking. It would be at that point that I would have to obey what God was showing me and move on the opportunity and activate or implement that insight by faith. Or, I could choose to hesitate, procrastinate, and ultimately disobey at that juncture of opportunity. I quickly discovered that postponed obedience was disobedience in the final analysis. You can't get by with just "placing an insight into the pigeon hole of suspended judgment."

As I learned to obey more quickly, each act of obedience would trigger another sequence of insight-opportunity-obedience. I would receive from the Holy Spirit another insight, and a short period of incubation time, and then suddenly another opportunity for obedience: insight-opportunity-obedience; insight-opportunity-obedience. That was the way Project C.U.R.E. was built.

It has not been a flash-in-the-pan phenomenon, but a sustained effort of twenty-five years and counting. When I think about what has happened, I am overwhelmed. I have been allowed to be a part of a present-day miracle. Who would have believed it twenty-five years ago? Project C.U.R.E. will ship in excess of $50 million in donated medical supplies and pieces of medical equipment each year into over one hundred and twenty recipient countries. Project C.U.R.E. has been honored with highest recognition around the world. Not long ago the office notified me that we had passed the one billion dollar mark in giving away medical supplies. Now we are shooting for $1 trillion! We have a long way to go.

In my pilgrimage from trading rabbits out of my Radio Flyer wagon, to traveling over the globe, I have learned much about myself. I would never get away from the stories my mom read to me when I was young about other boys in America who grew up to be great men of ability, determination, and integrity. They loved God, achieved success, lived lives of goodness, and helped other people to be better off.

I never saw wealth and money as evil or wrong, but as a tool that could be used to help other people. Even when I became addicted to selfish acquisition for a time, God allowed me to gain knowledge and skill in rearranging assets from a position of lesser value to a position of greater value. I then learned that I could take my entrepreneurial skills and apply them to help hundreds of thousands of other people. I pursued my childhood dream of doing well so that I could do good.

My thirty-year adventure exposed me to discomfort and danger. These acute challenges helped me to focus on the essential and the enduring. In places like Rwanda and Pol Pot's Cambodia, there was nothing that was "just going to happen" to change the world's dark side. There needed to be risk-takers who would choose to relinquish the selfish use of their God-given talents, using them to counter the world's greed and murderous lust for power.

Along the journey I encountered enough hypocrisy to make me angry and bitter, and prone to renounce the whole community of institutionalized religion and false friends. The worst of it was watching my family suffer. But God was ever so gently leading us into the incredible knowledge and experience of relinquishment. I learned to take my hands off the things that would last for a short time so that I could lay hold of the things that would last forever. The best business trade I ever made was to exchange what I could not keep for what I could not lose.

In the process, something transformational happened at my core. God helped me to see the futility of trying to accumulate enough material things to make me happy. I suddenly realized that I could never gain enough to make me satisfied and fulfilled. At that point I asked God to help me find a more excellent way. I was ready to pursue goodness and abandon selfish accumulation. I never took a vow of poverty or promised to wear a hair shirt. I just wanted to break the addiction to the power of selfish accumulation. From that time on, I have actively and sincerely tried to pursue the concept of "relinquishment." I changed from a person bent on "getting," to a person bent on "giving."

I ask you a simple investment question: Was it a good deal for Anna Marie and me to give away, back at the time of Jackson Brothers Investments, what in today's currency would be in excess of $70 million, for the possibility of seeing that gift grow to a billion? Of course, we didn't make it happen alone. God gave the increase, and thousands and thousands of volunteers and donors brought it to pass. We have never taken a salary from Project C.U.R.E. in its twenty-five year history, and yet God has repaid us over and over in an abundant life we could never have imagined. You just can't out-give God.

When I lay my head on my pillow each night, I realize that God has given me everything I once mistakenly thought I could purchase or secure through position. I have health, family, good friends, peace of mind, and heart. I now possess everything I would have said even then was truly valuable.

My journey helped launch Project C.U.R.E., and now, I hope and pray, a new wave of dedicated cultural entrepreneurs will be courageous enough to believe that with God's help they can change the world. That dedication and belief opens the door for God to display once again in history what He can do with and in and for and through and by a man or a woman who is totally at God's disposal.

Through my eyes of faith I see myself standing before the King with satisfaction beyond compare as I give back to Him what He gave to me, and its eternal increase. I did not bury my one talent in the ground, as the foolish servant did in Christ's parable of the talents (Luke 19:12–27). I cooperated with God's plan of divine multiplication.

I choose to delight the heart of God by living a life of kindness, justice, and righteousness on this earth.

I challenge you to give yourself completely to a life of relinquishment and dedication to helping other people become better off. You are part of something larger, and you are beautifully individual. Christ loves the world and longs to give it His life. You must do the same! You, too, can experience the transformational adventure and become the happiest person in the world.

Appendix

PROJECT C.U.R.E.
Recipient Countries

1. Afghanistan
2. Albania
3. Angola
4. Argentina
5. Armenia
6. Azerbaijan
7. Bali
8. Bangladesh
9. Belarus
10. Belize
11. Benin
12. Bhutan
13. Bolivia
14. Bosnia
15. Brazil
16. Bulgaria
17. Burkina Faso
18. Burundi
19. Cambodia
20. Cameroon
21. Chile
22. China
23. Christmas Island
24. Colombia
25. Costa Rica
26. Cote d'Ivoire
27. Croatia
28. Cuba
29. Czech Republic
30. DR Congo
31. Dominican Republic
32. Djibouti
33. Ecuador
34. El Salvador
35. Equatorial Guinea
36. Estonia
37. Eritrea
38. Ethiopia
39. Fiji
40. Gabon
41. Gambia
42. Georgia
43. Ghana
44. Greece
45. Grenada
46. Guatemala
47. Guinea
48. Guinea Bissau
49. Guyana
50. Haiti
51. Honduras
52. Hungary
53. India
54. Indonesia
55. Iraq
56. Israel
57. Jamaica
58. Jordan
59. Kazakhstan
60. Kenya
61. Kiribati
62. Kyrgyzstan
63. Laos
64. Lebanon
65. Lesotho
66. Liberia
67. Macedonia
68. Madagascar
69. Malawi
70. Mali
71. Mauritania
72. Mexico
73. Mongolia

74. Montenegro
75. Morocco
76. Mozambique
77. Union of Myanmar
78. Nagorno Karabakh Republic
79. Namibia
80. Nepal
81. Nicaragua
82. Nigeria
83. North Korea
84. Panama
85. Papua New Guinea
86. Pakistan
87. Palestine/West Bank
88. Paraguay
89. Peru
90. Philippines
91. Poland
92. Romania
93. Russia
94. Rwanda
95. Saba, Netherland Antilles
96. Samoa
97. Senegal
98. Serbia
99. Sierra Leone
100. Somalia/Somaliland
101. South Africa
102. St. Lucia
103. St. Vincent
104. Sudan
105. Swaziland
106. Tajikistan
107. Tanzania
108. Thailand
109. Tokelau Islands
110. Togo
111. Tonga
112. Trinidad
113. Tunisia
114. Turkey
115. Uganda
116. Ukraine
117. Uruguay
118. Uzbekistan
119. Venezuela
120. Vietnam
121. Zambia
122. Zimbabwe

The Project C.U.R.E. Distinctive

Over the years Project C.U.R.E. developed a list of distinctive characteristics that guided the policies and behavior of the organization. We believe this list can be utilized as a transferable model.

ECONOMIC:
- Ensure everyone involved ends up "better off"
- Utilize "leverage"—multiplication of assets and outcomes
- Share the glory—let others share the photo ops
- Insist on good stewardship 1) frugality 2) ask for help

ETHICS AND TRUST:
- Conduct mandatory on-spots Needs Assessment
- Pursue excellence
- Insist on integrity
- Remain independent of governments and denominations

POLITICAL:
- Remain politically neutral
- Pursue venues without regard to politics
- Work with the top leaders ... but get the goods to the people

PARTNERS:
- Go only where invited
- Enable existing endeavors

VOLUNTARISM:
- Accept responsibility of offering worth-building activities
- Customize entry threshold levels of volunteers

POLICIES AND PRACTICES:
- Pursue insistence on persistence—"Can Do" attitude
- Strive for singleness of purpose
- Continue development of systems
- Expect accountability and follow-up

THE WHITE HOUSE
WASHINGTON

July 22, 2005

Dr. James Jackson
Dr. AnnaMarie Jackson
Evergreen, Colorado

Dear AnnaMarie and Jim:

Congratulations on your selection as the 2005 National Parents of the Year by the National Parents' Day Council.

Parents are the most important role models for their children. As parents, we help our children understand that they are the future of our country and America's next generation of leaders. By providing guidance, support, and unconditional love for children, parents like you shape the character of our Nation. Your good works demonstrate that each of us has the power to make a profound difference in the life of a child.

Laura and I send our best wishes to you and your family. May God bless you, and may God continue to bless America.

Sincerely,

George W. Bush

The President
REPUBLIC OF RWANDA

Ref.: No 141/01/AP.01/04

03 May 2004

Dr. Jim Jackson
Founder and Chairman
Project CURE
Denver

Dear Dr. Jackson

I write to thank you most sincerely for your hospitality and friendship. My delegation and I felt at home in Denver because of your personal effort in making our stay worthwhile. I would particularly like to express our gratitude for the donation of 10 million dollars worth of medical supplies to Rwanda.

My friend, as a true man of God, you have let God's will be done through your service to Project CURE; touching so many people's lives along the way. May God continue to bless you and Anna Marie.

I look forward to a future of continued partnership with Project CURE and look forward to welcoming you once again to Rwanda.

Sincerely,
P. Kagame.

Dig a Little Deeper

Reader's Discussion Guide

Chapter One—The Question
1. List what is in *your* "bag of tools."
2. Recall a "stepping stone" that someone created for you.

Chapter Two—Snakes on the Road
1. What may have encouraged the doctors in Kimpese to risk performing the innovative orthopedic procedures when other doctors would not take the risk?

Chapter Three—Childhood Promises
1. Recall a story from your childhood and share how it impacted you.
2. "You can take anything you have and make it into what you want." How does this statement relate to the idea of making everyone "better off?"

Chapter Four—I Was Afraid You Were Going to Ask
1. Evaluate and discuss the statement, "It's not the set of circumstances in which you find yourself, but how you respond that makes all the difference in the world."
2. Discuss examples where *individuals* or *institutions* disappointed you beyond measure.

Chapter Five—Hardball Banking
1. What would be the value of the exercise for finding "*ten ways to tie your shoes?*"

2. What experiences have you had when your *perceived defeats* ultimately turned into *successes*?

Chapter Six—Making Money
1. What factors would have to be considered when dealing with the question, "How much is enough?"
2. Explain the difference between "doing *well*" and "doing *good*."

Chapter Seven—The Garden of Gethsemane
1. Share an incident when you were challenged to make a *life-changing decision* knowing the cost would be extreme.

Chapter Eight—Closing the Gate and Opening the Word
1. Describe one *economic principle* espoused in the Bible.
2. How would you explain the statement, "Growth starts where blaming stops?"

Chapter Nine—The Turning Point
1. What are some of the most common motivators that stir feelings of *compassion*?

Chapter Ten—Paradox and Reversal
1. Describe what you think is meant by the statement, "The *perception* of your obligation will determine your *behavior*."

Chapter Eleven—Devils and Angels
1. What are the *risks* involved in trusting God to provide when you assume the challenge to do something *great*?
2. "God can do a lot with a little when He has *all* there is of it." Explain what difference it should make that God has "*all* there is of it."

Chapter Twelve—Beyond Brazil
1. Give an example when you have felt compelled to be a part of *change*.
2. Describe the importance of accepting *personal responsibility* when cultural change is needed.

Chapter Thirteen—Up Close and Personal – Always
1. Explain the statement, " ... whatever was considered 'free' was somewhere along the process considered 'without value.'"

Chapter Fourteen—The Challenge of Neutrality
1. Why was "honesty, sincerity and concern" so effective for building trust with the North Korean officials?
2. Explain why the response, "I want nothing in return" was so *unusual* in Dr. Jackson's circumstance. Where would it be unusual in your life?

Chapter Fifteen—Avoiding the Pitfalls—and the Thugs
1. How is it possible that the government officials were influenced by the *good spirit* that was stronger than words?
2. How can *charlatans* so easily become gate keepers who can block acts of *goodness*?

Chapter Sixteen—Partners and Networks
1. What advantages are there to learning the art of *receiving graciously*?
2. Describe the differences between *collaborating with others* and demanding *personal recognition*.

Chapter Seventeen—A Short Course in Changing the World
1. Explain *wealth*, in your own words.

2. What are some factors that would either stifle or encourage *individual incentive*?
3. Make a list of attributes for, and compare the two categories: "free will creative compassion" and "planned controlled compassion."

Chapter Eighteen—Cultural Economics
1. Discuss the usual responses when faced with the *pain* of witnessing suffering and brokenness.
2. Why is it difficult to speak out against *cultural inequities*?
3. What are some *consequences* of treating all views as equally valid truth?

Chapter Nineteen—Despair
1. Why is despair so crippling?
2. What advice do you have to counteract *despair*?

Chapter Twenty—Cost of Petrol Just Went Up for You
1. Why do think *physical danger* and *fear of the unknown* make it difficult to respond to truth?
2. Can you give examples of people who have come into your life who you might consider "angels?"

Chapter Twenty-One—Empowering Others
1. How do you suppose Daniel reacted when his *dignity* had been recognized and his dream was being *fulfilled*?
2. How is it possible that even volunteers could be considered "international change agents?"

Chapter Twenty-Two—Darkness Comes to Call
1. What are the indicators of holding on to an *identity* or position too long or too tightly?

2. What in your life has become your *identity* and how would it make you feel if you were stripped of that identity?

Chapter Twenty-Three—The Final Surprise
1. Everyone's journey includes concepts or incidents that can be shared for the *benefit* of someone else. Give some examples that you have observed.
2. List some reasons that a person might be reluctant to make *life changes*.

Chapter Twenty-Four—A New Wave of Global Transformation
1. Recall the quote, "… the only ones among you who will be really happy are those who have sought and found how to serve." Discuss how *serving* is the key to happiness.
2. What in *your* life are you being asked to relinquish?
3. How can *you* become dedicated to helping other people become "better off?"

Notes

1. Oswald Chambers, *My Utmost for His Highest* (New York: Dodd Mead & Company, 1965).
2. James W. Jackson, *What'cha Gonna Do With What'cha Got?* (Denver, Colorado: Winston-Crown Publishing House, 1982).
3. Graham Hancock, *Lords of Poverty* (New York, The Atlantic Monthly Press, 1989).
4. Marta Davidovich Ockuly, Joy of Quotes "Quotes by Authors", (www.joyofquotes.com)